A Coach for your Heart

5 Steps to Improve your Life Now

Ed McShane & Grant Gavin

Denver, Colorado

ISBN-13: 978-0692528327 (Ascent Production)

TABLE OF CONTENTS

Chapter 4
Reaching to the Heart of Another

Chapter 5
Regenerating your Heart

AUTHOR'S NOTE

A Coach for your Heart was written as a team. It would not be possible without both the efforts of Ed McShane and Grant Gavin. Each author had a separate, yet essential role in creating A Coach for your Heart. The following are what each author contributed:

Ed McShane
Key Introductions
A Story from the Heart
How it Works

Grant Gavin
Organization of both the Chapters and Keys
Chapter Introductions
Why this is Important

DEDICATION

Ed McShane

To Lisa Coast, to whom I owe my reconstruction, reclamation, and regeneration of spirit, soul and life. Without you at this time in my life, this book would never have been written.

Grant Gavin

To my wife and best friend Kandi, for your Love & Enthusiasm, and Insight.

To my parents, Linda and Paul, for all the big and small things you have done to help me become the person I am today.

FORWARD

"The best and most beautiful things in the world cannot be seen or even touched. They must be felt with the heart." –Helen Keller

"It is only with the heart that one can see rightly; what is essential is invisible to the eye." –Antoine St. Exupery

What you hold in your hand –these pages– will change your life.

They will help you live a purposeful life, illuminated by feeling and made sturdy through love, presence, compassion, patience, empathy, forgiveness, and joy.

Life's journey has an infinite number of paths. It is up to you to shape, mold, and improve your life to create the experience and results you wish. This requires you follow the path true to your heart. Knowing and using the gifts you bring to this world are the key ingredients to a meaningful life. Our goal is for your gifts to flow directly and passionately from your heart.

Your heart is like a seed. When watered with mindful attention, it will grow, expanding beyond what you ever thought possible. No matter who you are, no matter how many failures you have had, your heart is a source of infinite power. This power is yours to find. We will help to guide your journey within.

We are all human. We have all had chronic bouts of anger, impatience, and frustration, all fueled by selfishness, creating an inability to focus on the needs of others. We fly into our ego and leave behind the balancing energy of our heart. This will always get us into trouble.

This book changes all that. Lead a life from your heart, from this moment forward!

Our goal for this book is to help you discover researched-based paths to life's meaning and true, lasting happiness, while helping you avoid illusory pursuits.

Some ideas presented in the book will strongly resonate with you. Others might not. Keep your mind open to what is possible for the rest of your life.

It is never too late to live a life with meaning. We will show you how your heart can set you on a new path of fulfillment, insight, and love.

We'll show you how and what to practice. Your results will give you reason to continue. This practice will become second nature. And quickly!

You'll care. You will turn off the autopilot on your thoughts - and instead choose consideration and possibility.

When you learn to pay attention to your heart's issues, you'll be able to choose between a treasure chest of responses. It will be within your grasp to experience a crowded, uncomfortable, noisy situation with the same grace and peace that you find in silence.

We wish you to be free to choose your reality, guided by the wisdom of your heart. Listening to your heart helps to develop and sustain the awareness and focus to care for yourself and for others, building up yourself and your relationships in ways you've never considered. You'll see immediate changes. And you'll feel better than you ever have.

We ask only that you keep moving forward. Keep turning these pages! Visit them when you feel yourself falling back into the same anger-laden, ego-driven, impatience-soaked, automatic thought processes that contribute to your resentment, impatience, and frustration. Refuse to live with the clawing sense of having missed life's important and meaningful moments; they are always within your reach.

Close your eyes and imagine yourself with the perfect body, perfect career, and perfect wardrobe. Externally, you would have met all of society's standards. But, in reality, happiness does not come from anything external. Past the fabric of consumer culture, you are the same person no matter what the wrapping. Living up to these standards is fundamentally reactive; you are responding to a culture that dictates what you should or should not do. By removing the blinders, you are able to pursue a life of meaning, a life lived from the heart. True satisfaction comes from living from your heart, finding meaning in the depths of relationships and experiencing the present moment.

Shift your actions from external pursuits to actions rooted in your heart. You don't have to quit your job, grow a big beard, or go chant in a mountain-side cave. You can do all this in the life that you have. Right here! Right now! Be fully present in your relationships, accept reality for its endless flaws, forgive people who are plagued by their egos, and give from a place of abundance.

In the mind-made story of your life you may feel scarcity. Once you tap into your heart, though, you realize the connections between everyone and everything, and that scarcity does not exist. Scarcity is part of your mind-made past, and the past is gone; it lies in the wake of the present moment. It is a figment of your imagination subject to a multitude of interpretations. There is no tangible past, only interpretations of events in the present moment; internalize this belief and use it to create a better reality where painful events increase power instead of limiting or blocking your heart.

You can do all of this by shifting your awareness to your heart.

Feel everyone around you! Feel your relationships! Feel the world! Offer your heart! Stand open to the present moment. Right now, as you read this, release any tension you feel to be holding you back. Whether it's emotional pain, health problems, financial, or social issues.

Begin your life now by connecting with your heart. Your new perspective will allow you to live with wisdom, faith, and love.

And this is our promise: We will make it possible, tangible, and far easier than you can imagine.

Here's to your journey of the heart.

We're with you! We are here for you!

CHAPTER 1
THE HEART'S FOUNDATION

In this section, we focus on the foundation of the heart, your sense of me. Treating yourself well is important to have a healthy self-worth. You must create a positive relationship with who you are and who you wish to become. These keys will help you create, maintain, and repair this relationship:

Key One: Be Present

Key Two: Know Thyself

Key Three: Develop Self-acceptance

Key Four: Maintain Integrity

Key Five: Develop Understanding

Key Six: Establish Solitude

Key Seven: Meditate

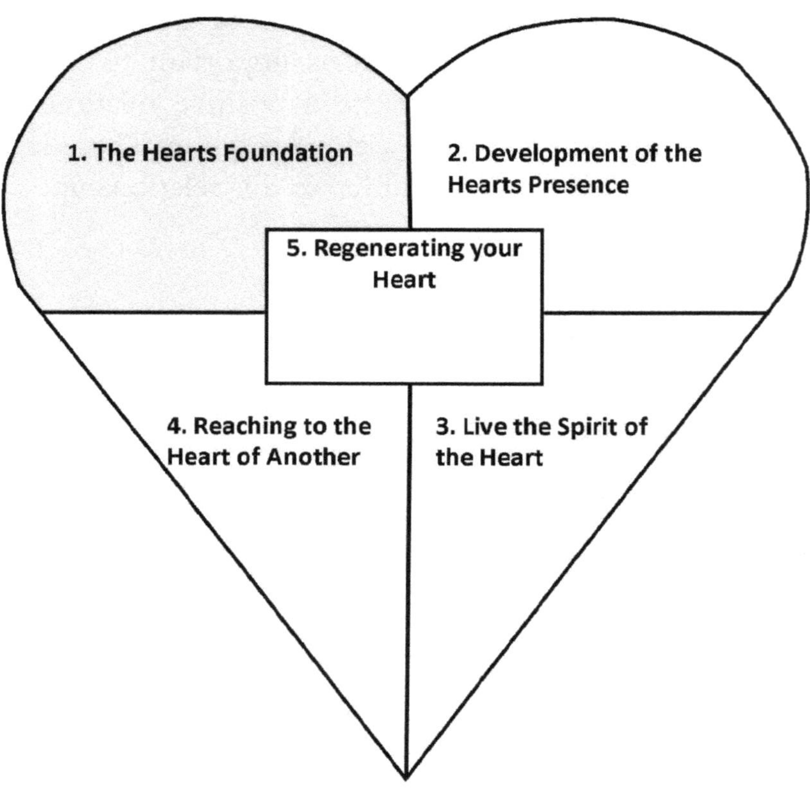
1. The Hearts Foundation
2. Development of the Hearts Presence
5. Regenerating your Heart
4. Reaching to the Heart of Another
3. Live the Spirit of the Heart

KEY 1
KEY ONE: BE PRESENT

Most of us spend our days thinking of the past or dreaming of the future, and we miss what is happening right in front of us. Being present in your life is the first step to living a meaningful life.

To recognize, to hold, to feel, and to express our most complex and deepest feelings with meaning, strength, and intention, one must be present. To be present we have to do two things right off the bat: be calm and be attentive.

Now, I want to pause right here and mention that, when you hear the words "calm" and "attentive," go with what you know. There are a variety of synonyms that work just as well. If it is easier for you to relate to the words "chill" or "rest" or "relax" instead of "calm," that's fine.

If it is more familiar for you to use the words "focused" or "engaged" or even "hunker down" instead of "attentive," I'm good with that, too. Doesn't matter. Whatever you reach into when you read those two words, "calm" and "attentive," use what's familiar. I will get into further explanations of both points throughout the book.

This calm and attentive state is the first place we want you to go. This is the starting point, the center, from where you begin.

Look, it's easy. It just takes a little–a little, mind you–practice.

A Story from the Heart

A guy came into my office, sat down and began complaining about stress. Intense guy, going ninety miles an hour. He told me that his life is hectic, his pace is constant, he can't relax, and he doesn't know how to keep from being tense. I explained the idea of being present to him, told him how important it is, but he didn't get it. He nodded his head, gave me a little lip service, then carried on with his complaint.

Now, outside my office window I have a bird feeder. Goldfinches gather on these two long nylon feeders full of seed, crashing into each other and eating like there's no tomorrow. I've had these feeders up for years, largely because they're just so pretty you can watch them for minutes at a time and forget about everything else going on in the world.

As my client was speaking, I looked out the window and, pointing at the feeders, I said, "What do you think about those?"

I looked back at my client, and as he's looking at the birds, I looked back at the birds and listen for his response. He says, "You mean the birds?" I told him that, yes, I was referring to the birds, and I said, "These guys have been coming since 2005. It took them about six months to find the feeder. But once they hit it, they brought their family, their friends, finches they haven't seen since high school. I mean just about every goldfinch in the tristate area comes and visits these bird feeders."

Now the client was looking at the bird feeders. And to hold his interest, I pointed at one particularly well-fed goldfinch. I told him that this one comes here often and eats his weight in seed.

He laughed a little then, just before he goes back to his complaint, I stopped him and said, "Did you notice what just happened?"

He said, "What? What happened?"

I said, "You stopped to notice the goldfinches. You saw the fat one I was pointing to, observed the seed in the feeders, and stopped articulating your issues long enough to look outside of my window and see the goldfinches bash into each other."

He said exactly what I thought he was going to say: "So?"

"When I guided your focus over to the birds, you paid attention. You calmed down. You were present only with the birds and their feeding. For about 20 seconds, your thoughts changed. No distractions, just you looking at those little yellow balls of feathers pigging out outside of my window.

"In the moment that I redirected your attention, you became present. You were with those birds. They were the only thing that mattered, the only thought in your head."

I looked back at this man, and he had calmed down a little. I saw it in his breathing and I noticed it in his expression. I said, "What you did just now? That's what 'being present' is all about. Just focusing on something outside of yourself, giving it a little bit of attention, and allowing yourself to feel the calm that the focus facilitates. When you begin to think outside of yourself, and notice for a moment just what's in front of you, you are present, focused only what you are seeing and experiencing. Keep noticing, and you'll find yourself becoming a little more calm, a little more relaxed."

He went on to describe his feelings and his issues, but came back to being present as a way to take the anxiety and strain from his emotional responses, becoming more at peace and, as a result, more effective in addressing all of the issues that brought him to my office. After a few sessions, he saw the world and, more importantly, himself and his environment very differently. His problems decreased. And his attitude toward his life improved. And just from knowing how to be present.

How It Works

Start by wrapping your head around this quote by Eckhart Tolle, "All you really need to do is accept this moment fully. You are then at ease in the here and now and at ease with yourself." Several people I know use this method, whether they are driving or on the phone or standing in line at the grocery store. When you follow their example, you are taking the first step toward living in your heart.

First, find a phrase that helps you move toward the present. Father Greg Boyle, head of Homeboy Industries, uses a mantra from a Broadway play to become present. His mantra is "Now. Here. This." As in, Be "Now," Be "Here," See "This." Find the words that suit you best and put them somewhere you can see them. I wear a bracelet on my wrist, with the words, "Exhale Gratitude" where I can always see it. You might decide to make your mantra your cell phone screensaver, tape it to your fridge, write it on your mirror, or something else.

Secondly, focus on everything else around you. Take an inventory of everything you see and hear. You could even say the things you see out loud. If you're driving, for instance, just notice the cars. Observe the billboards, maybe even read them. And make an observation like "interesting billboard," "nice car," or something along those lines. These statements just identify that you are giving your attention to the world around you, not to your worries or inner monologue. Do the same thing when you are in a store. "That lady has a lot of cabbage." "That guy parts his hair on the side." "They play a lot of music from the seventies overhead."

Now you've got the attentive part. The calm comes from doing. Your focus is outward. It's being observant. It isn't on you, your schedule, or anything that has to do with you. Just seeing, just paying attention, just noticing the things around you, pulls you away from your stress and puts you into the world; your focus is outward, not inward. This is where calm kicks in. When we think about everything we are engaged in–all the action, the lists, the endless stressors in our life– we stay tense. Putting our focus elsewhere, just noticing life outside of ourselves and truly focusing on the world around us, calms our tension.

Some parts of life–even the most mundane, like doing the dishes–can be rewarding when fully present and accepting. When we're truly present, we see the task, and only the task. We're not thinking "I hate these gross dirty dishes, I want to be sitting, watching TV, reading, sleeping, anything but this!" Instead, we feel the warm water, we see the piece of food being rubbed off by the sponge, rinse, examine, and repeat. By not attaching anything to the task, there is not resistance to it, there is only the task. This, inherently, is less urgent, and less agitated. Thus, every task becomes an opportunity for calm.

Your senses connect you to the present moment. To immediately access your present, do a quick inventory of your five senses:

Sight: What do you see around you? What can you notice?

Hearing: What can you hear? Become aware of all sounds around you.

Taste: Generally, unless you're eating, there's a rather neutral taste in your mouth. Probably didn't know that until just now, huh?

Smell: Air has a distinct smell to it. Move from room to room and the smell changes.

Touch: Feel your shirt against your arm. Just as you're sitting there, focus on that feeling.

Why this is Important

Remaining in the present keeps you in touch with reality. Being in touch with reality allows you to truly give and receive from the heart, unobstructed by limitations and conceptions of past and future. "Nowness is the sense that we are attuned to what is happening. The past is fiction and the future is a dream, and we are just living on the edge of a razor blade."[1]As real as the past seems, it is mind made and limited, influenced by perception and faded by time.

Positive or negative, appreciate the present because it is the only thing that is real. Right now. Any "memory of an event cannot pass for the event itself. Nor can the anticipation. There is something exceptional, unique, about the present event, which the previous, or the coming do not have. There is a livingness about it, an actuality; it stands out as if illumined. There is the 'stamp of reality' on the actual, which the past and future do not have."[2] Being in touch with reality allows you to truly give and receive from the heart, unobstructed by limitations and conceptions of past and future.

We have to be attentive to all of the good, all of the beauty, and all of the love around us. It is only possible when we are present, when we pay attention.

Being attentive is easy when the present is pleasing. But suffering is a part of life, and a lot of life is hard. Being present doesn't mean that you have to remain in a bad situation; "you have three options: remove yourself from the situation, change it, or accept it totally. If you want to take responsibility for your life, you must choose one of those three options, and you must choose now. Then accept the consequences. No excuses. No negativity. No psychic pollution. Keep your inner space clear."[3]

Learning to enjoy life in the present moment, the process of being alive is where "the real juice of life, whether it be sweet or bitter, is to be found, not nearly so much in the products of our efforts as in

---

[1] Trungpa, Chögyam, and Carolyn R. Gimian. Ocean of Dharma: The Everyday Wisdom of Chögyam Trungpa. Boston: Shambhala, 2008. Print. pg 151

[2] Nisargadatta, Frydman, M., & Dikshit, S. S. (2012). I am that: Talks with Sri Nisargadatta Maharaj. Durham, N.C: Acorn Press.

[3] Tolle, Eckhart. The Power of Now: A Guide to Spiritual Enlightenment. Novato, Calif: New World Library, 1999. Print. pg 90

the process of living itself, in how it feels to be alive."[4] All life occurs in the present moment; there is nothing more than right now.

[4] Leonard, George. Mastery: The Keys to Success and Long-Term Fulfillment. New York: Plume, 1992. Print.

KEY 2

KEY TWO: KNOW THYSELF

The big question, the one worthy of consulting the Oracle of Delphi, is this: Who am I?

As we grow, we find uniqueness within ourselves. Although we start to answer this question in our teens and twenties, as our values evolve and strengthen, our attachment to our identity, or the self, strengthens, too. We develop the ability to empathize. Our beliefs are challenged and deepened as we encounter new information, people, and circumstances. The pain of death, the joy of birth, and the struggles in life offer emotional perspective that further shape our identity. We strengthen a sense of what we feel is right and fair. We begin to hold fast to a view of who we are, and grow into a sense of comfort and predictability with our view of ourselves. We begin, often in our thirties, to truly feel comfortable in our own skin. We not only "know" who we are, we actually begin to like the person we see in the mirror.

A Story from the Heart

Ken is a fantastic psychotherapist and life coach. At 77, I've been humbled to sit at the feet of this masterful, kind, and compassionate man, learning a trick or two of his along the way. Ken has helped people "Get to the bottom of themselves," he says, for over fifty years.

"When someone sits down with me," he says "I generally ask them to tell me about themselves. And, invariably, almost every person asks the question, 'Well, what would you like to know?'

"This is a very reasonable response. And it's a hard question to answer. 'Please tell me about yourself' is often the first question in a job interview. I don't wish to make them uncomfortable or defensive. So when I ask this question of my clients, although it's my attempt at finding out who they are, I leave it open ended. I don't ask for specifics.

"What I find is people are, at first, very vague, but they initially tell me about their faults or areas of life where they don't feel they measure up. I sometimes chalk this up to their trying to be humble. But when they continue to be self-critical, I interrupt the process and ask them, 'Would you tell me three things about yourself you truly like, three things that stand out either in your character or in the things you're proud of?' I'm not doing this to get them to brag about themselves, rather to balance out descriptive scales of interpersonal assessment. If a person is going to tell me who they are, the good points are often harder to reach.

"Now," Ken continued, "if they're still unable to expand on their good points, I ask for some history, things like 'Who is your greatest influence, and especially, whom do you consider having been the most kind to you?'

"When I find out the answer to that last question, I ask them, 'How would that person, the one who has been so good to you, describe you to me? What would they say about you to me if they were sitting right here?'

"That always helps them see the best of who they are.

"But to get to this point," Ken said, "like I mentioned, at first I ask general things. I ask what brought them to my office, then expand into more personal things to get an autobiographical look into who they are, and who they think they are.

"I'll give you an example," said Ken. "One time, a guy came into my office and, after he told me why he was there, I asked him to tell me a little bit about himself. He said, 'Why do you want to know about me? Sooner or later you're to find out that I'm just a big nobody, and that whatever I tell you will evoke the same reaction as everybody else. I'm just a cog in the wheel of the universe. I'm a big nothing.'

"Well, I immediately understood why he came to see me, and I couldn't help but feel badly for this man. So I asked a second question, hoping I would elicit a better response. 'Can you tell me one person that you know that really loves you or appreciates you?'

'Yeah,' he said, 'my Mom.'

"I then asked him, 'Could you describe yourself as if your mother was describing you? I mean, on a day that you haven't gotten in trouble?' That brought a smile to his face. After apologizing profusely over the words he was about to say, making sure I knew that these were words his mother would say, not necessarily how he would describe himself, he embarked on a fifteen minute description about who he was, beginning in his childhood, bringing himself to the past year.

"At the end of this description, he stopped for at least a minute. He looked out my window, looked back at me and said, 'You know, I didn't realize I knew all that stuff about me. I mean, I think I'm better than I thought.' "

Ken looked at me and said, "To know yourself will translate into loving yourself. So, to learn to know yourself, refer to those who have known you with affection. Your opinion of yourself will improve."

<u>How it Works</u>

We'd like to say something like "OK, just make a list of all the things about yourself you like and all the things you don't like and then grade each one from one to ten, one being not much and ten being a lot. Then, you'll know who you are. Isn't that cool?" But if we said that, then you'd know we were a couple of morons and you would stop reading right about here.

Yet, that list is what we all gravitate to, even though we're sure that it's a finite and restrictive gauge. Knowing yourself is a contiguous and continuous process. It's difficult to put your finger on exactly who you are, because, at any given moment, your feelings can change your attitude or mood. Sometimes, you are just "beside yourself" with anger or frustration or feeling "outside of yourself" with worry. Does this mean you're not being yourself? Or maybe you are yourself, just not the person you're used to being? If that's the case, was that you who just got through running around the room with his hair on fire? Or, who is that person who picked up their car when their child was trapped underneath? That had to have been somebody else. Because I can tell you, up to that point, they didn't think they could pick up a car without a good jack and some directions.

To know thyself is often related to the way we express ourselves, and by identifying our feelings and how we articulate them. Upset, confused, bewildered, amused, angry . . . the list of feelings is endless. Each one can be expressed internally or externally, with different degrees of intensity, given our style of communication and the depth of these feelings. It's enough to make your head spin.

Begin the process of knowing who you are by finding out what means the most to you in life. Instead of making a list of things about yourself, identify your list of important values. And see how your identity branches out from those tenets. You'll begin to get a grasp on that ever elusive, ever changing you.

Why this is Important

Sun Tzu, in The Art of War, says, "If you know the enemy and know yourself you need not fear the results of a hundred battles."[5]

Identity makes a person unique, and it also reflects who that person is right now, not in the past or future. Having a clear perception of who you are as a person shapes your actions and decisions.

People remain consistent with their identity, even if it is limiting, because people's definition of themselves creates the boundaries within which they live their lives "Our beliefs about ourselves are among the strongest forces that shape our lives. We will always act consistently with our view of who we truly are - whether that view is accurate or not. In other words, the strongest force in human personality is the need to remain consistent with how we define ourselves." [6] Some identities are constraining and some are empowering. Osho urges us to "drop all comparison. Drop all these stupid ideas of being superior and inferior. You are neither superior nor inferior. You are simply yourself! There exists no one like you, no one with whom you can be compared. Then, suddenly, you are at home."[7] It is important to see the false limits your identity places on you. Then you can remove those limits to affirm a more empowering identity.

Luckily, "Our personal identities are in a constant state of evolution. We all contain the power to reinvent ourselves and create a new, empowered identity that expands what is possible in our lives. The key is to take conscious control of the beliefs we are creating about ourselves, so they can propel us toward what we desire most." [8] Understand that your identity and you as a person, will

---

[5] Tzu, Sun. Sun Tzu: The Art of War. S.l.: Pax Librorum Pub. H, 2009. Print.

[6] Robbins, Tony. RPM

[7] Osho, The Book of Understanding: Creating Your Own Path to Freedom. New York: Harmony Books, 2006. Print. pg 85

[8] Robbins, Tony

continue to grow, to evolve, to become better. Accepting this change must be part of your identity, too.

In your gut, who are you? How do you define yourself? Are you a leader or follower? Are you a person who makes a difference or a victim? A person who looks to grow or a person who looks for an excuse? Are you your past, or who you are now? Are you a collection of your past patterns or something deeper? What are you capable of?

Much of your identity will come from your life's purpose. What are you here on earth to do? How do you find out about your life purpose?

Act as the person you want to be. Do not lock yourself into the finite self who lives by your old rules and boundaries. Establish a clear positive, empowering definition of who you are. You are not your past; you are who you decide to be NOW. You are Spirit, never ending, not your finite beliefs about yourself. You have the capacity and wisdom to do anything you decide in life. Be open to redefining yourself. The way you define yourself affects everything you do, so define yourself without limits.

Choose to be the best you possibly can. "Go to your Highest Thought about yourself. Imagine the *you* you would be if you lived that thought every day. Imagine what you would think, do and say, and how you would respond to what others do and say . . . Change your thoughts, words, and actions to match your grandest vision. It will involve choice-making- consciously . . . When you have a thought that is not in alignment with your higher vision, change to a new thought"[9]

What is your highest vision of yourself?

Who do you want to be?

[9] Walsch, Neale D. Conversations with God: An Uncommon Dialogue. New York: G.P. Putnam's Sons, 1996. Print. pg 177

Choose now, to see yourself as all of these things all the time. Make an effort to be this person. This is who you are, on the inside, and whom you can truly be.

KEY 3

KEY THREE: SELF-ACCPTANCE

We throw the word Acceptance around a little bit in this book. But first, we want to start at the fundamental and most important level of acceptance: yourself.

And a small disclaimer: We understand that we are organisms striving and awakening. We get that we are thinking and acting and hoping that we become and evolve into a good person. We are learning more, achieving more, and unfolding into a higher version of the person we were yesterday.

But without knowing that who we are–right now and in this very moment–includes all of the good and grace and kindness that we have learned up to this point, we aren't going to be all we want to be tomorrow.

The bottom line is this: if we don't accept ourselves today, we won't understand the point of achieving our goals and sustaining that vision of who we want to be tomorrow.

Self-acceptance is critical for understanding the essential goodness of our being. Our hopes and vision of a future need self-acceptance as a jumping off point.

A Story from the Heart

Years ago, Dr. Leo Buscaglia wrote the book Love. It's an absolutely beautiful book, based on the stories and experiences from a course he taught at the University of Southern California. He called the class "Love, 101."

He often told the story of a group of students discussing that week's assignments. During a discussion about self-acceptance, a young woman had shouted out the word, "Insight!" It was Dr. Buscaglia's rule that if a student came upon an awareness or a new perspective about an issue, they had permission to scream out that word and share with the class what they had just learned. Hearing this, the rest of the students paused and waited quietly for her to speak.

"I'm not a banana," the woman said. The rest of the group, startled, broke into soft giggles. When they saw her begin to giggle too, they all burst out into laughter.

"What I mean by that is, for a long time, I've tried to be a banana. I've tried to do everything I could to make myself into something I'm not. To carry this metaphor forward a little further," the young woman said, "I'm more of a plum.

"What I'm saying, I guess, is that I've tried to be what other people have wanted me to be for a long time. Instead of accepting the fact that I'm small and round and purple, I've tried to stretch myself, reach outside of myself, and even try to paint myself a variety of different colors."

Not a sound was heard among her classmates. A few had tears in their eyes. "I know," she continued, "that this may not be the most graceful metaphor, but I can't be tall, tanned and sleek. No matter how I try, no matter how I change my outside appearance or my inside substance, I will always be a second-rate banana.

"I'm a plum. And if I can truly accept myself, I'm going to be the best plum I can be. I know I can do that well. And I hope that I find people in my life that really appreciate plums. Because I just can't be a banana anymore and stay on the path of genuinely loving who I am. I'm going to be a plum all my life. I may as well start appreciating and accepting myself now. Better to be a happy plum than an unsatisfied banana."

The class laughed and applauded. And they all knew exactly what she was talking about. "Self-acceptance," she said, "begins in knowing who you are and continues when you try to be just that, not striving to please or to be what you can't."

"I am what I am," she said, "And, right now, that's really good enough for me."

How it Works

If you really want to enjoy your life tomorrow, love yourself today.

And self-acceptance isn't giving yourself a pass on the things you did today. It's just acknowledging that you're still OK and, for the most part, you did your best. In spite of all your fears to the contrary, you're good, you have meaning, and you belong here. It is a basic tenet of humanity. If you exist, you matter. So, accept yourself as being a part of this existence.

And you're not alone in this struggle. We are all climbing Jacob's Ladder. We are all "Bozos on this Bus." We are making our best effort. And we screw up. We fall short. We feel badly. That critical voice inside of our head seems to be equipped with a really big bullhorn, the one police use from a helicopter.

Self-acceptance means we keep our perceived weaknesses in perspective. We all are who we are. The things that we criticize ourselves about are the same thing that everybody else does, too.

Whenever I become self-critical, a dear friend of mine says, "Don't say that about my friend." She reminds me to be kind to myself, as kind as we would be if we were talking to our friend. It's such a beautiful gesture.

A person who knows you and loves you would describe you positively. Now all you have to do is be that person for yourself. This is what self-acceptance is about

In the past, when we discussed self-acceptance at seminars, we've been asked about the line between conceit, arrogance, and acceptance–that's a fair question. Conceit and arrogance reside in in the ego, where we rationalize and we make excuses. Self-acceptance takes account of all of our personality flaws, as well as all of those things that are loved by others and that we learn to love about ourselves. Self-acceptance doesn't ignore or embellish any part of who we are. We see it all, and we understand and embrace every single thing.

And we know we need to do better. That's part of it. You won't find that in conceit. Self-acceptance recognizes the good and the bad, and loves all of it, placing emphasis on tomorrow's journey to correct some of the flaws and enhance some of the goodness.

Self-acceptance means to see yourself, all of yourself, and know you're really good today. Know you will be better tomorrow. And the more you accept yourself today, the better tomorrow will be.

Why this is Important

Self-acceptance is the ability to embrace all aspects of yourself. Nobody's perfect; we all can change for the better. We all have weaknesses, problems, and have made big and small mistakes. To accept yourself is to accept the parts of yourself that are less than perfected because "happiness and self-acceptance go hand in hand. In fact, your level of self-acceptance determines your level of happiness. The more self-acceptance you have, the more happiness you'll allow yourself to accept, receive and enjoy. In other words, you enjoy as much happiness as you believe you're worthy of."[10] You are worthy of complete happiness.

Many people are much more tolerant of other people's faults and weaknesses, but are very hard on themselves. Do not allow an adversarial relationship with yourself; be on your own team. Release your inner critic. The more you judge yourself, the more it becomes a habit. Talking to yourself in a negative, judgmental way perpetuates negative thinking, and negative thought processes cut you off from all the world's possibilities. Forgive yourself.

To accept yourself is to love yourself. Your ability to love others is determined by your ability to first accept and love yourself. Leo Buscaglia says, "To the extent to which you know yourself, and we are all more alike than different, you can know others. When you love yourself, you will love others. And to the depth and extent to which you can love yourself, only to that depth and extent will you be able to love others."[11] Accept your authentic self. Many people put on a show or change themselves to fit what they think will gain them social acceptance. Lower your guard; realize this is you not accepting yourself.

Do not mistake self-acceptance with lowering your standards. With determination and discipline, we must commit to being our best selves. Do not accept anything less than your potential.

Self-acceptance can also be accepting your strengths and individual talents, and nurturing both. "We can run not only from our dark side but also from our bright side—from anything that threatens to make us stand out or stand alone, or that calls for the awakening of the hero within us, or that asks that we break through to a higher level of consciousness and reach a higher ground of integrity. The greatest crime we commit against ourselves is not that we may deny or disown

---

[10] Holden, Robert. Happiness Now!: Timeless Wisdom for Feeling Good Fast. Carlsbad, Calif: Hay House, Inc, 2007. Print. pg 92

[11] Buscaglia, Leo F. Love. Thorofare, N.J: Charles B. Slack, 1972. Print. pg 101

our shortcomings but that we deny and disown our greatness—because it frightens us. If a fully realized self-acceptance does not evade the worst within us, neither does it evade the best."[12] It is a scary proposition for many people to try their best because there is no excuse if they fail. Practice self-acceptance when pushing yourself. No great person started out an expert in their field.

[12] Branden, Nathaniel. The Six Pillars of Self-Esteem. New York, N.Y: Bantam, 1994. Print. pg 103

KEY 4

KEY FOUR: MAINTAIN INTEGRITY

When our behaviors consistently match our ideas of what is moral and right, we are acting with integrity. Our level of integrity validates our identity and strengthens our interactions with one another.

Integrity is often associated with a moral code, a belief system, or a format of operations. It is found in the laws of religion, government, and military, but can also be a personal code. We are taught about integrity from the time we're a child, and these limits are set forth to establish a sense of safety and carve out roles within a family. Integrity is an integration of our code; a balanced continuity of being our best.

These rules dictate our personal code of behavior. In following this foundation, we begin to create what is important and meaningful in our lives, families, and relationships. We particularly take account of what we see as good and bad to create a personal code of ethics.

We think and behave in a manner that is consistent with our belief system, along with tenets of faith and societal norms that support our behavior. Although we live in a world of billions and billions of people, our feelings of what is important begin with ourselves and extend to our families and friends.

Integrity is following and adhering to this ethos.

A Story from the Heart

A friend of ours is a personal trainer, and she's rather exclusive. She is exceedingly popular. She only takes one person at a time for 90 days. She's very expensive and she also spends about four hours a day, when possible, with her client. Hundreds of people want to study with her and will spend thousands to do it.

So, to find the best person to work with, our friend the trainer has developed a unique selection process.

At the beginning of the 90 day training period, she goes through about 300 applications, then narrows the field down to 25 to 50 people and interviews all of them. From these interviews, she arrives at ten candidates.

She determines who she wants to train using series of challenges.

"It's simple," she says, "I take the person with the most integrity. It doesn't matter how young or old, how fit or out of shape the person is. I just want the one that demonstrates the most integrity."

We asked her how she determined who had the most integrity.

She said, "I put all 10 of these people in the room. Think a room the size of your living room, maybe a little bigger, like a yoga studio. In this room are a series of challenges marked in bold letters on ten different exercises, each with their own apparatus.

"I tell each person that they are to complete the exercise, but I tell them that they are difficult and some require a great deal of time. Some exercises are quick, some are more deliberate, and some may be nearly impossible for just about anyone to complete, including me. I ask that each person sign a paper saying they give their word that they will complete each exercise."

I piped up and said, "Wait a second. You said that some of the exercises are so tough, even you have difficulty completing them. Isn't this setting these people up to fail?"

"No," she said, with a little bit of firmness in her voice, "this is a test of who will keep their word. Integrity is one thing, and one thing only: You do what you say you're going to do. And," she paused, "it's doing it when nobody is looking. It's doing it when you're on your own, when you know you could quit, but your word and your promise to push on is stronger than your pain.

"When I find the one who lasts throughout all these exercises," she says, "that's the one I train.

"Oh, and I should mention," she said, with a sly little smile creasing her lips, "that I have cameras in the studio. I have them hidden everywhere in the room. I watch them go through this process. And I continue watching them until the last one remains."

Two days later, she called me. "Hey, I want you to meet somebody." She had selected her new student.

She introduced us to John. He was a middle aged guy, about my age, and he reached out to shake my hand. When I grabbed his hand, I noticed that two fingers were missing, and that burn marks covered his skin.

"Come on into my office." We sat down, and with John sitting to my right, she brought down a movie screen. She took a remote control from her desk and, turning to John, she said, "John knows I videotaped this, and he gave me permission to share this with you."

In the video, she skipped around some, and pointed out places on the videotape where people had given up. Some had left. Some were yelling and cursing the equipment. "But not John," she said, "Here, look at this."

She showed us John trying to lift barbells, do pushups and even climb a rope with his right hand. "That last one?" The card said, "Climb this rope only with your legs and your right hand. And you see John here? Not only is he trying to climb, he was the last one at the rope. He never gave up. He even tried to help the other people with the exercise."

"That's integrity, gentlemen. John kept his word. And he helped others as well. Integrity and heart. How could I say no?"

As we got up to leave, our friend said, "Integrity is just doing what you say you're going to do. No matter what, no matter where you are, no matter the impediments. You commit and follow through. Integrity, my friends, is as simple as that."

How it Works

Once you say something and commit to your intention, your integrity is sustained by dedication, concentration, and follow through. In short, Integrity is doing what you say you're going to do. It is a must.

The operative words of that last sentence are "say" and "do."

Our words and behaviors are dictated by a belief system. Integrity is following this system with our words and our actions. When we move away from this standard, and act outside of this interpersonal system of beliefs and protocol, we are operating outside of, or without integrity.

Integrity is a complex and important word, but when you break it down, it means knowing what you should do, saying what you'll do, then doing it.

Why this is Important

Life flows between the two banks of polar opposites: positive or negative, success or failure, good or bad, happy or sad. Life's circumstances are always in constant flux. The one thing that remains consistent through change is the strength of one's character, or integrity. Integrity is living life within your values and life purpose. In his book The Six Pillars of Self-Esteem, Nathaniel Branden says "Integrity is the integration of ideals, convictions, standards, beliefs— and behavior. When our behavior is congruent with our professed values, when ideals and practice match up, we have integrity. Observe that before the issue of integrity can even be raised we need principles of behavior—moral convictions about what is and is not appropriate— wisdom about right and wrong action. If we do not yet hold standards, we are on too low a developmental rung even to be accused of hypocrisy. In such a case, our problems are too severe to be described merely as lack of integrity."[13] The Latin root of the word integrity is the adjective "integer," meaning whole or complete. Integrity is acting one way, with consistency of character, even when nobody's looking and no one will find out.

Emerson, in his essay "Self Reliance," says "Nothing is at last sacred but the integrity of your own mind. Absolve you to yourself, and you shall have the suffrage of the world."[14] The essential theme in much of Emerson's writing is thinking for oneself; not merely taking the word or tradition of others. Integrity is being fully committed to your values. This attitude offers liberation from the confines of culturally, socially, or religiously imposed values. However, as Ayn Rand says, "Integrity is the ability to stand by an idea. (Integrity) presupposes the ability to think. Thinking is something one doesn't borrow or pawn." [15] This does not mean completely dismissing traditional value systems; a person with integrity must assess all value systems with an open mind and fully commit to their chosen set of values. A person with integrity embodies these values with their life.

Being a person of integrity means choosing actions based on values instead of selfish desires or personal gain. A person living with integrity, despite the outcome of the situation, knows they have done the right thing. Negative emotions like regret, shame, and

---

13 Branden, Nathaniel. The Six Pillars of Self-Esteem. New York, N.Y: Bantam, 1994. Print.

14 Emerson, Ralph W. Self-reliance. Seattle, WA: Domino Project/Amazon.com, 2011. Print.

15 Rand, Ayn. The Fountainhead. New York: Plume, 2005. Print.

embarrassment do not cripple a person living with integrity because they know, in the face of any outcome, that they have lived their values.

KEY 5

KEY FIVE: DEVELOP UNDERSTANDING

Understanding is the cognitive form of acceptance. When we accept, we see and recognize the good in another person from our heart. Understanding is recognizing this good from our mind.

We start on the path of understanding through our logic; we stay on that path through our emotions. Logic leads us toward reasoning. Acceptance pulls us toward the heart of the matter. Understanding is triggered by a deeper, intuitive wisdom that gives us knowing beyond just outer facts and thinking.

Understanding does not always result in acceptance. In fact, it can be separated from it completely. We have heard people say that, although they understand why someone engages in an activity or adheres to a belief system, it is emotionally difficult to accept.

Yet, we see an overlap. Understanding begins to open us to acceptance. We can recognize something for its logical merit but not truly feel an emotional closeness to the concept or the person holding the belief. Understanding makes ethereal concepts more concrete. It takes things that are somewhat vague and makes them tangible.

The more we try to understand, the better chance we have of developing relationships. Friendships start with understanding. Acceptance blossoms. And love grows.

A Story from the Heart

About a quarter-mile from my office is a trailer park. Most of the residents are over 55.

Every morning of every day, an older man with a wild shock of white hair, dressed in a white shirt and black pants, would walk up and down the sidewalk, waving at the oncoming traffic.

I tried to reach for some reasonable conclusions. Maybe he got up early. Maybe he was lonely and was trying to make a friend. Or maybe it was a tradition that was carried from another part of his life. Or maybe he was just a little eccentric.

In any case, I never quite understood what he got out of this. I didn't see how it benefited him. He would be out on the street in all manner of weather. I saw him walk in a blistering rainstorm and in the blazing sun. No matter the condition, he showed up every day.

So one morning I got up the nerve to walk down from my office and introduce myself. I told him that I'd seen him everyday. Looking out of my window and watching him wave, I was curious as to why he continued this practice, day in and day out.

"I always see you smiling," I said, "and you never miss a day. "Breaking out in his customary grin, the man said, "Oh, and I never would. I think I would be missed."

I was puzzled for a second, and I thought he was talking about me. Awkwardly, I responded, "Oh, well, yes, I would absolutely miss you."

His smile never wavered, but his voice softened a little and said, "Well, thank you, but I was referring to them."

When I turned around, I saw the traffic coming toward us. From the vantage point in my window, I could only see my white haired friend facing me, waving at the cars.

But when I saw the cars from his perspective, all I saw was a sea of smiles. Behind every steering wheel, in every driver's seat, every person in their car was smiling and waving back at him.

"I offer a smile to all those starting their day," said my friend. "I know how hard it was for me, driving the long slog to work every morning. So, I figured, I'd try to brighten up a few people's days, bring a smile or two to their faces. It makes them feel better, and it gets me out for my morning walk. So I decided to combine the two."

He looked at me and said, "I'm glad to meet you. Thank you for wanting to know and understand why I do what I do. To some, I suppose, it would appear that a doddering old fool is just randomly waving at strangers. But, to me," he said, pointing at the cars, "I put smiles on their faces. It matters to them. And it sure means something to me."

"Thanks again for taking the time." I shook my friend's hand and watched him further his morning activity, hand outstretched, the smiling man moving along his appointed course.

How it Works

Think back to a time that you said to yourself, "I just don't get it!" Here's what happened:

First, you tried to understand something. An incident, a person, or an event. And something didn't quite gel. You weren't confident in your observations or your conclusions.

Your task is to find a way to look at this fact or opinion a little differently. Not necessarily from your own experience, but possibly from the thoughts and history of another. Empathy, a byproduct of understanding, opens our intuition. You can ask somebody about their perspective, maybe get a feeling for their history and the perspectives that helped them arrive at their conclusion. This allows you to place yourself in someone else's mindset and ask "What do they think and feel about this?" Both help open your preexisting pool of logic to other possibilities. You can begin to draw from a different place in your head.

Mind you, this is a gathering of data. It's an effort to learn more about the person or circumstance. It bypasses your initial gut feeling or instinct in order to–and here's the key word–help you learn about what's being presented. In other words, to understand you must investigate before forming an opinion.

Secondly, go at understanding deliberately. Try to respond instead of reacting. The road to understanding begins in our ability to pause before acting. Developing understanding is cumulative; each piece must be looked at in the context of the others.

Lastly, ask questions that get to the meaning or the feeling behind the data. Asking "Could you tell me what you mean by that?" generally means you're open to more information, the emotional significance, and especially the perspective that supports their view or feelings. Be sure to phrase it with enough gentleness that the person answering the question is willing to respond with compassionate awareness.

Why this is Important

To act with understanding, you must understand yourself, understand others, and understand the world. To understand, your perspective should be "having no particular, fixed view, which means seeing that all views are limited, that no particular view is the only view. They're all restricted, they're all limited, they're all fragmented. Actually, the right view is no view."[16] Understanding this, you become less attached to your own limited point of view, and approach the world with an open mind. Einstein says, "The mind that opens to a new idea never returns to its original size."[17] Rigid thinking and narrow-mindedness create illusions which are barriers to insight and true understanding. Lack of understanding, or wrong views, is the cause of

[16] Merzel, Dennis G. Big Mind, Big Heart: Finding Your Way. Salt Lake City, Utah: Big Mind Pub, 2007. Print.

[17] Einstein, Albert

suffering. Jesuit priest and psychotherapist Anthony De Mello says, "Suffering occurs when you clash with reality. When your illusions clash with reality, when your falsehoods clash with truth, then you have suffering. Otherwise there is no suffering."[18] Understand that wrong beliefs cause suffering; keeping an open mind, instead of maintaining a fixed perspective, allows a person to understand the nature of reality.

Living with understanding is living and practicing knowledge. "You see, knowing the words is not the same thing as living the meaning. Suppose I memorize the printed instructions on a first-aid kit. Does that mean I can give first aid? No. The full meaning comes when I admit I know nothing and then try, practice, succeed." True understanding starts from knowing that any one perspective is limited but, through practice and experience, insight is gained. Insight is to see inside, into the inner core of what is and respond as fully as possible.

---

[18] De, Mello A, and J F. Stroud. Awareness. Collins Fount, 1990. Print. pg 74

KEY 6

KEY SIX: SOLITUDE

Unlike the other behaviors, attitudes, and perspectives we ask you to adopt to connect with other people, Solitude is very different. It is a stepping back. It is a withdrawal from stimulus and activity. Solitude is the sanctuary for the heart.

Solitude is an opportunity for us to be alone with ourselves, but solitude is not an opportunity to analyze our thinking. Rather, it is a pause or respite from our engagements, our activities, and other people, quieting the mind so that ripples settle into a window for the soul to shine through.

Solitude is a chance for us to regenerate our spirit. This is an important distinction. Solitude can offer time for study, but it is more often a time of reflection and self-examination. Solitude is a path through quiet and peace. Within that peace, we reclaim our spirit and our life's energy.

Solitude allows us to slow ourselves. It does not demand that we engage in any task or pastime. Although we may be alone, solitude requires us to withdraw from the pace that ordinarily dictates our lives. It is a break in the action. We step away from our routine and regain balance and calm. Therefore, within the state of solitude, we keep distractions and demands to a minimum. There are no schedules or appointments in a state of solitude. There are no obligations or deadlines.

<u>A Story from the Heart</u>

A friend of mine is a famous television personality in the area. He has been on the air for over 30 years.

We have often found ourselves together in small gatherings and large functions. Whether he is the center of attention or just one of many gathered, he generally does one thing consistently anytime he's with a group of people.

He leaves.

My friend will get up in the middle of whatever is happening, and just leave. I have seen him walk around the block and stand out on a balcony. I've even seen him go to the bathroom and lock himself in the stall.

He's not rude about it. His timing is really good. When there's a lull in the activity, that's when he makes his exit. Many people don't know he's gone until five minutes before he returns. He's got this down to a science.

One day, he and I were driving to an event and I couldn't help myself. Because we did so many things together over the years, I finally had to ask about these temporary escapes he performs in the middle of these gatherings.

As we're pulling up to the front door, I asked him, "I don't want put you on the spot, but I noticed that you always take about 10 minutes in the middle of any of these things to disappear. I was just curious about that. Are you uncomfortable? Do you get anxious when you're with a lot of people?" I was really going out on a limb here, but he been my friend for a long time, so I didn't think that he minded me asking such a direct question.

Instead of getting uncomfortable, he started to laugh. "No, it's not like I have a disorder or something." Shaking his head, he said, "I try not to make it so noticeable, but since you asked, I leave because I just need a few minutes of solitude.

"I like being around people. But sometimes I find myself listening to about 12 different things at a time. When these events are in the evening, it's particularly distracting to me."

"So, I take a few minutes. I disengage in order to re-engage more deeply. It's kind of a meditation, and it helps if I'm alone. It doesn't matter really where I am. I can disengage while I'm riding the bus or walking through the shopping mall. But when there is something expected of me, when I am either the center of attention or among several people, I'll take that solitude for just a few moments to reset myself.

"And, like I said before, it's not that I'm anxious or disturbed. I just know that when I get a few minutes to myself to draw my energy inward, my spirit is regenerated. And I can be my best self again."

So we went into the event, found our places, and became one with the activity. After about an hour or so, I looked around and he was nowhere to be seen. As I turned to my left, the woman who organized the event reached out her hand and introduced herself.

Just as I was about to apologize for my friends momentary absence, she looks to my right, extends her hand, and there he is. The two of them shake hands, and she goes about her business.

Just then, I hear this whisper in my year, "That was 10 minutes, and you didn't even know I was gone, did you?" We both started laughing out loud. My friend left my side and reengaged the crowd.

How it Works

To kick start this process, engage with nature as much as possible when embracing solitude. If you are in a city, open a window. If you are close to a park, walk through it. If you are able to drive to a field, a lake, a river, or anywhere with trees, spend time there. There is nothing quite like engaging in the outside world to support a sense of peace. Within solitude, recognizing our natural surroundings facilitates balance. Nature gives us contrast to everything that creates frenetic pace of our lives.

Anything natural can symbolize and anchor our feeling of solitude. A window box full of flowers, a breeze through the curtains, even the wind outside your front door assists this focus. Although we cannot completely eliminate the sounds of life, nature can help turn the volume down. If we are fortunate enough to have some natural life and beauty nearby, practice your moments of solitude there.

If you are unable to find solace in nature or to reach the natural world, find a quiet place. It can be in your home or it can be in your heart as you walk around the block. If you can find just some little bit of quiet, rest there. Let go temporarily of all expectations of work, of your demands, and all that may be required of you. Think only of your immediate environment. Observe all that is around you. If you like, close your eyes. Solitude need not take a long time. It just gives you a chance to be on your own terms, with yourself and your feelings. Let solitude draw you toward that inner light and rekindle that glow of your spirit. Ease down into solitude, and recognize it as a chance to be away, not to solve any problems or evaluate pressing conditions. Think only of that which keeps you at peace. Turn your thoughts toward appreciating the way your body is relaxing and your mind is quieting down. A few minutes can make all the difference between tension and calm.

Schedule this as you can, but it's more important to know what and how to engage a state of solitude when you need it. If you have to ask for a moment of solitude, let those around you know how important it is to your well-being. "I need to take a pause, a little bit" is a perfectly acceptable way to ask for solitude. If you have family, let them know that you need, on occasion, these times of regeneration. Solitude is not meant to be a permanent state, but rather a break from life's rigors and a chance to disengage in order to re-engage more deeply later. Use this time judiciously; you will see lasting effects supporting happiness in your relationships and in your attitude.

Why this is Important

Humans, being social creatures, learn from others and are able to pass on knowledge from person to person, generation to generation. However, our modern society bombards us with external influences, conditioning us to live according a mesh of digital information, Hollywood plotlines, and advertising. Ralph Waldo Emerson, in his essay "Self Reliance," says "It is easy in the world to live after the world's opinion; it is easy in solitude to live after our own; but the great man is he who in the midst of the crowd keeps with perfect sweetness the independence of solitude."[19] It is essential, now more than ever, to make time to connect with your inner self.

Being alone helps you access inner strength, but it may be challenging at first. The ability to be alone means you are sufficiently happy in yourself, that you accept yourself. People who are not comfortable with themselves maintain a constant stream of external distractions to avoid themselves, their thoughts, and their emotions. You do not need to "seek for seclusion in the wilderness, by the seashore, or in the mountains–a dream you have cherished too fondly yourself. But such fancies are wholly unworthy of a philosopher, since at any moment you choose you can retire within yourself. Nowhere can man find a quieter or more untroubled retreat than in his own soul; above all, he possesses resources in himself, which he need only contemplate to secure immediate ease of mind–the ease that is but another word for a well-ordered spirit. Avail yourself often, then, of this retirement and so continually renew yourself." [20] Look inside yourself and listen to the inner wisdom.

---

[19] Emerson, Ralph W, and Brooks Atkinson. The Essential Writings of Ralph Waldo Emerson. New York: Modern Library, 2000. Print.

[20] Marcus, Aurelius, Charles R. Haines, and Aurelius Marcus. Marcus Aurelius. Cambridge, Mass: Harvard University Press, 2003. Print.

Painful memories, regrets, and other negative emotions will come up. Just sit. Let them pass! Watch them go by! Bless them on their way. This process of solitude allows the psyche to heal. "Spend time every day in solitude, with no distractions. Just sit, for ten minutes. No fidgeting, no channel surfing, no magazine thumbing. Just be, exactly as you are, not trying to change anything. Stay with your suffering, until you fall through it and intuit the groundless source of your life."[21] This independence of thought keeps you true to yourself. Solitude, although challenging, allows the individual to connect with the source of their self.

[21] Deida, David. The Way of the Superior Man: A Spiritual Guide to Mastering the Challenges of Women, Work, and Sexual Desire. Boulder, CO: Sounds True, 2004. Print.

KEY 7

KEY SEVEN: MEDITATE

Yeah, well, we figured you saw this one coming.

Look, you just have to. It's not that hard. Yes, it takes time and practice, but if you don't add this to your life, much of what we've said up to this point will have less impact and even less meaning.

And, we know: Meditation always meets resistance.

In a rather unscientific survey, we asked about 100 people "Why don't you meditate?" They generally answered one of two ways: "Because I can't stay with it long enough for it to make a difference" or "Because I get too distracted." The occasional outliers were along the lines of "It's going to make me too mellow" or "It's going to change my personality." One guy said, "I need my edge. I have to stay sharp. I have to stay aggressive."

Meditation, to this man's credit, probably won't make you aggressive. But it will make you sharper, more attentive, more observant, and far less likely to be reactive, impulsive, and angry. You'll learn things more easily. You will be less anxious and afraid. You will find that you can handle things with more ease. You will be more thoughtful and alert. You will look at life with a lighter, easier perspective. Studies have even shown meditation has the ability to prevent dementia and, believe it or not, slow the aging process.

And the most important thing as far as this book is concerned: It furthers and deepens your sense of understanding and compassion.

If you can do only one thing to calm your center and continually access the fullness of your heart, meditation is it.

Guatama Buddha, our greatest authority on meditation, says during mediation "the mind is deliberately kept at the level of bare attention, a detached observation of what is happening within us and around us in the present moment. In the practice of right mindfulness the mind is trained to remain in the present, open, quiet, and alert, contemplating the present event. All judgments and interpretations have to be suspended, or if they occur, just registered and dropped. The task is simply to note whatever comes up just as it is occurring, riding the changes of events in the way a surfer rides the waves on the sea. The whole process is a way of coming back into the present, of standing in the here and now without slipping away, without getting swept away by the tides of distracting thoughts."

Surya Das further says "Breath by breath, moment by moment, we sit motionless, training ourselves not to fixate on transitory distractions such as bodily discomfort, emotional turmoil, and our virtually ceaseless mind chatter. Eventually we work free on these entanglements that cause so much anxiety and suffering in our day-to-day lives and begin to cause to experience stretches of pure awareness. To our amazement, refreshment, relief, and even enlightenment, we stay focused clearly and totally on the present, unencumbered by past baggage or fantasies of the future–just totally, unequivocally, wholeheartedly here and now. How delightful."

A Story from the Heart

When I first learned to meditate, I went to a real authority. The guy who ran the class had been taught directly by the internationally-famous spiritual leader Thich Nhat Hanh. The classes were expensive and had a huge waiting list.

They were terrible.

I then heard about a woman named Clara who had taught a colleague of mine, and I called her to find out if she'd teach me.

"Yeah, sure. But I only teach in the morning. I'm an old lady, you know."

I met Clara at her door, but I didn't know if the woman at the door was actually her. She didn't look old at all. "Are you Clara?" She looked at me and said, "I'm the only one living here, honey."

Clara said she had been teaching meditation for twenty-five years. "And I'm 80, so you can do the math on when I started."

I asked her what got her interested in meditating at this late point in her life. "I started when I was in prison."

I laughed because I thought she was kidding. "I'm serious. I started meditation when I was in prison. My cellmate taught me how to do it."

"You're serious?" I said.

"Yes, absolutely so. In fact, it saved my life. But if you want me to tell you, it's going to take a while. Want some tea?" Clara poured me a little tea, poured herself some, sat down and said, "I had gotten in an accident. I drank pretty heavily then. Not every day, but a lot on the weekends.

"I remember it was St. Patrick's Day, and I started drinking in the morning. I took a nap, went to a party, got pretty drunk, then got into my car. That was my first mistake. I got lost, I called a friend, I didn't know where I was. The next thing I know, I'm being handcuffed and put into the back of a car. And I passed out. When I woke up, I was in a jail cell. I asked what I was being charged with, and the officer said, "Assault with a deadly weapon. And if the woman doesn't make it out of the hospital, you'll be charged with murder.

"Now, I'm not going to bore you with the details of my incarceration, trial, and sentencing. Suffice it to say, the woman lived but she was in occupational and physical therapy for quite some time.

And I was put in jail for a seven year sentence. I served three and a half years.

"But the first few weeks, I was a wreck. I was put in a cell, I had a cellmate, and all I remember doing was crying. I cried my eyes out for weeks at a time. I couldn't eat, I didn't sleep, I just had this awful, heavy depression hanging over me. And it never seemed to lift.

"Well, one day, my cellmate Sheila, who was a very large but quiet woman, turned to me and said, 'Lady, I'm going to tell you what. You've been crying for weeks now, and I've been very patient. But, honey, right now I'm about on my last nerve.' "Clara sipped a little more of her tea. "Now, I should mention, that my cellmate was in jail for her second time, both for the same charge: Assault with a deadly weapon. She was serving a ten year sentence. Oh, and I should mention this, too: she was about six feet tall and she weighed about 200 pounds. So when she spoke, I paid attention.

"Now, Sheila didn't say this like she was upset. I wasn't afraid she was going to hurt me. No, Sheila was very kind but firm. She said, 'Lady, I'm going to teach you to meditate.'

"When she said that, something came over me. Something really peaceful. It's hard to explain. But I knew something important was about to change in my life."

Clara smiled and said, "Sheila sat me down and helped me concentrate on my breathing. Then we would sit together, just ten minutes at a time, and meditate. She gave me tips on focusing, sitting, and just being. Sheila said that she learned in prison after her second arrest. In her first year, Sheila told me that she could handle her anger better than she'd ever been able to before. She said she forgave the people that had hurt her in her past, forgave the men that hurt her, too. Sheila said it even helped her lose weight." Clara began to giggle and said, "That woman must have been really large before I showed up.

"In time, I could do this on my own, and I felt a sense of peace. I'm not going to sugarcoat the process, though. Meditating in prison is a little like meditating on a street corner at rush hour. The noise can be a bit much. But that was good training for me. I was able to shut out the noise, and really increase my focus.

"When I got out of prison, I started teaching ex-cons meditation. I'd get referrals from probation officers. Then, when the probation officers saw what a change took place in their cases, some of the probation officers wanted me to teach them. Before I knew it, I was teaching classes in the courthouse to a bunch of these folks.

"You have to do it, though," said Clara. "Think of it like playing an instrument. You don't have to be perfect, but you have to practice a little every day. But when you do," Clara said, clearing away the tea cups, "you'll see yourself and the world differently. Before I started meditating, I was a woman with a record who couldn't stop crying in a prison cell. Now, I'm living a peaceful life."

Clara moved into her living room, lit a candle and waved at me to follow. "Come on now, honey. Let's get started on changing your life."

How it Works

Jack Kornfield, a brilliant psychologist who has written extensively on meditation, says that learning how to meditate is "like teaching a puppy how to sit." That's about the size of it. You sit, you concentrate on your breathing, and then you go off into thoughts of your financial situation, whether or not you locked your car or wondering why your butt itches. Then you go back to your breathing and start over again. In the beginning, that's how it is. Your mind is trained to think about a hundred things at once, and to pretty much be on its alert setting nearly all day long.

Meditation, at first, slows the mind from 80 to about 55 mph. You still can go fast, but you see more along the way. As you continue your practice, Meditation can keep your thinking deliberate, your reactions measured, and your emotions balanced. In short, meditation is the best way we know to keep a sense of awareness and peace, to make better choices, to check your responses to tense, uncomfortable, angry or challenging stimuli, and, above all else, to feel comfortable in your own skin.

Meditation helps you know and love yourself.

Why this is Important

A major skill successful people possess is the ability to control their consciousness. Mihaly Csikszentmihalyi, in Flow, says "The mark of a person who is in control of consciousness is the ability to focus attention at will, to be oblivious to distractions, to concentrate as long as it takes to achieve a goal, and not longer. And the person who can do this usually enjoys the normal course of everyday life."[22] Meditation is not part of any religion. Meditation is simply a method of training the mind and building your power of focus. Meditation has many physical and emotional benefits. Physically, meditation is shown to lower high blood pressure and reduce the risk of anxiety attacks. Meditation also decreases stress-related pain like headaches, ulcers, and insomnia. In one researched-based study, "Meditators showed a marked decrease in the thickness of their artery walls, while the non-meditators actually showed an increase. The change for the meditation group could potentially bring about an 11 percent decrease in the risk of heart attack and an 8 percent to 15 percent decrease in the risk of stroke."[23] Meditation can increase serotonin production, which improves mood and your immune system.

---

[22] Csikszentmihalyi, Mihaly. Flow: The Psychology of Optimal Experience. New York: Harper & Row, 1990. Print.

[23] http://www.psychologytoday.com/articles/200105/the-science-meditation

Emotionally, meditation is also shown to decrease anxiety, tension, anger, and frustration, and increase emotional resilience, improve creativity, increase clarity of thinking, and improve overall mood.

Meditation is the "direct observation of the mental continuum moment by moment [leading] to the discovery that the continuum is constantly changing. In this sense, direct special insight into impermanence naturally arises from mindfulness. Attempting to apply nonreactive, pure awareness to whatever arises also naturally leads to an appreciation of the mind's incessant reactivity to whatever comes into awareness. Mindfulness leads to direct experience of attachments and aversion as they operate moment by moment in the mental continuum."[24] Practicing this process of observation, leads to an increasing understanding of how your mind works. Once you understand that the mind is constantly changing, you naturally become less reactive to these changes. You become less reactive to ordinary sensory experiences, increasing your ability to control your consciousness.

---

[24] Brown, Daniel P. Pointing Out the Great Way: The Stages of Meditation in the Mahāmudrā Tradition. Boston: Wisdom Publications, 2006. Print.

CHAPTER 2

DEVELOPMENT OF THE HEART'S PRESENCE

To develop the heart's presence is to be willing to engage the challenges of life. A present heart does not retreat inside itself as a turtle pulls into its shell. A truly present heart is open and exposed, fully present in each moment– a challenging task! Events can trigger a person to withdraw from the moment, to escape into safety. Just as a body digests food, your heart digests experience in a positive or negative way, a healthy or unhealthy way. The following keys will increase the effectiveness of this emotional metabolism, helping you authentically experience your life, both the good and the bad.

Key One: Know Happy

Key Two: Practice Optimism

Key Three: Practice Patience

Key Four: Know your Calm

Key Five: Have Faith

Key Six: Engage Acceptance

Key Seven: Exhale Gratitude

Key Eight: Express Appreciation

Key Nine: Keep a Diary

Key Ten: Learn to Let Go

Key Eleven: Express Forgiveness

Key Twelve: Know your Anger

Key Thirteen: Know Fear

Key Fourteen: Be Sad

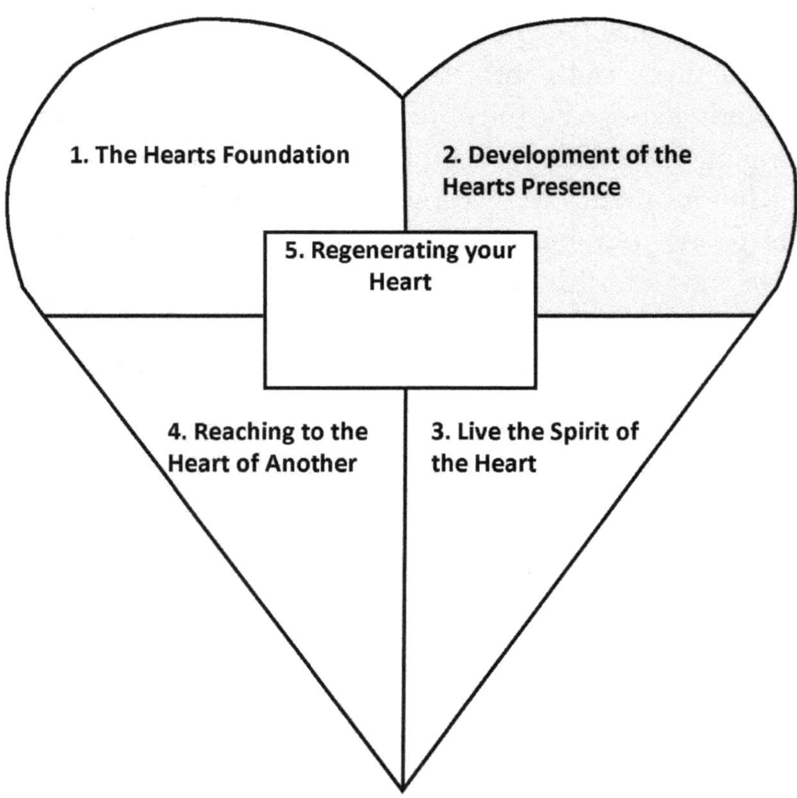

KEY 1

KEY ONE: KNOW HAPPY

When you consider the word "happy," the magnitude and diversity of definitions can give you a headache. It's a big word. Nothing in our reading–and there's a ton of it to swim through–has satisfied either of our ideas of happiness. Most literature tells you what to do to get there, but none of it tells you what it is.

And our lives are no different. In taking a shot at happiness, we miss the mark by miles. Some sources tell us happiness is a byproduct of engaging in virtuous activities, being grateful and embracing mindfulness. Some theories say happiness is a conscious decision, and others assign it to a default mechanism in our brains, determined by our preexisting neurological makeup.

Happiness is transient. We are affected by a thousand different things on any given day. If we stayed happy in spite of life's variety of emotional stimuli we would be, at best, one-dimensional and, at worst, numb. Life cannot stay solely in one emotional state. We are moved by pain. We are afflicted by sadness. And we can be struck by grief.

To make this all the more challenging, what makes you happy may not make somebody else happy, and so on. Trying to encapsulate all the feelings, thoughts, behaviors, situations, and encounters that relate to happiness appears impossible.

In writing this, we got stuck, so we took a deep breath and sat there. And after stepping back from this struggle, we found the one thing that universally makes us happy. Use this method, and you'll know you're happy. So here goes:

Write down three things, every day, that were good about that day. Make sure that, when you write them down, you include the circumstances surrounding them.

Simple, we know. But it absolutely works.

A Story from the Heart

Leon has been a community organizer and fundraiser for the last fifteen years. We met in his office. He says he sees "examples of happiness every day," and told me a story of when it clicked for him–when he first really saw what he, in his words, "had been missing all these years. But on the day I'm about to describe, I found it again. I always refer to the memories of that day to get me back into gear."

Leon closed his office door, sat back in his chair, and said, "Years ago I found myself on the board of directors of the local YMCA. I was on the childcare committee."

"One of our functions was to go around to the different child care sites and check on the condition of the facilities. We had to look important and peruse the facility, making notes on a checklist as we went.

"During our last stop, clouds had formed and the temperature began to drop. When we unloaded from our bus, we all just wanted to get through the facility and get back on the road before the rain came.

"My colleagues were looking around the place, seeing if there were enough materials, desks, or if anything needed attention or replacement. All of these folks looked very official, nodding their heads and speaking under their breath.

"I found myself wandering through the place. It was the last facility, and I'd stayed with the group for the trip, but I decided I wanted to do a little investigating on my own.

"I ended up in the play area, behind the main building. There I saw a merry-go-round, one of those old metal ones that you held onto and ran in a circle, taking turns pushing the big circular frame around and around.

"Now, remember, this is day care. Most of these kids, at the oldest, were no more than six, maybe seven. And there were about ten children all together. Three of them were sitting on the merry go round, two were attempting to push.

"I just stood there, looking official with my clipboard, when I saw one of the children trying to push this heavy circular piece of equipment. He was just straining against this monstrous merry-go-round when he stopped, looked straight at me and said, 'Mm, mm, mister? Would you pease' –not please. He said, 'pease' – 'help me push them?'

"This I could not turn down.

"I got next to the kid and slowly pushed this thing. My knees and my back told me it had been a while since I pushed a merry-go-round.

"The boy who had been pushing jumped on. They wrapped their tiny hands around these metal bars on the merry-go-round, and looked at me.

"These kids smiled like they were going to Disneyland. And here I am, some middle aged guy with a clipboard, pushing this thing around and around in circles. Upon hearing the words, 'faster, faster' I gave the bars one last hurl and I saw these children, looking long into the air, past the clouds and into the sky.

"I mean, my word, these kids were happy. I just sat back and looked. Here this thing is spinning around, and I'm holding my clipboard, mesmerized by their faces and the sounds and the sheer happiness these kids felt. I thought, 'This has got to be the most amazing thing I've ever seen.' And, I'm telling you, I really felt that. But the next sentence that came into my head was, 'How in the hell did I lose this? Where is that feeling? Is it still with me? Can I still retrieve it?' I mean, I'm standing there, and this battle of explosive joy and the beginnings of anxiety starts in the corner of my head at the same time, they're ready to duke it out with each other, and I don't know what to do. I'm laughing, I'm looking at the magic of these kids, and I'm thinking, 'I have to keep this feeling! I have to get this into my skin, my cells, my everything, right now.' "

Leon stood up from his chair. "So, the kids were starting to slow down, and the rest of the board members started to congregate by the front door. They were ready to go.

"So I looked at the kids, and I looked at the board members, and I said, 'Hey, little help?'

"I leaned over, grabbed the metal bars, and sat myself between two kids. I said, 'We could use a push.' The Board members looked at me like I was the third moon past Uranus. They started mumbling to themselves, and a couple of them crossed their arms over their chest. When I saw that, I brought in the reinforcements.

"I said, 'Kids, on three, say, We need a push! We need a push!'

"Now the Board Members are really looking pissed. And I'm loving it. So as loud as I could, I said, 'One, two three,' and these kids absolutely screamed, 'We need a push! We need a push!' I mean, we're talking on the scale of one hundred and thirty decibels here. It was incredible! Then I stood up, and I started in, screaming with these little kids, 'We need a push.'

"And, the Board Members didn't move. The staff didn't move. They stood there, at the door, with even more horrible expressions than before. I'm sure, at this time, that they are all thinking of their next opportunity to vote me off the board.

"And, right then, it starts to rain.

"Here I am, sitting with these kids, on a merry-go-round, in the rain, and we stopped yelling for them to give us a push. We got quiet. And then the most wonderful thing happened. A little girl, sitting next to me, looks up at the sky and says, 'Oh, rain. I love the rain.' And she stands up, holds her hand open with her palms toward the sky, looks up and says, 'Rain. It makes me so happy.'

"Then, we all stood up, all on the merry go round, and looking up toward the sky, stretched out our hands, catching the raindrops in our palms. We looked at one another, and we held the hands of the person standing next to us.

"We held hands, in the rain. Me and ten little kids, just standing there, holding hands, not saying a word, getting wet, being happy in the rain, on the merry-go-round."

Leon looked out the window and smiled. "Right at that moment, I knew what happiness was. Being with those kids, on the merry go round, holding hands, yeah, that's the poetry of life right there. But that moment wasn't exactly what made me happy.

"It was when I decided, right there, to stay on the merry-go-round, to hold the child's hand in the rain, and to be OK with a bunch of pissed-off adults. I had an opportunity to be happy, and I took it. Yeah, the opportunity came to me, but it was my decision to stay with it, to step further into that feeling."

Leon smiled, "That's what you have to do. Move into it. Be with it. It's hard to explain, but you get the idea. I decided to be happy, I guess. I hate to put it into that simple of a term, but that's pretty much what happened.

"And I should say," Leon said, "the Board fired me, but the staff at the daycare? They invited me back the next day. Now the kids call me 'Mr. Leon.'

"I mean, is that just the best, or what?"

How it Works

By simply writing down those three good things, you change your perspective to focus on what is good, and right, and of inherent value in your life. You can take a step back and move away from the life's difficulties. Do it for a while, and you'll feel better. It works.

The Greater Good Science Center at Berkeley came up with exercise. In their course The Science of Happiness, Dr. Dacher Keltner and Dr. Emiliana Simon-Thomas make this simple assertion: If you focus on three good things and the circumstances surrounding their occurrence, you reset your perspective. Do this every day, and this perspective becomes a way of life. You begin to look for the good and emphasize its value.

We know this to be true. In our coaching practices, this technique has helped clients reach a positive outlook and focus on the good, supporting their goal of happiness.

Here's another: Consciously say a positive word about everything. Think "I like the (and find something positive around you right now)."

This is a little more difficult, but it's nice to keep in mind. Try putting a reminder on your mirror, your desk, or your steering wheel. This exercise in consciousness helps contribute to a good perspective.

To be happy is an active, daily practice. But we're not asking you to put on your sweats, strap on your shoes and go jogging around the block. This is WAY easier. Writing down three things at the end of the day will develop your ability to say something positive about everything. You will condition yourself to be a more positive person just as if you were conditioning yourself to become a better jogger. Takes practice, sure. But the benefits are too many to list.

Why this is Important

Many great thinkers, from Aristotle to the Dalai Lama, have cited happiness as the meaning or goal of life. The Dalai Lama says "I believe that the very purpose of our life is to seek happiness. That is clear. Whether one believes in religion or not, whether one believes in this religion or that religion, we all are seeking something better in life. So, I think, the very motion of our life is towards happiness."[25] Everyone is looking for happiness, often indirectly by pursuing goals like a better job or a new relationship, more money, or a flatter stomach. These false beliefs won't help people reach that elusive feeling. Goals like these are actually the cause of unhappiness, because situational improvements in life do not increase an individual's overall happiness, since "there is only one cause of unhappiness: the false beliefs you have in your head, beliefs so widespread, so commonly held, that it never occurs to you to question them."[26] Understanding that the goal of life is happiness, true lasting happiness, will allow you to recognize happiness in your life, in the present moment, and align your goals more directly with things proven to produce happiness.

So what is happiness? Harvard professor Tal Ben-Shahar says in his book Happier, "I define happiness as 'the overall experience of pleasure and meaning.' A happy person enjoys positive emotions while perceiving her life as purposeful. The definition does not pertain to a single moment but to a generalized aggregate of one's experiences: a person can endure emotional pain at times and still be happy overall."[27]

Understand what happiness is. Understand that unhappiness and happiness are both the direct result of the beliefs and rules that you have for life. "I'm not talking about wishful thinking, or simply deciding to be happier. That's like pasting a smiley face over our pain or spreading a layer of icing over cake that's burned to a cinder. The

---

[25] Dalai Lama and Howard C. Cutler. The Art of Happiness: A Handbook for Living. New York: Riverhead Books, 1998. Print. pg 13

[26] De, Mello A. The Way to Love: Meditations for Life. New York: Image, 2012. Print. pg 4

[27] Ben-Shahar, Tal. Happier: Learn the Secrets to Daily Joy and Lasting Fulfillment. New York: McGraw-Hill, 2007. Print. pg 7

bad stuff is still there. What I'm talking about is accessing the higher center of your brain, your neocortex, to reverse the negativity bias and override your primitive alarm system."[28] Becoming happier takes effort; being happy is the practice of taking steps that bring happiness, while mitigating actions that cause unhappiness for yourself and others. Becoming happier in the moment requires completely changing your overall thinking process by cutting off negative thoughts when they occur and actively being positive. To become happier, you must assess if your goals are bringing you toward happiness.

Working toward your own happiness is not a selfish goal. Sonja Lyubomirsky, in The How of Happiness, says that "In becoming happier, we not only boost experiences of joy, contentment, love, pride, and awe but also improve other aspects of our lives: our energy levels, our immune systems, our engagement with work and with other people, and our physical and mental health. In becoming happier, we bolster as well our feelings of self-confidence and self-esteem; we come to believe that we are worthy human beings, deserving of respect. A final and perhaps least appreciated plus is that if we become happier, we benefit not only ourselves but also our partners, families, communities, and even society at large."[29]

---

[28] Shimoff, Marci, and Carol Kline. Happy for No Reason: 7 Steps to Being Happy from the Inside Out. New York: Free Press, 2008. Print. pg. 89

[29] Lyubomirsky, Sonja. The How of Happiness: A Scientific Approach to Getting the Life You Want. New York: Penguin Press, 2008. Print. pg 26

KEY 2

KEY TWO: PRACTICE OPTIMISM

Being optimistic is often equated with being naïve. It is almost a given that, if you are optimistic, you are overlooking so much that is awful in this world: hunger, poverty, war, selfishness, and ignorance. To be optimistic means to be unfeeling, unaware, and uninformed. It is shortsighted. It means to be one dimensional, without depth, emotionally blind. And, at the very least, it means to be unwilling to grasp the breadth and scope of reality.

Nonsense.

Optimism is the foundation of what we see as good and possible. Optimism is love's vision. It opens us up to see all we can do if we apply the right thoughts, perspectives, and beliefs.

To be Optimistic is to believe in the good in spite of all the bad. It is to see the better beneath the lesser, and work to awaken it in the world.

Optimism is rising above the pain that surrounds us, and choosing to focus on the beauty of life within the fog of darkness. It is realigning our perspective on what we've done, believing in what we can do; it is not stopping at what is, but seeing the good that could be.

It is the smile within our minds. Optimism is the perspective that keeps us looking forward, but also looking at the beauty in life, all that is underneath our feet and around our life, to the heavens and beyond. Optimism sees all that is, viewing it as beautiful; as each moment passes, we see it grow increasingly so.

To be optimistic is knowing that all can be good with time, love, and understanding. To be optimistic means to be inclusive. You take in all of life, and love it for all it is, maintaining the belief that who you are and the conditions you create have the potential for good.

A Story from the Heart

I visited my childhood neighborhood several years ago, and one of my stops was the neighborhood bar.

I had heard it was run by an old friend of mine, a classmate from grammar school who I had lost touch with over the years. When I heard that he was in the bar that day, I was embarrassed and a sense of shame washed over me. There was no reason that I lost touch. I just neglected to write. We get busy. College, marriage, family, and my career took the focus away from my roots, my childhood.

John bought the bar in 1993. I heard that he always arrived around 10 o'clock in the morning to set things up for the afternoon rush. I looked at my watch. It was five minutes after 10.

John always struck me as the happiest kid in class. I never remember him without a smile on his face, and we are talking from first through eighth grade. From six years old to adolescence. In my neighborhood, there's a lot that would take that smile straight off your face and throw it down the block. But not John. Scolded by a teacher or fell down and skinned his knee, he always came back smiling.

So when I stuck my big Irish head through the door, I saw that smile. Before I could say, "I don't know if you remember me, but..." that smile turned into a bellow of, "Oh my gosh, what's it been, 40 years?" And he started laughing. Then I started laughing. Then he hugged me so hard I thought I would need to be placed in intensive care.

He poured us a couple of beers and we exchanged a lot of stories. I sat there about three hours. He had the same smile, the same demeanor, that he had when we were young.

"John," I said, sheepishly, "you were always the happiest kid in school. No matter what happened to you, no matter the season, the grade, the weather, you always had a smile on your face.

"Can you please tell me how you did that? I've never met anybody since with that optimism, that light in their eyes like you've had."

John shook his head, giggled a little, took a pull on his beer, and said, "Interesting that you use that expression, the 'light' in my eyes. See, my dad died when I was five years old. I remember it was dark outside. People had left our house after paying their respects, and I remember distinctly being scared by the nighttime. I knew my father would never come back.

"My Mom and I sat on the couch, by ourselves, looking out the window onto the street. Only one small light was on in the living room. The room was dim. The only sounds were the traffic in the street.

"I was beginning to get scared, and the lights outside were fading. So I asked, 'Mom, is it always going to stay this dark?'

"My Mom looked at me, smiled and said, 'No, tomorrow the sun will shine. But then it'll be dark again, honey. We can't always find the sun where we want it. So we have to look inside ourselves to find that light.'

"Then she took her finger and put it on my heart. She said, 'There's your light, Johnny. It's so bright, and it's always there. I can see it. Johnny, we have to always remind ourselves that light is there, letting us know that everything is going to be bright and good and happy.'

"My Mom said, 'All we need to do is smile. The light comes on when we smile, Johnny. And the more we smile, the brighter that light. The light shows us all the good there is in this life. So smile, Johnny, and see how beautiful this world is.'

"So," he said, "I've smiled because of her. I've been an eternal optimist. No matter how hard she had it, working two jobs, dealing with so much difficulty in her life, she lived with a smile on her face, sharing her light with me. So I've always done the same. I followed her directions from the time I was small and I've been doing it all my life."

We finished our beers, we hugged, promised to stay in touch, and I left.

I've had a smile on my face ever since. I want my light to show. I will be an optimist. And I will share my light with you.

Thank you, John. Thank you so much.

How it Works

Being optimistic begins with yourself. The first step is assessing who you are and the beauty within you. An optimist sees the good in themselves as part of their daily routine. They know that they are intrinsically good and believe that life will unfold in front of them accordingly. That said, most of us aren't always that optimistic; most of us need a little help.

We suggest doing what optimistic people do every day: They notice the good around them. They give people the benefit of the doubt. They see the good in things that, to everybody else, doesn't appear so obvious.

They make it their routine. And, although many optimistic people seem to be hardwired, most weren't born that way. There are strategies to become an optimist: "essentially, all optimism strategies involve the exercise of construing the world with a more positive and charitable perspective, and many entail considering the silver lining in the cloud, identifying the door that opens as a result of one that has closed. It takes hard work and a great deal of practice to accomplish effectively, but if you can persist at these strategies until they become habitual, the benefits could be immense. Some optimists may be born that way, but scores of optimists are made with practice."[30] In short, they develop and maintain optimism as their mode of interpersonal operation.

Optimists see the benefits of keeping a positive outlook, and so it becomes their way of life. And they will be the first to tell you that they get sad. They grieve. They become troubled by problems in their family, their friendships, or their work. But they universally give themselves only a short period of time to engage in those feelings. A friend of ours once said, "I can have a bad twenty minutes. But if I have a bad day, it's my decision." His focus is on that deliberate positive expression. He makes himself look at things in a good light. He posted the phrase "Say something nice NOW," in six places: His bathroom mirror, his wallet, on his desk at work, in his kitchen at home, on his coffee cup, and on his dog's collar. We asked him about that last one. He said, "Well, it's one of the last things I do every day, and I used to just cringe at the prospect of walking him. So, I put my quote on his collar and when I put it on him before our walk, I looked at it and felt better. I say something nice to the dog. Haven't had a bad walk since."

Why this is Important

Optimism is simply having confidence or hopefulness in a better future. The optimist sees a problem as an obstacle to overcome, whereas a pessimist sees a problem as a warning sign to stop. For the optimist or the pessimist, life is filled with disappointment, embarrassment, and mistakes. One must learn from these when they occur, and then let go, rather than dwelling on a negative situation. An optimist knows how to change their internal dialog from negative to positive when problems occur. Mihaly Csikszentmihalyi, in Flow, says "A person can make himself happy, or miserable, regardless of what is

---

[30] Lyubomirsky, Sonja. The How of Happiness: A Scientific Approach to Getting the Life You Want. New York: Penguin Press, 2008. Print. pg 110

actually happening 'outside,' just by changing the contents of consciousness. We all know individuals who can transform hopeless situations into challenges to be overcome, just through the force of their personalities . . . it is probably the most important trait not only for succeeding in life, but for enjoying it as well. To develop this trait, one must find ways to order consciousness so as to be in control of feelings and thoughts. It is best not to expect shortcuts will do the trick."[31] With confidence in oneself and the future, a person can take on challenges and face difficult situations with poise, since they know the outcome will be positive.

Optimists aren't blessed with a special way of thinking. Optimism is a skill and habit that can be learned. Like choosing to eat healthily, optimism is an ongoing practice, however, "unlike dieting, learned optimism is easy to maintain once you start. Once you get into the habit of disputing negative beliefs, your daily life will run much better, and you will feel much happier."[32] Cultivating an optimistic mindset makes a person open to possibilities, not fearful of problems. When problems do arise, as they always do, the optimist can overcome the challenge. Since outcome is dictated by focus, people with an optimistic viewpoint are much more likely to attain better results because people with a positive view of the future are much more likely to persevere past difficulties.

---

[31] Csikszentmihalyi, Mihaly. Flow: The Psychology of Optimal Experience. New York: Harper & Row, 1990. Print. pg 24

[32] Seligman, Martin E. P. Learned Optimism: How to Change Your Mind and Your Life. New York: Vintage Books, 2006. Print. end of chapter 12

KEY 3

KEY THREE: PATIENCE

Think on this for a second.

In I Corinthians in the New Testament, it is written "Love is patient, love is kind" instead of "Love is kind, love is patient." Why is that? Here's the answer: You cannot impart kindness without patience. Not possible. To engage in a loving act such as kindness, a person has to steady their emotions. This is the genesis of patience: a pause, a collecting of the spirit, a decision to engage in civility, affection, kindness, or love. It may be instantaneous.

But trust us on this: Without patience–in attitude or response–there is no kindness.

Patience controls our emotions. It is the brake pedal to our feelings. It slows us down. It keeps us from giving way to urgency and impulse. Our responses are softened. Our desires take a backseat.

Patience stops reactions. Patience is the first step toward a civil response and peaceful communication.

A Story from the Heart

Patience has never been high on the list of virtues of any of my friends, family members, children, coworkers, or, for that matter, anyone I'd ever met. It's not that they didn't possess the capacity for being patient; they just didn't always display that virtue when needed.

When I was about 22, I had recently had my first child and become the stepfather of two more. I was faced with being a father as young man, knowing that patience was essential to being a good father–but my reference points for patient parenting were few.

I lived in an apartment complex for families with children on the university grounds. The students had set up a garden between a row of flats and a playground.

On a clear day in early autumn, I rolled my new daughter in her stroller to the playground. As I got closer, I could see the hands of a woman reaching for something tall and green. The stalk of this plant bent toward her, then bent back. The motion was deliberate. The plant didn't snap back; rather, it was placed back to its original position.

I picked up my daughter and, instead of putting her in the swing seat, I walked closer to the garden. There I saw a woman with slightly greying hair tying the stalks of sunflowers to a post, helping them grow a little straighter.

I commented on how beautiful the garden looked, then I paused and told her that I noticed her working with the sunflowers on the walk to the playground. I mentioned how I found it interesting that the stalks returned to their place with ease. "I noticed that you were very careful in positioning the flowers."

"Well, gardening takes some care," she said, "and it's a deliberate effort." She turned toward me, smiled at my daughter and, while trimming the leaves from another plant, said, "I don't mean that it's hard. It's very simple. And this is the fun part. The plants you see all around you were planted from seeds last autumn."

This garden, as thick as any jungle, was higher in some areas than my head. "It must have taken a lot of work," I said, thinking her efforts were no doubt pretty arduous.

Smiling again she said, "Work? No. A little patience, I suppose. And that's not really work, it's just practice."

Then, with a philosophical tone in her voice, she started to talk. "I find gardening a metaphor for life. You begin with seeds. We all do, at different stages of our lives. We look at something so insignificant about our lives, ourselves, that we aren't sure what to make of our future. So, we plant something. School, career, a family, we all start out as a seed.

"But," she continued, "to carry on a rather worn out metaphor, we cultivate our efforts with consistency and attention, and something comes of it. We're never really sure exactly what, but our efforts bring forth results.

"To me, the greatest effort in any continuous course is being patient. Not just with your efforts, but with life itself. There is so much we can't control. Look around you." She stretched out her arm toward this avalanche of growth. "The sun. The rain. Wind. Earth. Not in my control here. But my patience is.

"I live life deliberately. One step, then another. Bend the stalk, put it back. Kneel down, dig a little dirt. Each action is dictated by patience. Each step is a move forward down the path. Patience is accepting what is, and following the path as it flows in front of me."

She took a couple of steps toward me, looked at my daughter in my arms and said, "You have begun planting your own seeds. And look at this beautiful creation. Your path has been set. See the beauty in everything about her, from the diapers and the tantrums to the smiles and laughter. Accept this creation with love, and apply great patience to her life. The patience I use with my garden is how I show my love. And trust me, the patience you show your child? Well, that's how she'll know you love her."

Taking one last look at my daughter, the woman kneeled down in the dirt and said, "Be patient in your 'gardening!' "

I thanked her, and she returned to her digging. I walked to the playground, sat my daughter in the swing, and gave her a gentle push, watching her hair whisk in the crisp autumn air.

How it Works

Essentially, patience works in two fundamental ways. The first is the attitude of patience. You have seen people who exude a sense of peace. They actually exist. They offer the benefit of the doubt to everyone. Understanding underscores their communication. Speaking to them never results in conflict.

Patience is their demeanor and a part of their cellular makeup. They live patience.

We're pretty sure, for the most part, that they are aliens.

For the rest of us, we have to calm ourselves. It is against our nature to be patient. We tend to want things our way.

The best and first step is to pause. Stop. Back off. Think. Then engage. The first step in this process of reconsidering emotional stimulation is to stop.

It's conditioning. It takes practice, and it takes investment in the concept of patience. We have to value allowing ourselves to be patient. This seems overly simplistic, but it's of great importance. So much of the time we slip into thinking we are right when, in fact, we have instead become self-righteous. We defend our principles instead of listening to the other's perspective. We become too caught up in our needs, truly believing that we are the center of the Universe.

See if this exercise brings it home for you. Try being patient in line. At the store. At night. When you're exhausted. The first thing is to consider, however remote, that the person in front of you counting their pennies and taking forever to move the line along is afraid that they may have to make another trip to the store. That they have very little gas in their car and these pennies have to be exact to make sure they cover their bill.

Then see the expression on the checkout person's face as one penny after another gets counted. They have been there all day. On their feet. You have no idea how their legs must feel. Or their back. Or the fact that their job requires them to continue to hold their form and countenance against the most difficult and challenging people, day after day.

Look at those two people. Now look at yourself. Find your patience now. And become acquainted with how the patience within you feels. If it's still hard, think a little further.

If you're a parent, remember when you held an eighteen-month old. That you're trying to get to sleep. For the last hour. At two in the morning.

Or the time you tried to teach your dog to sit. Repeatedly. Time. After time. After time. After . . . you get the idea.

Or when you were with your really boring Uncle that you love and had to endure the same story, every month, month after month because that is what you did. You would never want to hurt his feelings. So you listened, and you smiled politely, even laughed because that's just what you did.

This is where it really matters. And the existence of patience within you is exactly within that context.

You have it. We know you do.

Be aware of other people. That's your first step. Be present and hold your calm. Remind yourself of times that you have been patient in the past, because you've been there, you really have. And keep those reminders handy–you're going to need them.

That's patience. We all know it. We all have it. We know how it's done.

And it is so worth it.

Why this is Important

True patience allows a person the space to be above the grips of a problem. In psychological terms, patience refers to deferred, or re-directed, gratification. Deferred gratification is the ability to wait for a later reward instead of giving in to a lesser, more immediate reward. A person must build this skill over time; it does not come easily.

Short-term sacrifices are necessary to grow as a person. Stephen Covey says "Be patient with yourself. Self-growth is tender; it's holy ground. There's no greater investment. It's obviously not a quick fix. But I assure you, you will feel benefits and see immediate payoffs that will be encouraging."[33] Be it patience with yourself or with the world, it all comes down to the ability to control yourself.

Having patience will insulate you from many hasty mistakes. Although cliché, it's crucial to understand the meaning of the adage "Rome wasn't built in a day." In reality, nothing happens immediately. Hard work and sacrifice are required; both are a result of patience.

A crucial barrier to patience is one's relation to Time; have faith that by taking correct actions, the desired result will be attained. But, "without patience as your sword and shield, your timing will fail and you will inevitably find yourself a loser."[34] We need to be aware that, when being patient, we will wait. We will watch the hands of the clock pass ever so slowly. To be patient is to think a little more deliberately.

"Time, then, depends on perception, which, we know, can be willfully altered. This is the first thing to understand in mastering the art of timing. If the inner turmoil caused by our emotions tends to make time move faster, it follows that once we control our emotional responses to events, time will move much more slowly. This altered way of dealing with things tends to lengthen our perception of future

---

[33] Covey, Stephen R. The 7 Habits of Highly Effective People: Powerful Lessons in Personal Change. , 2013. Print. Pg 70

[34] Greene, Robert, and Joost Elffers. The 48 Laws of Power. New York: Viking, 1998. Print.

time, opens up possibilities that fear and anger close off, and allows us the patience that is the principal requirement in the art of timing."[35] Mastering the emotions calms inner turmoil, allowing a person the space to take correct actions, bringing about a desired result.

[35] Greene, Robert, and Joost Elffers. The 48 Laws of Power. New York: Viking, 1998. Print.

KEY 4

KEY FOUR: KNOW YOUR CALM

Be Present asserts that, when you're focusing on something other than yourself, you become a little calmer. When we focus on things outside of ourselves, particularly if we observe our immediate environment, we relax a little. This will "calm and clarify your mind and you will know yourself as you are, beyond desires, memories, and concepts."

Now, we need to identify this state. So often, we lose what we really feel like when we're calm. We can feel calm in a variety of degrees, too. There's a difference between the calm we feel when we're taking a deep breath with our eyes closed at work, as opposed to doing the same thing on the fifth day of a two-week vacation. But as long as we know the essence of what calm feels like, we know it when we get there. Calmness should feel spacious, not confined by pressing thoughts, plans, or desires. And we can, by familiarizing ourselves with this place, get there a little more quickly.

A Story from the Heart

Recently I had the chance to speak to a group of high school seniors on their Career Day about what it takes to be a writer, counselor, and life coach.

I should mention that this talk was in June, one week before they would graduate. Needless to say, the class was a little restless.

Their teacher was a friend of mine, and I watched him as he calmed the kids down. Approaching retirement, he's got another year or two with teenagers, then he will stop teaching. He's been at it for over thirty years.

As I approached the front of the room, the class was agitated, at the very least. I saw maybe two sets of eyes looking at me, the rest of the room was a collection of bobbing heads and students talking to one another feverishly.

My friend stood next to me, put one hand on my shoulder, and the other one in the air. Palm up, arm extended, his eyes focused on the clamber of voices, expressions, and movement that one often associates with twenty seven hamsters jammed into a cage . . . or, in this case, a classroom full of teenagers.

Not three seconds after he held up his hand, the class fell silent.

I spoke for about twenty minutes, took a few questions from the class, then met with my friend for a coffee after his classes were done.

After all these years, I wanted to know how he got to be so calm.

Now, I should mention, I've known him for years, and not once have I ever seen him get riled about anything, even though he's a pretty passionate guy. He feels strongly about things, is very sentimental, and shares my rabid involvement with the Chicago Cubs. I mean, right there, is a perennial reason for passionate displays of disappointment, depression and rage.

So he answered my question directly, without much explanation. "I have grown to like myself a lot. My sense of calm is a byproduct of a reasonably strong sense about myself, I guess." I asked him to explain.

"When you like yourself, you accept who you are and how you behave. So you calm down a little. You believe a little more in your abilities to take care of things, whether they are routine or within a crisis. You think a little more, react less and respond with more ease.

"I didn't always feel this way. And getting to that point of self-acceptance and appreciation took some time. But I forgave myself for my mistakes, strove to be a better person, and through that effort I suppose I felt, in time, that I liked myself.

"I made efforts to be calm. I meditated, did yoga for a while. It helps, sure, but it wasn't until I really gave myself a break about things, and felt that I was OK, that I mattered, that I wasn't such a bad guy, did a sense of peace begin to develop. And, as a result, I became much more calm."

My friend continued, "Look, I get angry. I get sad, anxious and depressed. I'm still a member of the human race, you know? But it passes. I go back to that place where I know that I'm enough. I got acquainted with it so often that I can now reach for it quickly. That feeling has become stronger than any problem that comes my way. Some people say it's their center. I'm not sure what that is, but I can tell you absolutely that the minute I started accepting and genuinely liking myself, I relaxed. And this is what you see."

He and I talked a little more. We finished our coffee and set up a time to meet again.

As he shook my hand to leave, he said, "Remember, lead with being OK with you. Keep reminding yourself that you're OK, that you're enough. You belong here. You're sufficient, OK? Just hang on to that concept. And trust me: The calm comes directly after."

How it Works

We suggest that you begin when you don't need to do much of anything. Maybe on a Saturday or Sunday - whenever you can take a little time to be idle. At least at first. Later, if you practice this a few times when you are at rest, you can do it in the car, at work, or even when you're being yelled at. We're serious. But first work at it.

Now while you're sitting, observe and take notice of the color and texture of the walls, the ceiling, and the floor. Then close your eyes. Just sit there for thirty seconds. Breathe. Feel your breath go in your nose, and out. As your breath comes out, feel tension leave your body. Feel your breath go in your nose, and out. As your breath comes out, feel tension leave your mind.

OK, that's a baseline. That's calm. It might only seem like a little calm, but it is a departure and a deepening of your spirit beyond what you felt just thirty seconds ago. Now you have a reference. Right there, you experienced a little bit of calm. And it's easy to retrieve, just in case you forget.

And that's one way, but certainly not the only way. This method is an accessible way to reach a calmer state. Anyone can do this. You can practice this anywhere and at any time.

Why this is Important

When searching for our calm, we learn how to access a state of mind that feels safe. When life gets chaotic, when we get too angry, too anxious, too lonely, too tired, too sad, or too frustrated, we need to be able to rise above these emotions without denying their existence. Initially this will be challenging, but over time, with focus and practice, we will be able to remain in the present moment, facing reality with calmness, not hiding from it. "As long as there is a lack of the inner discipline that brings calmness of mind, no matter what external facilities or conditions you have, they will never give you the feeling of joy and happiness that you are seeking."[36] Even if you get that job, that relationship, that 5% body fat, there will still continue to be a void, a feeling that something is missing. It is not the things or events in our lives that make us happy, it is our thoughts about the contents of our

---

[36] Dalai Lama and Howard C. Cutler. The Art of Happiness: A Handbook for Living. New York: Riverhead Books, 1998. Print.pg 26

lives. Unhappiness is still unhappiness in a shotgun shack or a mansion. "On the other hand, if you possess this inner quality, a calmness of mind, a degree of stability within, then even if you lack various external facilities that you would normally consider necessary for happiness, it is still possible to live a happy and joyful life."[37] By re-centering yourself into the calmness of the present moment throughout your life's struggles, you will feel more at ease in the world.

---

[37] Dalai Lama and Howard C. Cutler. The Art of Happiness: A Handbook for Living. New York: Riverhead Books, 1998. Print.pg 26

KEY 5

KEY FIVE: HAVE FAITH

We want you to apply the concepts from this book that resonate with you, in your life. And there is no perfect path to success.

So this particular key, Have Faith is important to practice right about now.

You're beginning a new path. You're setting out in a new direction. And now, you've gotten through this much of the book and, even though it's early, it's usually here that people begin to deal with being discouraged and upset, wondering if this effort is worth it.

Faith has many religious connotations, positive or negative. Suspend those thoughts for now. This section is not about blind faith. This is about practical faith; the faith necessary to live a life of meaning. We want to stress that faith is not a word that belongs only in the context of religion; here we are talking about faith in yourself and faith in the future. A faith based on the premise that the goal of a human being is to improve, to grow, to evolve, to become better.

Have faith.

Faith is belief and a little more. It's belief with a sense of peaceful or contented knowing. You just have a sense that things are going to turn out alright. "I believe…" are the first two words to establish a sense of faith.

It begins with a sense of faith in yourself. This is often the hardest hurdle to clear. Believing that you're good, that you matter, and that your efforts will bring forth something positive. Believing that your actions will carry you further down life's path.

Have faith in yourself and your actions. Mahatma Gandhi says, "Faith is not something to grasp, it is a state to grow into" built by wisdom and experience. The foundation of faith can be in your values, passions, abilities, and life's mission. Have faith in what you know to be true–that what you are doing right now will lead to a better life.

Have faith in your direction, whether it's knowing that going to school is the right thing for you, believing that if you keep practicing, you can learn an important skill, or even absolutely believing that, as your awareness increases, your sense of purpose and meaning will deepen and you will feel better about life.

Finally, faith in general is often supported by faith in a higher power. A belief in God, the power of the Universe, or simply that there is something bigger than yourself out there is the foundation of spirituality. Having faith in something greater than ourselves can help us in our most hopeless moments. If you have a spiritual practice, this would be a good time to examine its place in your life.

A Story from the Heart

Years and years ago, I went to middle school with a kid who lived in a foster home. I'd never heard of one before. I lived with my family on the north side of Chicago, and all I knew from my rather sheltered perspective was that kids lived with their own families in an apartment or a house.

But this kid didn't. He said his family was on the south side but he didn't get to see them. He didn't say why. I was too young to know what the reasons might be, and too afraid to ask.

We became friends, and one day he asked me to come to his house after school. I was kind of an anxious kid, so on the way, we talked about who might be there, what might be expected of me, that sort of thing. When I got there, my friend said "Momma McCormick is nice, but she's kind of strict, so be really good, OK?"

As a sixth grader, that's all I knew how to be.

As I walked through the front door, standing in the hallway was one of the biggest women I'd ever seen in my life. Hands on her hips and a smile that stretched into the kitchen, Momma McCormick said, "Well, who do we have here?"

I told her my name, and she said, "Well you just sit down right here and let Momma get you something to eat." I didn't dare tell her that I wasn't hungry. She was a formidable figure of a woman. I decided it would be best to just be quiet and eat.

My friend sat down next to me and pulled a picture out of the bag he carried home from school. "Momma, my teacher told me to draw a picture of myself when I'm older, me being what I want to be when I grow up." He handed her the picture and Momma's eight mile smile lit up the room. She said, "Baby, this is beautiful," and she taped it to the front of the refrigerator. My friend said, "Momma, do you think I can be a musician?" The picture was my friend playing the guitar. That's what he wanted to do when he grew up. "Honey," Momma said, "I believe you can. And God believes you can. Now, do you believe, too?"

My friend sat up in his chair as if the voice of the Almighty was ringing through the room. "Yes, Momma. I believe I can." And my friend left the table and ran up the stairs to his bedroom. The next thing I heard were the faint tones of what sounded like a guitar, only I wasn't sure of the tune. I wasn't really sure if it was a guitar or their cat fell down the stairs.

My friend never returned. After a few minutes, I thanked Momma McCormick and went home.

The next day I saw my friend. We talked about him being a guitar player. "Momma says I can, and she says God says I can, so I figure I can, that's all. I believe I can play. And I just started learning at Christmas." It was February. That explained the sounds I heard the day before.

After the school year ended, I lost track of my friend. I went to the home and Momma said he'd moved back in with his family. And up until about three years ago, I wasn't sure I'd ever hear of him again.

Then, by accident, I was looking up the tour schedule of a rather famous rock star to see if he was coming to the area. And when I got on his website, there was my friend, standing there, holding a guitar.

A few weeks later, I'd made contact with him and invited him to dinner. He remembered me. We talked about Momma McCormick and his time in the foster home. "Because of her, I made it," he said. "She instilled a sense of faith in me. She believed in me, and she taught me that God believed in me too. So I kept at it. If I had Momma and God behind me, I figured I couldn't lose. I believed without any doubt. No matter what happened to me throughout my life, from that moment on, I had faith. And I kept practicing. I knew I'd arrive at that place, the one she believed I could reach, if I just persisted."

"Here, let me show you something." He went back to his car and came back with a guitar case. He opened it up, pulled out his glistening six string, and flipped it over. "I have this engraved on the back of every guitar I play," he said, and showed me the engraving. It said, "I believe you can. God believes you can. Now, do you believe?"

"Faith is a belief, sure, but it's also a knowing," said my friend. "It's a sense within you that, if you just keep at something, the results you dream of will become a reality."

My friend put his guitar back in its case and said, "On the wall of my office is a picture my wife gave me a couple of years ago. The first two lines go like this: "It starts with a dream. Add faith, and it becomes a belief." I dreamed I could play the guitar. Momma gave me the faith, and it became a belief."

"And now, here I am." My friend, stretched out his arms, and smiled. He said, "Faith started me on the path of perseverance and patience. Given time, and a lot of practice, and it turned into a dream come true."

"But don't get me wrong," he said, "All of my dreams began with faith. Without faith, I wouldn't be with you today."

And with that, my friend held his glass of iced tea, held it to the sky, and said, "To Momma McCormick, and to the faith she brought into my life."

We clinked our glasses together, and the words of Momma McCormick came back into my head, "I believe you can, God believes you can. Now, do you believe?"

<u>How it Works</u>

In manifesting faith, consider the words "Life is unfolding for my highest good." Keep these words close. When we assess ourselves, our actions or our path, these words engage our faith and keep us believing.

Live and be your best in each and every moment. Believe the best is with you, at this moment, and will continue with you on each step on the path of life. As Dr. Rev. Martin Luther King, Jr. says "Faith is taking the first step even when you don't see the whole staircase."

Faith inspires us and keeps us moving. Whenever we make a change, our faith brings forth all that we can dream about. It is the first reference in manifesting our goals. Faith shifts our direction to the basic good of ourselves and our intentions.

Prayer to a higher power as you understand it is a frequent vehicle for faith. We pray for so many things. We pray for our life to change in a thousand different ways. But the act of prayer engages our faith. We reach outside of ourselves and engage the possibility, praying for a better or higher result. As Rabbi Heschel says, "Prayers may not save us, but might make us worthy of being saved."

Another approach is to use affirmations to remind us of the things we believe. Affirmations like "I know my decisions are good" or "I can do anything I put my mind to doing " help ground us, and keep the doubt from creeping in.

Prayer and Affirmations are statements of Faith. They stir our belief, give energy, and propel our lives to the place we wish to be.

Meditation, as we discussed in Section One, is another approach. It calms your mind and helps you hear the voice of faith.

Why this is Important

Faith in yourself and your actions establishes faith in the future. While hope is passive, faith implies acting with wisdom and courage. Franklin D. Roosevelt, who led the United States through World War II says, "The only limit to our realization of tomorrow will be our doubts of today. Let us move forward with strong and active faith."[38] Austrian neurologist and psychiatrist Viktor Emil Frankl survived multiple concentration camps during the Holocaust, including the infamous Auschwitz. In these horrific life-or-death conditions, Frankl analyzed what separated those who survived from those who did not. Frankl says "the prisoner who had lost his faith in the future—his future—was doomed. With his loss of belief in the future, he also lost his spiritual hold; he let himself decline and became subject to mental and physical decay."[39] Frankl goes on to say "just as a small fire is extinguished by the storm whereas a large fire is enhanced by it–likewise a weak faith is weakened by predicament and catastrophes whereas a strong faith is strengthened by them."[40] Life is unpredictable

---

[38] Roosevelt, Franklin D.

[39] Frankl, Viktor E. Man's Search for Meaning. Boston: Beacon Press, 2006. Print.

[40] Frankl, Viktor E. Man's Search for Meaning. Boston: Beacon Press, 2006. Print.

and the trajectory of growth and improvement is never a straight line. Have faith in what you know to be true in your heart. When obstacles arise, faith helps you overcome them. After overcoming these obstacles, your faith will be strengthened through concrete evidence that your faith is formidable.

Without faith in yourself, your ability to evolve as a human wanes. Evolve to become wiser, more knowledgeable, more caring, and more confident. Faith makes you a more effective you.

KEY 6

KEY SIX: ACCEPTANCE

Acceptance is part of Being Present. It places us at the center of our emotional being. It puts us at the starting gate of the decision-making process. And it's the most effective and most reliable coping mechanism.

Acceptance steps away from evaluation and expectation of an outcome, situation, circumstance, or event. It takes us out of conflict and hostility by avoiding the angry engagement caused by inner resistance.

To accept means to suspend judgment. It is identifying what is while forgoing positive or negative evaluation. Acceptance is to see and identify what is real, without assigning any value to it. For the moment of acceptance, everything is fine. It may not be optimal. It may not be anything near what we wanted or expected. But, for the moment, it's enough.

Acceptance means telling yourself "everything is as it should be right now, this is the best I know how to respond in this moment, and I'm OK with that." It's not surrender, it's not resignation, it's not even compromise. Acceptance means knowing "It is what it is." Acceptance does not engage your mind in solutions, not right away. First, acceptance is pausing to acknowledge the situation and, secondly, sitting with what the circumstances are in that moment. Acceptance is the breath before we take the first step, and that breath may take a while.

Acceptance sounds a bit like a holding pattern, but it's not. Acceptance is a place to be. It's a destination, a perspective that a situation is as it should be, at least for the moment.

A Story from the Heart

My friend Amelia is a former Catholic nun. She lived in a convent just outside Bogota, Colombia for ten years.

When we sat down some time ago, we talked about Acceptance. She said, "I had been a nun for about three months when I was assigned to a convent in a poorer section of town. Our job was to work with the locals to help rehabilitate the structure of the church, the rectory and the convent. As nuns, we didn't do the heavy lifting. But we could swing a hammer and hold a nail, and we could feed the workers as well. So anytime we had a chance, we would pitch in."

"The problem was that the convent, where the other nuns and I slept, was in complete disarray. The stairs were nearly gone, the walls had holes in them, and the roof leaked. Now, in Bogota, it gets a little wet. It rains. And there are nights when the rain just pelted the church and the surrounding buildings.

"The convent was a one-story adobe structure. We all slept on the same floor. Because I was the youngest, I was assigned a bed, the last one available, right underneath a leak in the ceiling.

"Most nights, this wasn't a problem. The hole was small and the roof was to be repaired sometime soon. I thought it might rain a time or two, but it shouldn't be a big deal. A little drip here and there, and it will pass.

"And it rained once. And then it rained again. And I found myself adjusting. I moved my pillow a little, put a towel down close to where the water dripped through the ceiling. And I was OK.

"But after about a week, the construction stopped. For some reason, one I was not aware of, the workers were needed in another part of town, so the repair on every part of the church was left undone. A couple of days, then a week, then two weeks, and then the weeks became months. And nothing.

"Throughout this time, a new group of nuns were supposed to come and help with the construction but, since there wasn't any, they never showed up. And, as a result, my bed didn't move.

"In short, I was stuck with sleeping right underneath the hole in the roof. For two years."

Now, I'm thinking this was pretty awful. And I asked her a few questions about whether she asked to move her bed, fix the roof, or have some kind of bucket next to her head. Questions about how this could be fixed screamed through my head and, as I was about to start the barrage of inquiries, my friend said, "And you know? It was the best thing that could have happened to me."

I looked at her with the expression that a dog gets when there's a high frequency in his ear.

She smiled and said, "Yes, I tried to move. I asked for another bed. None was available. I moved a little to the left, and then to the right, but because we were in such close quarters, I kept running into my friends, interrupting their sleep.

"About this time, the Mother Superior took me aside. I thought I was in trouble. She wasn't the easiest woman to be with, let alone to answer to.

"She walked with me back to where we've all been sleeping, stops by my bed, and looks up. She squints a little, looks down at the floor, then looks right into my eyes. And she smiles. She put her hand on my shoulder and pointed to the ceiling. 'Amelia, love this as best you can.' She didn't say, 'Accept this,' although that's what she meant. She took it a step further. She told me to offer my love to this condition. She knew that, given my youth and my frustration, that acceptance would only come if I truly offered my heart, my love, to that crummy little leak over my pillow."

Amelia said, "You know, that's how I accepted my leak. I learned to love it. I grew fond of it. I even, at times, looked forward to the rain! Isn't that something? I looked forward to my little leak saying 'hello' to me, letting me know it was there, waiting for me to love it all over again.

"And it was so strange," she said, "but when the hole was fixed, I thought I'd be relieved. But the next time it rained, I was sad. I missed my leak. I'd learned to accept my condition by offering it love, and when it left me, I had to adjust."

Amelia said, "That old nun talk me that the only way to accept a condition, a circumstance, or even part of ourselves is to love it the best we can. An amazing lesson, don't you think?"

How it Works

When you begin to accept a situation just for what it is, it may feel like you're giving in, but that's not the case. Although, if you are not used to just being okay with something, suspending judgment and evaluation for a minute or two, a percolating sense of urgency begins to build within you. When faced with an obstacle, it is entirely normal to want to DO something, right now, this second, and hurry up about it.

Let that pass. 99 times out of 100 this feeling will occur, but it interrupts your ability to accept the reality of a situation.

Accept the circumstance, the feeling or the situation "for the time being." This is the hand you're dealt, but it's not the cards you'll play forever. It doesn't mean that change can never happen. It's just that, for the moment, it is better to either suspend judgment or withdraw from it entirely.

All of us have encountered traffic, sometimes every day. We all have to accept, to a certain degree, that traffic is going to flow at the pace it's going to flow. We can be the most skilled driver on the road.

We can dart in and out of the cars in front of us to get ahead a little bit. But, bottom line, we're all pretty much stuck.

Acceptance means that you can only drive one car a time. You do your best. You breathe a little. And, for the moment, that's more than enough.

Why this is Important

Acceptance means surrendering "each moment to the reality of that moment. Knowing that what is cannot be undone–because it already is–you say yes to what is or accept what isn't. Then you do what you have to do, whatever the situation requires. If you abide in this state of acceptance, you create no more negativity, no more suffering, no more unhappiness. You then live in a state of nonresistance, a state of grace and lightness, free of struggle." [41] Sometimes bad stuff happens. Our minds struggle against it, we disconnect from the present moment, and we feel even worse. If we accept the situation instead of judging it or struggling against it, we become able to deal with it in a more positive way.

Without acceptance, an inner resistance to the situation occurs; this creates additional suffering and your mind becomes distracted. Your full attention is not on the present moment. It is wrapped up in thoughts or labels about what is. It is this abstraction that denies the present moment, hindering the individual from seeing the situation clearly. In a life or death situation, action is imperative, not dwelling on fears or potential pain.

Eckhart Tolle uses the word "surrender" interchangeably with acceptance. The inner bravado in us says "I will never surrender! Surrendering is for the weak." This is not the white flag, lay down your

[41] Tolle, Eckhart. The Power of Now: A Guide to Spiritual Enlightenment. Novato, Calif: New World Library, 1999. Print. pg 220

weapons type of surrender. This surrender is simply accepting what is, and moving forward toward a solution.

127 Hours tells the true story of Aron Ralston, an adventurer who had an 800 pound boulder fall on his arm while rock climbing alone in a Utah slot canyon. Accepting the circumstance that his arm is trapped, he has two choices: either die a slow death, or risk death by severing his arm. He says, "knowing the alternative is to wait for a progressively more certain but assuredly slow demise, I choose to meet the risk of death in action."[42] To survive, Ralston emotionally and intellectually accepted that his arm was permanently stuck. Once he reached the point of acceptance, he was able to focus his mind on the solution that eventually saved his life.

Learn to practice acceptance, as "in any moment, you have the capacity to breathe deeply, relax, and let go. Allow rather than resist what arises in the present moment—inside or out. Let it be interesting rather than good or bad."[43] Acceptance is the opposite of giving up. Acceptance does not hinder action, but allows the individual the ability to dedicate complete attention to the present moment and find the most inspired solution.

---

[42] Ralston, Aron. 127 Hours: Between a Rock and a Hard Place. New York, NY: Atria Paperback, 2010. Print. Pg 280

[43] Millman, Dan, and Dan Millman. Body Mind Mastery: Creating Success in Sport and Life. Novato, Calif: New World Library, 1999. Print.

KEY 7

KEY SEVEN: EXHALE GRATITUDE

We usually think of gratitude as being thankful for something. But actually gratitude is more like an emotional state: "I am in gratitude" is like any other state of being, such as "I am in trouble" or "I am in love." It is identifying where you're standing. It is what you are: "I am in a state of thanks and gratitude." Gratitude is an acknowledgement, a "thank you" within your heart.

It's possible to feel gratitude for life, the universe, and everything, and live in that state of gratitude all the time.

A list of things you are thankful for is a great way to bring forth your initial feeling of gratitude. This practice will kick start your awareness of gratitude. But once it is in gear, once are aware of being grateful with every thought, gratitude rises. It is almost like a sense. You have a sense of smell, you have a sense of taste and you have a sense of gratitude: Gratitude is an aspect of perception. It evolves from taking an inventory of things you are grateful for to becoming a part of you. Gratitude, at this most evolved level, defines our relationship with literally everything.

Gratitude allows us to hold tight to the notion that all of life, every part, is to be perceived as a blessing, a gift. It lives in the now. It is a combination of how we see the world and, then, how we meet the world with our presence.

A Story from the Heart

I know a career cop. One of the sweetest guys you could ever know, but he has very definite opinions on things. And when you ask him his opinion, he will tell you, without holding back. And he will keep railing on until he's done.

So if you ask a question, be prepared to get a very full, detailed, (and often loud), answer.

We were out for a cup of coffee and he knew I was writing stories for this part of the book. I asked him if he could share a story about something he was grateful for, or maybe sometime he felt grateful.

He took a sip of his coffee, grabbed his napkin, wiped his mouth and looked straight at me. I could see the floodgates begin to open.

"You know" he said, "I have no idea what this whole gratitude thing is about and I'm still not sure. I'm not sure it matters, either.

"I think, frankly, it's a bunch of crap, people going around noticing how wonderful everything is. I mean, you need to practice this?"

He leaned into me a little. "Gratitude is like a big ladder. And as you move up each rung, you climb into a more exclusive club of gratitude. I'll explain as we go.

"Let's start at the bottom. You want to talk Gratitude, huh? Look at it this way. You, my friend, are a billion to one shot. Seriously and literally. One billion sperm, and you hit the egg. Slam dunk. You got the brass ring. Take up step up the next rung.

"Now let me put this out there. Let's say you're lucky enough to have been born into this country. You have made another one in a billion shot and now take your next step up.

"Go further up the ladder here. Look at me: You can hear what I'm saying, you can see my face, you can touch my hand. You have all of your senses working for you. And you can understand what I'm talking about. You know my words, you can understand my speech, right? Put yourself higher on the odds board of existence. You are increasingly rare, and we're not even close to being done.

"Now let's go to this point. You got a mother? How about a father? Know who they are? Keep going up. Are you in touch with either or both of them? Really? Keep climbing.

"You went to school? Another rung on the ladder my friend. Take a look at the statistics. You learned to read while you were in school, right? Yep, keep climbing. And you can read a magazine article from start to finish? Hey, here's one for you. How about an entire book? Keep going, man, and you're still miles away from getting near the real gratitude yet.

"Now let's go here, and these are going to get your attention.

"You drink water today? Oh, that's nice. Another step up. Oh, and it was clean? And it came out of a tap? Two big steps up, pal. You're into another galaxy of gratitude now. But we're not done. You eat today? Yeah, how many times? More than once? Keep going, keep going. But we're not done yet. Not even close."

The man was on a roll. I didn't date to interrupt. I just kept nodding.

"What's that you're wearing? A shirt? Honestly, is that what they call that thing? Keep going. Oh, and it fits, too? Like, the right size and everything? And you've only had it for a year, huh? Keep going.

"You have a job? Really, now. No, I don't want to know about it. I don't care what you do or if you like it or not. I just want to know that you have one. You have an actual job.

"So I'm thinking this: You had money to buy the food? And pay for your water? Amazing. Reach on up there. Keep climbing, my friend, because we only have two things left to go over. And you're going to really love these next two.

"You have transportation where you live? No, I don't mean a car, I'm talking about any transportation. A bike, a bus, a cab . . .

anything? Really now? Another step up the ladder. And this next one, oh, man you're going to love this.

"You get shot today? No? Oh, well, let me put it to you this way. Were you afraid of getting shot? Or stabbed? Or beaten? None of the above? Oh, that's great. You felt kind of safe today. How special. You are now so far up on that freakin' ladder that you have nearly left the galaxy.

"Now, we've got one more step. The last and most important step of all." He sipped his coffee and I could tell he was really reaching down for this one.

"Have you ever felt that somebody loved you, or that you loved somebody else?

"This is the high point of the ladder, my friend. You've ascended to the top. You've gotten the most wonderful thing you could ever have.

"Now let me tell you something. When you really realize how high you've climbed on that ladder, you'll never have to try and feel grateful about anything ever again. You'll just know it. In your heart, in your spirit, you'll just know it. It will be as much of a part of you as breathing. Every breath, you'll exhale gratitude."

I had never heard my friend speak this way. Not ever. Not once.

He sipped his coffee and leaned back in his chair. And he was silent. His eyes seemed to look past me, over my shoulder at some far off place. I was nearly dumbstruck by the way he articulated gratitude. Rapid fire, point by point.

And I figured this was as good a time as any to ask him a question.

"How did you know all of this? I mean, putting this list together, right off the top of your head."

He leaned in, and almost in a whisper, said, "Because the opposite of every one has happened to me."

He finished his coffee, got up and began to leave. And as he was about to walk away, he leaned in. Smiling at me, he said,

"That's why I know. And that's why I'm grateful. Every second of every day. That's why I'm grateful."

How it Works

Sometime today, get out a piece of paper and a pen. Then lay on your back in your bed, and imagine it's the first moment you woke up. OK, got this so far? You're in bed. Lying still. Head on your pillow. Your eyes open. You wake up.

Now, if you're like us, your first reaction is "I have to pee."

Instead, frame that as an expression of gratitude.

"I am grateful that I have to pee."

Today, do this. As much as you can, begin all that you do with thinking "I am grateful that . . . " "I am grateful that I lost my keys. It reminds me that I don't have Alzheimer's. I am really grateful I can think and retrace my tracks. And I am intensely grateful that I have found my keys."

This step will begin training you into a reflexive, automatic sense of gratitude. From your first thought, to everything else. Literally everything. To be "in gratitude" is akin to being "in school." You're paying attention to the world around you, with deliberate focus and pause. By purposely cultivating this attitude, repeatedly for a time, it becomes natural.

Now, if this doesn't work, look at it this way:

For a moment, imagine your life is ending. You've been told to put your affairs in order. What would you do now? What in your life becomes petty, insignificant, without meaning? What would change in your reactions, your encounters with other?

What matters now?

The answer? Everything. Everything matters. Everything becomes a reason to be grateful. Every. Single. Thing.

Contemplating your mortality is a severe exercise, but it will jump start your gratitude.

<u>Why this is Important</u>

The Dalai Lama says, "Every day, think as you wake up, today I am fortunate to be alive, I have a precious human life, I am not going to waste it. I am going to use all my energies to develop myself, to expand my heart out to others; to achieve enlightenment for the benefit of all beings. I am going to have kind thoughts towards others, I am not going to get angry or think badly about others. I am going to benefit others as much as I can."[44]

Gratitude has a synergistic effect on a person's life, as when a person recognizes and is be grateful for the positive things in their life, the person becomes happier. Research has shown "People who are consistently grateful have been found to be relatively happier, more energetic, and more hopeful, and to report experiencing more frequent positive emotions. They also tend to be more helpful and empathic, more spiritual and religious, more forgiving, and less materialistic than others who are less predisposed to gratefulness. Furthermore, the more a person is inclined to gratitude, the less likely he or she is to be

---

[44] Dalai Lama

depressed, anxious, lonely, envious, or neurotic."[45] Being grateful focuses the mind on the positive aspects of life, instead of what is lacking. Instead of feeling Gratitude, if a person focuses on what they do not have, they experience lack, which becomes desire. Desire blocks happiness by causing a person to wait for happiness at some later time, not find it in the present moment.

Two Princeton professors, economist Alan B. Krueger and Nobel laureate and psychologist Daniel Kahneman, collaborated on a study to determine if wealth is related to happiness. "Despite the weak relationship between income and global life satisfaction or experienced happiness, many people are highly motivated to increase their income."[46] The study found that people who are motivated by money are more likely to misallocate "their time, from accepting lengthy commutes (which are among the worst moments of the day) to sacrificing time spent socializing (which are among the best moments of the day)."[47] People who lack gratitude are constantly trying to fill a void, believing that if they had something more, they would be happier. Lack of gratitude causes people to overlook the present moment with the hope that in some future moment, when they have more, they will finally be happy. Happiness becomes a distant fantasy rather than a present reality.

Of course, there's a case to be made that some material possessions, like more money, a bigger house, or a safer car can help you attain your goals, protect your family, and increase your overall happiness. But consider a higher level of gratitude. If your goal is really to grow, evolve and become a more resilient, happier person, then we must even be grateful for challenging situations. "Consider it pure joy,

---

[45] Lyubomirsky, Sonja. The How of Happiness: A Scientific Approach to Getting the Life You Want. New York: Penguin Press, 2008. Print.

[46] Would You Be Happier If You Were Richer? A Focusing Illusion Daniel Kahneman, Alan B. Krueger, David Schkade, Norbert Schwarz, and Arthur A. Stone Science 30 June 2006: 312 (5782), 1908-1910. [DOI:10.1126/science.1129688]

[47] Would You Be Happier If You Were Richer? A Focusing Illusion Daniel Kahneman, Alan B. Krueger, David Schkade, Norbert Schwarz, and Arthur A. Stone Science 30 June 2006: 312 (5782), 1908-1910. [DOI:10.1126/science.1129688]

my brothers and sisters, whenever you face trials of many kinds, because you know that the testing of your faith produces perseverance."[48] Developing the ability to be grateful prepares a person to be positive, or at least resilient, in any situation.

---

48 Niv Bible. London: Hodder & Stoughton Ltd, 2007. Print. James 1:2-3

KEY 8

KEY EIGHT: APPRECIATION

Appreciation is the frosting on the cake of gratitude. Gratitude is to appreciation what "thank you" is to " . . . and that was amazing." It's saying "Thanks for making dinner, and by the way, it was delicious." It is noticing the particularly special, the out of the ordinary, even the unexpected, as adding depth to our lives. Appreciation is happiness and sheer excitement over how spectacular life can be.

When you see someone dance with steps barely sweeping the floor, or hear poetry that makes you weep, or watch a sunset where the clouds and color and reflection combine into a canvas unlike any painting you've ever seen, you can't help but sit back and feel a sense of awe over the wondrous life before you.

Appreciation is also finding value or goodness in that which draws your attention, even in the most routine and seemingly unnoticeable things. For example, a friend once told me that he "appreciates how smoothly the light switch moves up and down every time he turns on the light." He said he had never actually paid much attention to this until his wife told him that, when she returned from a small town in South America, the thing she noticed was how light switches were metal and, when switched from "on" to "off," made a rusty, stiff clicking noise. After that, our friend considered so many things he had taken for granted, in every part of his life. From driving a car to the way his head hit the pillow, he began to notice and offer appreciation for hundreds of small aspects of his life, every day.

Sometimes appreciation is seeing what you've missed and finding a new, more pronounced perspective. We often begin to appreciate life when we come close to losing it. We awaken our appreciation of things we used to take for granted. Life has a little more sound, more color, more light, and more energy. When something we are used to is taken away, we realize how much we miss it, and if it returns, we appreciate it more.

A Story from the Heart

As I was told the story, there was this writer for TV shows in Hollywood. He wrote for a few shows over the years, and had contributed to several others. He'd been a writer for nearly thirty years.

His friend was a really big fan of the TV shows he'd written for over the years. So, one year for his friend's birthday, the writer decided that he'd show the man around the studio and let him see how a TV show was put together.

When his friend showed up, he couldn't believe it. As they drove to the front gate of the lot, the writer introduced the security guard and got his friend a pass for the day. The friend was so overcome with excitement that he got out of the car, went right over to the security guard and shook his hand. He introduced himself and said how wonderful it was to meet him.

Now, the writer was a little uncomfortable. His friend just got all gushy over the guy in the booth who checks IDs. The writer had seen Norm, the security guard, every day for nearly twenty years – he was nobody special. Norm handed the writer back his ID as he had a thousand times before, and the writer rolled his eyes at his friend's excitement. Norm offered an understanding smile, and the writer drove to his office.

His friend's attitude didn't stop with the security guard. Everybody and everything they saw was met with "Wow." The studios, the writer's office, the sound stages, and the lights (seriously, the lights) were met with awe.

After the day was done, the writer and his friend went out to dinner.

After the meal they had a cup of coffee, and the writer asked his friend about his trip. He said it was one of the best things he'd ever seen. "It was so cool!" he said, and he described everything he'd seen and how it made him feel. "I couldn't say 'Wow' enough."

Now the writer thought about this. His friend seemed profoundly affected by just about everything. Even the writer's office. So the writer asked a question.

"Just throwing this out there," the writer said, "you were even impressed by my office. No window, piles and piles of papers, and it smells like an ashtray. My chair has stuffing coming out of the upholstery, and the walls still have calendars on them from three years ago.

"So, I have to ask: Why were you so awestruck by everything you saw today?"

The friend sat back, smiled, and said, "In the past year, I lost my brother and my uncle. I saw a coworker succumb to cancer. And my daughter lost her job and moved in with me.

"Then, I was diagnosed with cancer myself, and made the best of it throughout the process. I got good news last week."

The writer was speechless. His friend had never shared any of this with him.

"It's cliché to talk about how you appreciate things once you know you may never see them again. But this wasn't like that. I started saying 'Wow' inside of my head years ago. I would make a point of saying 'Wow' just once a day.

"The first thing I decided to say 'Wow' to was my toilet paper roll. I'm sitting in the bathroom, thinking about life, and I came up with the idea of looking at one thing every day and saying 'Wow' about it. And then there it was, right in front of me. I just never realized how cool toilet paper was. Those little serrated sheets that keep each piece easy to pull apart, the way it fits on the roll, and if you look at it really closely, you can see the weave in the paper, ever so slight."

The writer started to giggle, and the friend said, "No, really, I'm serious. It's quite beautiful. But, you know, I thought if the toilet paper, something I see every day, can make me say 'Wow,' all I have to do is adjust my focus a little.

"And it came just in time, too," the friend continued, "I needed that change in perspective to see the beauty of things. It kept me sane through the pain. I had to appreciate the good in this life, or I would have lost my mind."

The writer got quiet. His friend said, "I say 'Wow' a lot now, mostly inside. It's profound appreciation. It's like gratitude with laughter."

They left the restaurant. Both of them promised to stay in better touch. And the writer, as he drove home, kept thinking about what his friend said, about looking at things differently to really appreciate more about all there is in this life.

The next day, the writer was cleaning, when he went into the bathroom. He leaned over picked up a roll of toilet paper.

He thought of his friend. And looking back at the toilet paper roll, he smiled to himself and said, "Wow."

How it Works

It doesn't require a loss, a change, or a death to realize how different your life would be if you gave the time and attention to something as routine as, for instance, a light switch. Appreciation focuses and elevates gratitude by recognizing something and then assigning value to it.

We remember and take notice of the spectacular, and we express awe at that moment. Our focus is drawn to the act, the sound, or the scene. But that's just the one aspect of appreciation. We can appreciate the everyday by focusing, setting our gaze and attention on something that has often escaped our notice.

We truly can, if we listen, appreciate the sound of the wind, the birds, even the traffic by our window. In every step we take, we can appreciate how the floor creaks and bends as we walk softly around the room. We can appreciate the colors and dimensions, the texture and the position of every single thing within our sight.

And, if we look a little more closely, we can appreciate the presence of everything within our senses, the forehead-slapping amazement of the journey of life itself, with each piece fitting into the grand puzzle of our room, our home, our friends, our neighborhoods, and our lives.

It is easy to be bowled over by something extraordinary, saying "Wow" to any grand spectacle. But from within, appreciation is gratitude with focus and a smile. It is taking a moment to recognize how good even the most mundane can be. Appreciation, then, is saying "Thank you . . . and this has made my life so beautiful."

Why this is Important

Appreciating your life is a powerful tool to refocus on the positive–on what you have, not what is lacking. Appreciation starts with yourself. Appreciate your qualities and the things that make you original instead of criticizing yourself. Appreciating your life is key to happiness, whether you appreciate the roof above your head, clean air, family, a job, or a smile from a stranger. You can always try to get more and you can always find something wrong, but happiness is focusing on what you do have. It is impossible to have negative emotions like stress or sadness when you are appreciating yourself, others, and other aspects of your life. By having appreciation, you actively move your thoughts in a positive direction since, as Wayne Dyer says "When you change the way you look at things, the things you look at change."[49] You can even appreciate negative situations as a lesson, or a time to test emotional resilience. Zen master Gempo Dennis Merzel says, "That's the beautiful thing, that's the secret: to want what you get rather than trying to get what you want, because that seems like a never-ending battle, and a losing battle at that. We seem to always get what we need, though. So when we want what we get, it's really like wanting what we need." [50] By reframing your thoughts toward appreciation, you stop opposing life.

Along with appreciating yourself and your own life, it's also important to show others that you appreciate them, even verbally or in a simple note. This lets them know that they matter to you. Beyond setting the stage for a positive relationships with others, it makes them feel good. It brightens their day.

---

[49] Dyer, Wayne W. Change Your Thoughts, Change Your Life: Living the Wisdom of the Tao. Carlsbad, Calif: Hay House, 2007. Print.

[50] Merzel, Dennis G. Big Mind, Big Heart: Finding Your Way. Salt Lake City, Utah: Big Mind Pub, 2007. Print.

KEY 9

KEY NINE: KEEP A DIARY

Let's make sure we're clear on this. It's a diary. It's not a 'journal.

We detest journaling. Although there has been a wonderful outpouring of a thousand stories through journaling, it is usually just an account of your life. It is no more than a flat, poorly-detailed narrative of what you did today, what you hoped would happen, and whether you felt happy, or sad, or frustrated, or whatever.

Journals have no depth. They show little emotion. And reading one lends little more insight into who you are than you could get from reading your license plate. We could pick up ten journals and have no idea who wrote what about whom. They are interchangeable. One journal is no more significant, distinct, or different than another. Most amount to no more than a list of events, some description, and an occasional annoyance. It's akin to reading a book about traveling through a few small towns: they aren't terribly interesting, they have the same scenery, and after ten minutes they will bore you to tears and be soon forgotten.

This is why we make the distinction between writing a journal and keeping a diary. We also want to note the difference in verbs. You write a journal but you keep a diary.

A diary is you. When you are writing, you're writing to your diary. It is a conversation, not a play by play. Keeping a diary is an outpouring of emotion. Your diary listens to you. When you write in a diary, you're telling it your most personal, most intimate secrets. Why do you think so many diaries come with a lock and key? Ever seen a journal come with one of those? Yeah, we haven't either.

A Story from the Heart

"What I know," Julian said, sitting on his patio, "is that keeping a diary has saved my life."

Julian is sixty six years old. When I contacted him about why, (not what), he wrote in his diary, and after some pestering on my part, he agreed to speak to me about his process of writing over all these years.

I asked him how he got started.

"I watched my mother. She kept a diary.

"I lived near a farm. Not on one, mind you. That would have been great. No, my mother was a domestic worker on a farm. She had me out of wedlock. Back then, and where we were from, that was a pretty bad thing. So, her family sent her out of the house to make it on her own. It was a cruel thing to do, but my mother was a tough lady. She was only nineteen. But she took her clothes, stuck them in a bag, and went to make a life on her own.

"My first memory of her writing was when I was about five. My mother was a very reserved woman. She didn't have anyone to talk to anyway, so this was her way of processing her thoughts. After she came home from the farm, I saw her sitting on the edge of her bed, writing in a little book. I saw this key dangling from her hand, and I asked her about it. She said that the book had a lock to keep her thoughts safe. I didn't understand what she meant by that at the time, but I remember her locking the book with the little metal lock diaries have, then putting it in her drawer.

"Now, you should know that we had it hard. My Mom barely made enough for us to get by. We were dirt poor. And, growing up, I knew how hard it was for her to care for herself and especially me. She never mentioned it, but I always felt that I needed to do more to help. I tried to be as good of a kid as I was able, and I never gave her any trouble. Didn't have any friends, but I just kept to myself.

"Over time, from watching her, I started to write down my thoughts when I was about eight. I don't have those old diaries anymore, but I remember writing with my mother while she was writing in hers. After about a week, she told me that I should do mine in private, and that this process was a time to 'be still, and think about your day.'

"And it helped. Made me feel less lonely, less afraid . . . But, I told you that the diary helped save my life. Well, one day, when I was seventeen, my Mom didn't come home from work. Hours passed, and I finally called her work. They said that she'd been taken to the hospital that day, and the folks in the house went with her to the Emergency Room.

"I hitchhiked into town and got to the hospital. My mother was on life support. She had a stroke. The doctors were attending to her, but when I asked the nurse how she was, she shook her head and said, 'We probably won't know for another few hours.'

"Not an hour after the nurse saw me, the doctor came out to the waiting room and told me that my mother had passed away. I had never been struck with such profound sadness in my life.

"After the funeral, I was to supposed move in with my aunt and uncle, but I didn't go. I just stayed in the house. And the depression just deepend. My diary entries were short and very dark. So were my thoughts. The grief of my mother's death took hold and I wasn't able to shake it loose.

"Then, after a day or two, I decided it would be best to end my life." Julian looked at me, scratched his head and said, "With my Mom gone, I thought my life was over. And I didn't know what else to do. On my way to my room to go to bed that night, I passed my mother's room. Her diary was left out on her nightstand. I don't remember this ever happening. Maybe I just didn't notice, but there it was.

"So, I opened her diary. I had never done that before and I don't remember what compelled me to do it that day." Julian picked up the diary he had brought with him to our meeting. "Her last entry before she went to the hospital reads as follows: 'Dear Diary, My dear Julian is my greatest blessing. Please give him the strength to meet all his goals. Please give me the words to heal his heart, to let him know how much I love him, how much he means to me, and how empty my life would be without him.'

"That night," Julian said, "changed everything. I put down my mother's diary, and went back to my room. My entry for that night was, 'Dear Diary, I'll get through this. I'll keep moving forward. Please let my Mom know, wherever she is, that I'm going to be OK.'"

Julian started to cry, and said, "I tear up every time I read that. But I began a new life that day, one that my mother would be proud of.

"My diary continues to give me focus, to chart my path, and to bring my feelings to the surface. I write in it every day. It helps me think, it absolutely helps me get clarity on my feelingsI It makes me feel like my Mom is right next to me.

"And that night when I was seventeen," Julian said, "her diary saved my life."

How it Works

When you keep a diary, you are writing about the most personal aspects of your life: your feelings and your insights. You put down into words what you feel in your heart. And you lock this thing and put it away. It's between you and your diary.

A diary is a place where you can say things that you never want to share with anybody. You can place there any feelings, perspectives, opinions, and anything you've done. When you keep a diary, you give your feelings form. You have a record of not only who you are, but what you felt and how those feelings changed over time.

To open your heart to a diary, all you need is the willingness to be honest and detailed. It's a beautiful way to record your life. A diary is riddled with emotion. Sadness, grief, heartache, loss; joy, excitement, anticipation and achievement. Anger, frustration, disappointments, and letdowns. Wonder, appreciation, gratitude, and, most importantly, love.

A diary is more than just a place to put your memories. It is the story of your life and emotional history. When most people decide to give feelings form in a diary, they do it in spurts. Sometimes years pass between efforts. That's OK. Memories and feelings often require diaries to, if nothing else, make sense of how things are. A diary can make sense of your memories and feelings. Sometimes that takes a little time.

Get out your diary during the big events that evoke strong feelings. Start writing in your diary then. Soon you'll realize that everything in your life is a big event, and you can write about it as you feel the need.

A diary can become one of your greatest companions. It will show you who you were, how you've changed, and what you felt as you wrote. Your emotional organization improves with a diary, as does your ability to rely more on yourself and your instincts. As you become more accustomed to writing down your feelings with the honest abandon that diaries pull forth, you trust yourself a little more. A consistency forms in your view of your life and your feelings. And, ultimately, you become more comfortable with yourself. You know yourself better. And you like yourself better, too.

Begin this practice. And let loose when you write. A new world of insight about yourself and your life awaits.

Why this is Important

Life goes by fast. What was once easily remembered, fades. Lessons learned, often are forgotten. As Socrates says, "the unexamined life is not worth living for a human being."[51] A diary allows you to look at your life on a bigger scale, to examine your life. To see your thoughts and feelings, and see how they change and evolve over time. From this broad perspective, you can clarify goals, and see if where you are spending most of your time is creating the life you want.

On a day-to-day basis, a diary allows you to process thoughts and events in a written, linear way. By processing information in writing, you clarify your thinking. You are able to consciously and intentionally assign meaning to the events in your life, as well as providing a context to understand feelings. This connects you to your heart.

[51] Socrates

KEY 10

KEY TEN: LEARN TO LET GO

This next step seems counterintuitive to most of us, but it is placed in this book for a reason. To let go is to admit when our efforts will no longer result in progress, positive change, or improvement.

Human beings, by nature, are very cause-and-effect oriented. We take an action and we recognize a reaction. We have been raised to follow this basic law of physics. When we interact with our environment and the people within it, we expect to cause a response.

However, when we let go, we recognize that we have done enough. We have done all we can do, and no further action will improve the situation, but it will exhaust us.

When we let go, we realize our limitations. We have faith that the winds of life will affect the situation beyond what we can see and what we can do. To Let Go means to come to terms with life as it stands. It means to identify what we can and cannot change, and find peace in that release. It is not a surrender. Rather, it is stopping, evaluating, and allowing external factors to shape the circumstance. It is almost as if you are a momentary observer in your life. And in that moment you are at peace with who you are and what you can do.

To let go is to stand back and observe. It is a suspension of our involvement. It is the next step after we accept. We decide to release. We watch and wait. And we refrain engagement altogether.

We let go.

A Story from the Heart

"I'll tell you how I found out how to let go," said our rather straight in the face friend of ours, "I went out and got a dog."

Standing in our friend's living room, we all looked at each with the same expression on our faces: what does getting a dog have to do with letting go?

He must have seen our confusion.

"Tell you what I'm talking about. You've known me for a long time, right?"

He's looking straight at me. I've known my friend for a long time, but then, at my age, I've known most of my friends a long time. He was one of the first guys I'd known who had gone through a 12-step program and now he is thirty years sober.

I asked him what he meant by "letting go" and his usual pleasant demeanor became drawn. He became a little more serious, lowered his voice and said, "Letting go is one of the hardest things I've ever had to explain to anybody, let alone understand." When people talked about getting sober, they said that you needed to 'let go' and 'let God' and 'do the next indicated step' and all that stuff which, at the time I first became sober, was like trying to make sense of an owner's manual of an electron accelerator printed in Latin."

He was on a roll. "Let go. Yeah, sure. All our lives we're trained to 'hang on' and 'keep pushing' and now you're telling us not just to stop, but to release ourselves of this process? This was the most frustrating concept I'd ever encountered, and in the first couple years of my sobriety, I was worried that if I didn't get a handle on it, I would go out and get hammered. And that probably would've been the last time I drank, because I would have been dead.

"This thing had me over a barrel. I was such a controlling guy, I just didn't know how to let go. I studied the Serenity Prayer. You know what that is, right?" We said we did, but he recited it anyway: "God, grant me the serenity to accept the things I cannot change. Know what that is?"

We didn't answer fast enough.

"Everything! OK, then it goes, "the courage to change the things I can. Know that that is? Me! And the wisdom to know the difference rests on your ability to know what you are truly not in control of, and allow that to be a guiding principle of your life."

"Kind of like letting go?" I said.

"No, exactly like letting go." My friend's direct, but you probably picked that up already.

"So, let me get back to the dog. Twenty eight years ago, I had a girlfriend. She left me. And when she left me, she left behind a yellow lab named Bob. See, there's his picture." And on the mantelpiece over the fireplace was a picture of a really beautiful yellow lab, lying in the grass.

"Well, I wasn't too wild about the idea of taking care of a dog, but I didn't want to abandon him or give him away. And I was far enough into the program to know that if a gift comes your way, embrace it. But first, it helps to know that it's a gift. And, believe me, I wasn't sure whether Bob was the gift I needed, but I wasn't going to rest on my judgment, either. So, I kept him.

"First time I took Bob for a walk, we went down about two blocks from the house, and I saw another dog come right at him. And I'm holding on to Bob, and this dog starts growling. Well, Bob growled back and I kept walking. Bob gave him a look as he was passing us, and we walked on. He looked back up at me, got this big smile on his face, and started sniffing along the sidewalk, happy as he could be.

"I stopped. And I thought, 'That's what's letting go is all about. Bob just showed me. Right there, he had a conflict, it passed, and he let it go. He went about the business of sniffing and smiling and walking, just being a dog.'

"I finished walking Bob and I thought, 'That's it.' Letting go is precisely that. Letting things pass. Going about your business. Having the thought, whatever it is, then righting yourself and your focus into smiling and walking and sniffing, just like Bob.

"In the last twenty-eight years, I've had three dogs. The first, Bob, lived another twelve years. The second lived for twelve years, and . . . where's Bob?"

"He's in the picture," I said, pointing to the mantelpiece.

"Oh, no. I mean, Bob my dog. Because of Bob, my first dog, I've named the other two Bob in memory of him. Bob number two and Bob number three. But I've just called them all 'Bob.'

He whistled, and from the yard came a bounding mass of yellow hair, big eyes, and a huge smile. "This is Bob. The third of a line of dogs with a PhD in 'letting go.' "

<u>How it Works</u>

The first step is to realize that your involvement isn't making things better. You can recognize this when you feel increasingly frustrated at the lack of change in your relationship with another person or situation. It feels a little like you're pushing a rope. You can be the best rope pusher around, and you're exerting all kinds of energy toward that rope, but nothing is happening. All you're feeling is frustrated and upset, bewildered, and possibly a little anxious.

The second step is to stop. We must pause. We don't necessarily have to do anything at that moment; we just take a minute to step back or step away from the urge to respond, act, or offer input. Once that is done, we then recognize we have done enough.

The third step is to be okay with this distance. It is our nature to involve ourselves. We start to let go by disengaging for a period of time. Here, we revisit our sense of faith. Faith that other variables will, for better or for worse, result in the positive conclusion that we cannot bring about ourselves. It's faith that, even without our influence, things are going to be all right.

Why this is Important

Letting go is essential to happiness. By continuing to think about past pain, you relive it, and, the pain continues to be real. You give your energy to the events of your past, which feed them and keep them alive. Pema Chödrön says "We'd be wise to question why we hold a grudge as if it were going to make us happy and ease our pain. It's rather like eating rat poison and thinking the rat will die. Our desire for relief and the methods we use to achieve it are definitely not in sync."[52] To let go is not to be a doormat. Letting go is observing a situation, maybe even taking necessary action, but not keeping it alive in your thoughts. Like a computer's limited amount of processing speed, the mind only has a certain amount of thought capacity. When a person mentally relives the past, it takes energy away from their mind, sacrificing awareness of the present moment. Unless a person fully lets go of their past, they will continue to be affected by it. Letting go calms anger, hurt, and other negative emotions, leaving room to experience the positive in the present moment.

[52] Chödrön, Pema. The Places That Scare You: A Guide to Fearlessness in Difficult Times. Boston: Shambhala, 2001. Print.

KEY 11

KEY ELEVEN: FORGIVENESS

There's a reason forgiveness comes after letting go. To let go is recognizing that our involvement in a situation has reached the limit of its effectiveness. To forgive is recognizing that holding on to anger, resentment, and self-righteousness stops us from developing and sustaining inner peace. In Aramaic, the word forgive means to untie. In Latin, forgive means to release or to pardon. To forgive is to let go with your emotions and your spirit.

To forgive is to release the emotional pain caused by another's action. You recognize that continuing to hold resentment toward the person that caused you pain no longer serves you any purpose. Imagining how to rectify an injury, or pondering a counterattack, is no longer viable. You find yourself weighed down by sustaining your resentment. In forgiving, you disavow yourself from the emotional machinations that take up so much time and energy. You end your investment in evening the score.

Forgiveness brings freedom. In the release of this anger, the letting go of this inner tension, you recognize a calm. It almost feels like you've let go of a weight. You're lighter. And that person is no longer the center of your feelings. Through forgiveness, you reclaim your heart.

A Story from the Heart

I went to see my old friend, a guy I met in first grade. I sat down on his couch and he poured us a cup of coffee.

My friend was picked on. When we were kids, he was subjected to such cruelty that it hurt to listen.

I used to sit next to him in class. I'd listen to the whispers, the taunts, and the barrage of insults that came his way. I was too afraid to stand up and fight for him, too afraid of what would be done to me.

Although the childhood taunts stopped when we got a little older, he said he spent his teenage years preoccupied with becoming invisible. As he stirred the cream into his coffee, he said, "I didn't know who I really was, largely because I couldn't find myself. But I didn't let anybody else find me, either, so the pain from the outside stopped. The pain from the inside, not so much."

He didn't go to college, but he took a few classes to hone his skills, eventually becoming a computer hardware tech. "Originally, I knew that this would isolate me," he confessed," but the computer can't give me any grief. Well, most days it can't," he said, winking at me.

He said he wanted to make sure that he didn't interact with people. His life became entrenched in online contacts, virtual reality, and role playing games between faceless forms, known only by their screen names. No eyes to see, he explained, no presence to feel. Just the contact between the computer screens.

Taking another sip of coffee, he looked up at me, exhaled a little, and said, "Then something really odd happened. I was taking the bus to work. Regular day, nothing out of the ordinary about it. I sit in the back of the bus, as I have always done, every day. Nothing unusual.

"I look at this guy as I'm going to the back. He's sitting by himself, just staring straight ahead. But his eyes look familiar. Not sure where I could place them from, but something about him really stuck with me.

"Now, all of a sudden, it hits me. I'm thinking I'm living in an episode of The Twilight Zone. The guy who is sitting not two seats in front of me was the guy who gave me the hardest time in grammar school. This guy was the meanest, the most unkind. He didn't care. I remember him having hit me, spit on me, and pushed me down. Over eight years of my childhood, this guy made me most afraid.

"And here he was. Just sitting. And there I was, doing the same thing. The two of us, reunited as adults, in this random meeting.

"Right then, I felt afraid again. I felt like I was a kid. All that anxiety, all that fear came back. I felt my face get hot, and a tear rolled out of my eye and down my cheek."

He swallowed hard and kept talking. "Just as I was falling into the depths of this anxiety, I stood up. For no apparent reason, I grabbed on to the back of the seat in front of me, and stood up. I stared at the back of his head for what seemed to be a few minutes, but I know it was maybe ten seconds. Then I walked into the aisle. And I felt my feet move toward him.

"It was as if I was in a trance. I didn't know what I was feeling. I was almost having an out-of-body experience. I was walking up the aisle and I stopped. Right next to his seat. I stopped. Before I could say anything, he looked up at me, and his eyes widened. I don't know if he recognized me or not, but before I could say anything, he said, 'Hi.' And I froze. He looked away, out the window. I was struck with a feeling of rage that I'd never experienced before.

"I saw his face. And it wasn't the face of the child that hurt me. It was the face of a man, a person I didn't know, somebody who had lived their life through joys and trials, as I had. This was a face unfamiliar to me, a stranger's face.

"At that moment, my rage disappeared. I put my hand on the back of his seat, and walked back to the chair in the back of the bus. And I wept."

He started to choke up. "I cried not because I was upset, not at all. I cried because I had released him from my heart." He put down his cup, folded his hands in his lap. "I was no longer afraid, no longer angry. When I sat back down, looking out the bus window at the gray slate sky overhead, I forgave the child that tormented me. In the eyes of that man, whomever he had become, I forgave him for having lived his own life of anger, for having been raised in a family that may have been angry with him, or may have condoned his behavior. I finally forgave him for being such an angry little boy, and for turning that anger toward me."

Another deep breath came. My friend sat up in his chair, and leaned forward. Looking straight at me, he said, "Then I forgave myself. I forgave myself for not fighting back. I forgave myself for being afraid, and I forgave myself for holding on to the shame it caused me and the horrible drop in self-esteem I've lived with all these years.

"The bus stopped. I got off, wiped the tears from my eyes. I walked home.

"As I passed through the front door, I looked at my face in the mirror by the hallway. For the first time, I could see the person I was truly meant to be. I saw past my fear. And saw my face."

We were nearly in tears. I got up and hugged my dear friend and he said, "Forgiveness isn't something you do. It's not an action, it's an attitude. Forgiveness is knowing that you're OK now, you can take care of yourself. Forgiving yourself finally lets you off the hook." Sitting back down, with a smile on his face, he said, "Today, I'm me. And that's finally what I've come to be. And I'm good with that. Yeah, I'm good."

How it Works

To forgive is a coming to terms, of sorts. It is arriving at an emotional destination. You conclude that this feeling of resentment is counterproductive to your peace. You decide–from either a sense of spiritual awakening, or emotional fatigue, or a little of both–that these feelings no longer serve your purpose. In this context, forgiveness is something you do for yourself.

There is a feeling of vulnerability that goes along with this decision. You feel like you're dropping your weapon and surrendering your arms. And this is true. You are no longer in a state of alert or readiness against your enemy.

But, realize the enemy is you. The only enemy is the pervasive and continuing anger coursing through your consciousness. Nelson Mandela, after being unjustly imprisoned for 27 years fighting for racial equality says, "as I walked out the door toward the gate that would lead to my freedom, I knew if I didn't leave my bitterness and hatred behind, I'd still be in prison."

You decide to release, to untie yourself from the old angers. No more scores to settle, no more plans of retribution. You forgive the person for giving into their human weakness and allowing the darker part of their spirit to injure you. You impart to them a spirit of love in the release, and wish they ascend to their highest good.

You may have to repeat this a few times. This is a new conclusion for your spirit, and these resentments have a way of creeping back in. If it happens, continue to tell yourself that you wish to be free of the inner conflict. This is your new motivation.

Why this is Important

Forgiveness, fundamentally, is not about who or what caused you to hurt; forgiveness helps you. Ken Wilber says, "The theory behind forgiveness is simple: The ego, the separate-self sense, is not just a cognitive construct, but also an affective one. That is, it is propped up not just by concepts but by the emotions."[53] Your ego is

[53] Wilber, Ken. Grace and Grit: Spirituality and Healing in the Life and Death of Treya Killam Wilber. Boston: Shambhala, 1991. Print. Pg 159

the sense of identity your mind creates, using your thoughts and emotions. Emotional pain feels so real that it reinforces the ego, since ego identifies with and claims "My Pain." Negative events and insults reinforce this false sense of self. This pain grows because the ego "feed[s] on any experience that resonates with its own kind of energy, anything that creates further pain in whatever form: anger, destructiveness, hatred, grief, emotional drama, violence, and even illness."[54] The more this negative energy grows, the more it becomes part of your identity. Forgiveness is difficult because it requires letting go of this negative part of yourself, the part that feels alone, separated from others.

Forgiveness releases you from the bondage of your own thoughts and labels, and it's a powerful self-development practice. When you forgive, you are actually freeing yourself since, as Viktor E. Frankl says, "Each of us has his own inner concentration camp . . . We must deal with, with forgiveness and patience–as full human beings, as we are and what we will become."[55] We create this prison by holding onto negative energy and sense of separation. As Ken Wilber says, to forgive is to "uncoil the pain of my own self-contraction." [56] Forgiveness releases you from that contraction, the negative thoughts and feelings, freeing up energy you can use positively.

[54] Tolle, Eckhart. The Power of Now: A Guide to Spiritual Enlightenment. Novato, Calif: New World Library, 1999. Print.pg 37

[55] Pattakos, Alex. Prisoners of Our Thoughts: Viktor Frankl's Principles for Discovering Meaning in Life at Work. San Francisco, Calif: Berrett-Koehler, 2010. Print. pg 4

[56] Wilber, Ken. Grace and Grit: Spirituality and Healing in the Life and Death of Treya Killam Wilber. Boston: Shambhala, 1991. Print. Pg 159

KEY 12

KEY TWELVE: KNOW YOUR ANGER

One emotion will neutralize the presence and overtures of your heart, erasing the good you establish and your positive energy.

This emotion is Anger. Anger, no matter what, no matter how enlightened or spiritual you become, still arises. Anger is programed into our biology. Anger, like all emotions, has physiological, neurological, and cognitive components. Anger, like our temperature, has varying degrees, from warm to a searing blaze, from a mild irritation to a rage that cannot be repressed, denied, or ignored. Anger is the ego's defense mechanism and it takes over your mind like a parasite. If you feed it, it grows. Anger hijacks your world, contracts your focus to a single point of negativity, and warps reality to aggression and fearful pessimism.

Anger interrupts the motion and energy of the heart and turns it away. If the heart is where healing resides, anger has no place there, since anger heals nothing. Let us make this clear: When seeking to communicate with the heart, screaming and yelling doesn't make us heard. Anger prevents us from engaging with the spirit of another. In matters of the heart, the foundation of human existence, Anger helps nothing.

Anger disguises our feelings and disconnects us from who we truly are. So often in our lives, if we are afraid or sad, we become angry. Fear and sadness feel passive. We have no control. We are at their mercy. Anger, however, feels active; it is an adrenaline rush that gives us a sense of power and control. We mobilize these feelings away from our heart into anger, suspending genuine expression of our feelings.

Anger propels us into potential or intensified conflict. Relationships are destroyed. Hearts are broken. Wariness and apprehension replace trust and friendship.

Anger is isolating and self-righteous. It intrudes upon the peace of others and dissolves serenity. Anger destroys trust, supplants understanding, and displaces love.

A Story from the Heart

A video from Germany went viral not long ago, and at this point it's had about 5 million hits.

A friend of mine, a sociologist and a really smart, kind man, sat with me as I watched it. He asked me to make conclusions about the video after it was done.

The video opens introducing us to about six boys, around the ages of 10 to 15. Each one is told that they are going to meet someone.

Off from the side comes a girl about their age. She stands in front of them while the interviewer tells the boys to shake hands with her, give her a hug, even stroke her hair.

Then the interviewer tells each boy, "Now, I want you to hit her.

The camera then looks at the face of each boy, zooming in one at a time to catch their expression.

To a boy, their eyes show pain. An awkward smile, one of surprise, comes to each face.

And each one pauses.

Each of the boys say something like, "What?" or "Did you say, 'hit her?' "

The interviewer clarifies the question. He says that, yes, they should hit the girl. And, he says, he wants them to hit her in the face. "Just slap her," he says.

"Go on. Do it."

The boys stall.

"What's the matter? Why can't you hit her?"

Answers like, "I don't want to," or "it's not right" come in uncomfortable whispers from each boy.

The interviewer insists that each boy should hit this girl. "Now," he says, "Do it now. Stop stalling."

To a child, each one refuses.

And that's the end of the video.

Then my friend leaned over and asked me what I concluded from this video.

I told him that this was consistent with the old adage that the better you know somebody, the harder it is to hurt them. "You don't want to hurt your friends, and . . . "

He stopped me. "You're missing the point," he said. "Come on, what did you see?"

I told him I saw boys becoming acquainted with a girl and when the director said to hit her, they all backed down.

"That's not all. There was something else present within each one of those boys."

"Compassion?" I guessed.

"Yes, but something within them brought forth that compassion. Either most of them had never seen anyone get angry, which is somewhat possible, or they have all been the subject of someone's anger, which is far more likely.

"I would speculate that one or more of these kids have been the targets of someone's anger," he said. "Maybe a parent or a peer. And these kids, standing there in front of the camera, with an adult insisting to strike this girl, had enough time to think about how this anger had hurt them, and how they didn't want to hurt somebody else as they have been hurt.

"What you saw was a choice being made. Anger is a choice. Wherever it comes from, it is a choice."

My friend stroked his chin and, turning back toward me, said, "My sense is that their feelings of empathy and reference to pain, and least in some of them, guided their decision. But, even if that wasn't the case, they all chose to refrain from causing another person harm.

"In part," my friend continued, "you saw empathy in motion. But, bottom line, you saw a decision being made to turn away from harm and turn toward love. They all stepped away from an action of anger and responded with a gesture of peace."

My friend stood in the middle of the room and smiled, "You know what you saw? A decision."

"Anger is a decision. Each and every time. And you have the choice. Decide with anger. Or, as these children did, decide with peace."

How it Works

To understand anger, we need to understand that it is within our nature: Anger is part of who we are. It is a neurological response to a threat, part of the hard-wired fight or flight mechanism. For so many of us, there is no middle ground–we are programmed to fight.

We most often become angry when our expectations are not met. And this can be over just about anything: When we expect the water bill to be $50, but it's $100. When we expect our spouse to be home at 7, but they're home at 9. When we expect the toilet to flush first thing in the morning, but it overflows.

Another kind of expectation is how we expect others to treat us or respond to us. Anger comes when we expect others to recognize our needs. Whether it's by our family members or the clerk at the grocery store, if we are not treated the way we expect, Anger follows.

Anger suppresses fear and sadness. Instead of just being sad or afraid, and letting the feelings pass, we fall back on anger to propel us into action. Making this suppression a habit can, and often does, contribute to emotional problems and physical illness. If we do not, in calmer moments, return to the feelings that created the conflict, we never process our feelings. Anger becomes the only emotional route we travel when upset about a conflict over our wants and expectations.

To know how anger works, we must be aware of how we truly feel when our expectations are unmet. We must look at the value we place on anger in our lives, and conduct an inventory of the lives that have been hurt by our anger. This book's practice of cognitive awareness, spiritual focus, and behavioral change will lessen the need for anger by helping you see that anger no longer serves a purpose in your communication. Release your anger completely to let your life flow unfettered.

Resolve to let go of your anger. Feel your heart open to all of life.

<u>Why this is Important</u>

It's common to be angry at yourself over past actions, mistakes, or shortcomings, particularly when fighting to protect damaged parts of yourself. Anger comes when your psyche is damaged or experiences lack. "When you understand the roots of anger in yourself and in the other, your mind will enjoy true peace, joy and lightness."[57] From a place of understanding, anger is much easier to manage.

Aristotle said "anyone can become angry—that is easy. But to be angry with the right person, to the right degree, at the right time, for the right purpose, and in the right way—that is not easy."[58] To illustrate this point, consider a common scenario. A person says something hurtful, or just acts like a jerk to you; your ego could respond by feeling hurt or feeling angry at this jerk. The ego creates anger as a defense to protect itself from bad feelings. The Higher Self (the you that is not weighted down by limiting emotions or thoughts) on the other hand, would hear the hurtful comments, and accept the other person's inner chaos, without feeling insulted or even assuming that the other person had hostile. The Higher Self could even go so far as to appreciate that the hurtful actions were driven by the other person's inner turmoil, anger, and pain. I might then feel a deep sympathy, understanding that this thinking plagues all people.

Unbind your heart, live in openness. People living with closed hearts cause "a huge amount of unnecessary suffering in the world—unnecessary, because it does not arise directly from our life circumstances, but from the conditioned way in which we react to our own misunderstood inner feelings."[59] The root of anger, (just like fear and desire), is trying to control a situation, time, place, person, or anything else external. A person feels anger when the external environment does not cooperate with their projection of how reality should be, what they want reality to be, or when their reality is going to suffer a loss. Acceptance is the antidote to anger.

---

[57] Nhất, Hạnh. Teachings on Love. Berkeley, Calif: Parallax Press, 1997. Print. Pg 29

[58] Aristotle

[59] Mondo Zen Training Manual http://www.mondozen.org/_literature_118189/Mondo_Zen_Training_Manual_for_eReaders

KEY 13

KEY THIRTEEN: KNOW FEAR

We have given you a good start at finding light along the path of your heart. But if anything in life will extinguish that light and leave you stranded in the darkest part of your emotions, it is fear. We must know the potential derailing effects of fear well if we want to stay on our heart's journey.

Fear keeps us from living a fulfilled and happy life. It prevents us from taking risks, and from fully believing in ourselves. Fear fuels our misgivings, our self-doubt, our insecurities. It activates our prejudices and our addictions.

Fear is our withdrawal, our immobilization, and our lethargy. It is our depression, our pathology, our illness. It is our anger, our fury, our rage. It is our vigilance, our righteousness, our convergent conviction. It is our less than, our want to, and our I wish-I-could. It is our letdowns, our disappointments, our resentments.

Fear is ourselves at our worst.

. . . But you already knew that.

You would not have picked up this book without being acquainted, on some level or in some aspect of your life, with fear. You're not alone. Everybody–every single person, without exception–is sometimes afraid.

We're afraid we will fail. We're afraid we will be alone. We're afraid we will be poor. We're afraid we will forget. We're afraid we won't know what to do next. We're afraid we won't get there on time. We're afraid we will get lost. We're afraid we will get hurt. We're afraid we will get sick. We're afraid we will die.

So many self-help books talk about how to make your life better, but they don't get into how to release your fear. And it's not that hard.

A Story from the Heart

One July afternoon, a mother brought her eight-year-old boy into my office. She'd become frustrated because he wouldn't go to sleep at night. When she finally put him to bed, he would get up and wander into her bedroom; he was afraid, and he wanted to sleep in her bed.

He was afraid that aliens would come to his house and peer in through his window while he was sleeping.

This little guy gave me a great dissertation about this, and he claimed that as recently as last week he saw a UFO, and immediately told his grandfather about it. His grandfather said it was a bunch of balloons–he didn't believe him.

The Mom said she hadn't had a decent night's sleep in three months, and taking him to counseling was the last straw before she medicated him into slumber every night. She didn't want to drug him to sleep; after all, he was only eight. But she was at her wits' end.

So the boy sat on my couch and told me about the aliens. He said that he was sure they were looking at him through his window while he was sleeping. He said that this really scared him.

Here's what I told him:

"You're right. Sometimes aliens do come down to our planet, peer into windows, and go on to the next house and do the same thing. They do this a lot. It's their version of sightseeing."

"Aliens come down here for vacation. That's it. That's their only purpose. They come down, maybe land someplace or just hover for a while, and check out the planet. They live on other planets in other galaxies. They come down in order to get a little rest and relaxation from whatever they do day to day in their cities and towns, far away up there.

"And their spaceship? Think of it as a big RV. Kind of like taking the Winnebago out to the Grand Canyon. Except, in the case of an alien family, Earth is like Disneyworld to them, and looking into your window is just part of the show.

"And the aliens that look into your window? Kid aliens. The adult aliens know that it's not polite to look into somebody else's window and they know it's not polite to stare. That's why they don't stay long. They let the kids have a little look and then, that's it. They take off to see another house.

"So, bottom line, kiddo, you are probably a pretty interesting person for the aliens to want to stop by and have a look. And, remember, this is summertime. The aliens go on their vacations just like everybody else. Come first week of school, you won't see any of them anymore. They have to go to school just like you do."

I let the Mom know a little of the story, reframing the fear with understanding and perspective. I told her that he may even welcome the images now without fear and, instead, understanding and a feeling of patient curiosity.

Last night, I heard from his Mom. He slept in his room. The fear was gone. Now he's looking up at the sky hoping to see if the "kid aliens" show up so he can show them his room. And his room has never been neater.

Gotta love that kid.

How it Works

Every thought that inspires fear begins with the words "What if." Think about how you structure your thoughts when you're afraid: you'll realize "what if" is right in the beginning. Those two words keep you from moving forward in life with confidence and self-assurance.

The best response to these thoughts is another two words: "Oh, Well." That's it. "Oh, Well."

Every time you're afraid, identify the source of the "what if." It only takes a second. If you know you're afraid, and something is really causing you a great deal of anxiety, you have to go to the point where that sentence begins. Let's say you're in traffic. "What if I'm late for work?" This is common for everybody. Soon the "what if" sentences pile up: "What if I get there late and my boss is mad?" "What if I don't have enough time to do all of my work?" "What if I get there and I miss something really important because I'm late?"

Two words can bring your confidence back immediately. Just stop for a second, and go back to the very first principle Be Present. Think for just a second, then say "Oh, well, the boss is mad. She's been mad before and I've been able to handle it all right." "Oh, well, if I don't have enough time to do the work today, I'll pick it up when I can. I always do my work and I'm always pretty thorough. And what if I get there and I miss something really important? Oh, well, I'll make sure I get updated."

That "Oh, well" just gave you a boost of confidence and pushed away the fear. Two words did that. There's a sense of letting go in the words, "Oh, well." An inherent lightening of your perspective and increased confidence. Those two little words give you clarity. They switch and reframe your view, letting you know you can handle whatever makes you anxious or afraid.

"Oh, well." Keep those two words handy anytime fear begins to descend upon you. You may have to say it repeatedly, at first, to truly convince yourself that life will be OK. You don't need to be afraid. You can handle whatever comes your way.

Why this is Important

Fear never goes away, so to reach your full potential, you must be able to act in the face of fear. This ability gives people the opportunity to become more than who they were, even more than they could imagine themselves becoming. These people become heroes. The hero is an archetype, (a universally present, unconscious pattern of thoughts), who uses their courage to rise to the occasion and overcome fear. The hero takes on the world, faces demons, (both inner and outer), and conquerors them.

All growth is heroic, moving from the known to the unknown; conquering fear is always facing the unknown. To grow, Joseph Campbell says, "You enter the forest at the darkest point, where there is no path. Where there is a way or path, it is someone else's path. You are not on your own path. If you follow someone else's way, you are not going to realize your potential."[60] Everyone is on a heroic journey. The journey can be internal or external, but "in the process of becoming complete, integrated human beings, we are all Heroes facing internal guardians, monsters, and helpers."[61] First a hero takes the first step away from his ordinary life, away from old, reactive patterns, leaving the world of the ordinary and enters the path of the extraordinary. It is up to the individual to choose to face this opportunity with tenacity and drive, or cower back to safety. Framing your reality in this way makes life an awe-inspiring adventure.

All fear, even of external things, is rooted internally. "Fear of all kinds and sizes is a form of psychological infection. We can cure a

---

60 Campbell, Joseph, and David Kudler. Pathways to Bliss: Mythology and Personal Transformation. Novato, Calif: New World Library, 2004. Print.

61 Vogler, Christopher. The Writer's Journey: Mythic Structure for Writers. Studio City, CA: Michael Wiese Productions, 2007. Print.

mental infection the same way we cure a body infection—with specific, proved treatments."[62] To face internal challenges, to face the inner demons, you must shine a light on the problems and acknowledge they are there. Use the tools outlined in this book to conquer the beast lurking in the shadows. The first step is awareness–bringing the monsters out of the shadow. Seeing these beasts is terrifying, but the alternative is living a life in constant fear of them. If you waste your mind's capacity on repressing fears, you cannot fully face the current, real challenges. Feeling fear is uncomfortable, but to conquer fear, you must be comfortable feeling fear. You are more than the fear, the fear is not you. You feel fear, but fear does not paralyze your soul.

[62] Schwartz, David J. The Magic of Thinking Big. New York: Simon & Schuster, 1987. Print. pg 50

KEY 14

KEY FOURTEEN: BE SAD

We don't often really get sad. We don't allow ourselves. We don't often fully express sadness that requires us to feel deeply.

When we do become sad, the intimacy of this emotion stirs an unfamiliar vulnerability. We sometimes cry, and often these tears persist longer than we are comfortable with. So, we try to stifle our tears and withdraw from the feeling. We suppress it and become quiet. Instead of being sad, we often become angry, either at someone else or at ourselves. We either get angry and rage or give ourselves ulcers and migraines. Even worse, if we keep feeling sad, we instead become depressed, drawing our feelings of sadness further inward and expressing them through our perceptions and attitudes. Chronic depression deadens our emotions. We confine ourselves to an emotional prison. Our interest in things diminishes, our energy is reduced, and our unexpressed sadness becomes the source of our suffering.

And yet, this doesn't seem to make sense. We know what sad is, don't we? We've all felt sad before. We know it when we see it, and we should know it when we feel it. Sadness has been a part of our emotional makeup since we were children.

We remember how sadness is expressed, and we know what we looked and felt like when we were sad when we were younger. The difficulty for all of us is that we haven't found a more sophisticated or, dare we say, adult way of expressing our sadness. As adults, we don't know how to express, and therefore discharge, sadness. And without this method of expression, we lose the meaning of this emotion. Something so easy, so familiar when we were young becomes so remote, awkward, uncomfortable and even embarrassing as we age.

A Story from the Heart

I had lunch with a friend of mine a few years ago, and he told me something about being sad that has stuck with me ever since.

He's a physician, but he's also a practitioner of mindfulness. That is, he meditates regularly, and he has a particularly unique slant on the sadness associated with death.

He oversees the intensive care unit in the local hospital, so he sees people die nearly every day.

I have never seen him dour, never seen him drag. Speaking to the families of the dead, he deals with such pain and heartache every day that I had to ask him how he is able to cope with such sadness.

"Cope? I don't think that's the word you're looking for."

"OK, how about withstand?" I said.

"No, that's not it either. The word you're looking for is breathe. I was taught to breathe sadness."

Yes, as a matter of fact, I did ask him to explain what that meant.

"About three years into my career as a physician, I had to meet the family of a young Taiwanese man who was hit by a car.

"As I went out to the waiting room, I saw this family gathered in the circle. It was very quiet. You could hear them speak to one another, but in very whispered, low tones.

"I brought them the very sad news of their son's death. They spoke among themselves and became quiet. Then they all thanked me, one by one, smiling at me as they left. Smiling. Their smiles reflected such peace. You could feel the sense of calm within each of them, every single one of them just had a glow. It's hard to describe. But it was tangible, a palpable sense of goodness." He smiled himself, and said, "It's just a very hard thing to describe, but there it was. All these people being so centered, so peaceful, in the context of this terribly sad and tragic event.

"About a week later, a couple of the people in this circle–I think one of them was an older brother, and the other was an aunt or a grandmother–came by to sign something at the hospital. They went to the office two doors down from mine. As I passed them, they came down the hall. Very calmly, but quickly, they came down the hall and stood before me, took my hand and thanked me for my service.

"Now, I was a young doctor. And in a hospital, particularly in the Intensive Care unit, I had never seen such a display of unified calm. So I asked them how they were feeling. At the time, I didn't realize just how dumb the question was, but I asked it hoping they would tell me what I was really dying to know: How did they stay so peaceful? What was it like when they went home? And did they ever feel sad?

"For the next twenty five minutes, I was enrapt by their explanations of life, emotions, and peace. These two beautiful people sat there and told me that, yes, they were sad, but that they dealt with sadness differently than most people.

" 'We cry, of course, they said. 'But only for a moment. We only cry because our expectations of his presence are lost. Still, we remain sad, because we miss him.'

"Then the older woman spoke up. Putting her hand on her chest, she said, 'We breathe our sadness. With every breath, we think of him, and we breathe our sadness into the sky. Our breaths carry out sadness into the light. The light changes our breath from sadness to joy as it ascends to be in the place our boy lives now.

'By breathing out our sadness, we allow it to grow. It combines with all the breaths in all the world, transforming into the light of love for our son, helping him know how much we love him.'

She continued, 'To be sad is just to breathe. It lets it out of our bodies. And when we breathe, we think of our son. And we remember the peace we breathe back to him.' "

My friend put his hand on his chest. "I breathe my sadness, and let my breath rise to be transformed into the air, healed in the light of the universe."

He must have seen my expression. He looked at me, laughed a little, and said, "Yes, I am still a physician. And yes, I continue to be a scientist.

"But I'm a human being. And I see death and pain so much. It affects me just as it affects you. I have to be a person that cares and lives with the pain that these people feel. How could I do my job otherwise?

"So, when I see the families, almost all of whom are overwhelmed with grief, I breathe. Just like that family, I breathe. I exhale the sadness and let it rise into the sky, to be healed in the light of goodness and love. I absolutely believe that. I have seen the peace in the faces of those that believe the same thing. And, for them, I know it worked.

"And, now, I know it works for me, too."

How it Works

In order to be sad, as unfamiliar you are with this emotion, you have to express it.

So, when you get sad, cry. You just have to.

The word "cry" means "to let out." Sadness is not a contemplation. It is not meditative, it is not done in repose. Sadness is done with expression and a little volume. Its movement comes from within you.

You don't have to do this in a crowd. Sadness has become a private expression, and that's fine. But you should acknowledge sadness when you find something upsetting. Sadness is the first step in engaging your sense of empathy, because knowing you have the capacity to feel and express sadness is knowing you are affected by the unfair, unkind, and painful. Being sad brings forth a sense of connection. In an odd way, sadness reconfirms that you can feel. If you are moved by an image, a sound, a spirit, an energy, or a memory, this feeling might register as sadness. Sadness runs deeply. You might have to pause and notice when you are happy, but you know when your heart feels sad.

Crying is important, in part, because it reaffirms your ability to feel emotion like sadness deeply. It also helps you release these feelings.

Sadness is not meant to rest with you; it is meant to be felt, then released. You express sadness intensely, and then let it go.

Think of times you've cried. Although you may have thought it went on for hours, almost every time we cry, our tears last for no more than a few minutes. When you're crying and deeply expressing your sadness, just a few minutes can feel like hours, but it's rare to go on crying for very long period of time–sobbing uncontrollably is rarer still. Crying discharges sadness, and once the sadness is gone, the crying stops. The tears dry, and there is no further need to cry because the sadness is gone.

Sadness is meant to be felt and then released. You may still feel a little sad, but the release of crying allows the pain to heal. We can feel sad, certainly. But after our pain is past, we feel a sense of peace; crying facilitates that transition.

Why this is Important

Freely feeling sadness is important to maintaining a healthy psyche. Emotions are messages from your mind in response to the environment that, from our hunter-gathering past to our modern information age, have allowed humans to survive. Negative emotions can be helpful messages, a warning sign, or a call to action over something that needs to change.

Events in life will occur that will cause feelings of sadness to arise. No one likes to be sad; it is unpleasant. It is important to understand that our emotions are important messages from your heart. "Out of their need to avoid feeling certain emotions, people will often go to great, even ridiculous, lengths. They'll turn to drugs, alcohol, overeating, gambling: they'll lapse into debilitating depression. In order to avoid hurting a loved one, they'll suppress all emotions, end up as emotional androids, and ultimately destroy all the feeling of connection."[63] All of these activities are forms of denial. Numbing yourself to sadness cuts you from the world, and the important message contained in the emotion are lost.

Denying emotions shields you from pain in the short term, but in the long term it creates more pain. Denying emotions such as sadness creates a barrier between you and the present moment. It takes ongoing mental energy to keep this emotion out of your awareness. "Ignoring the message that your emotions are trying to give you will not make things better. If the message your emotions are trying to deliver is ignored, the emotions simply increase their amperage; they intensify until you finally pay attention."[64] Denying your emotions is not the solution. Feel sadness, understand the message of the sadness, and take action. Move your body, get outside, work, play music, and

---

63 Robbins, Anthony. Awaken the Giant Within: How to Take Immediate Control of Your Mental, Emotional, Physical & Financial Destiny. New York, N.Y: Summit Books, 1991. Print. Pg 246-7

64 Robbins, Anthony. Awaken the Giant Within: How to Take Immediate Control of Your Mental, Emotional, Physical & Financial Destiny. New York, N.Y: Summit Books, 1991. Print. Pg 246-7

remember your blessings are just beginning. Chose the closest path that frees your expressions.

CHAPTER 3

LIVE THE SPIRIT OF THE HEART

Living the spirit of the heart is navigating through life effectively. Our time here on earth is limited; we only have one chance at this life. All actions are choices, both big and small. To create the life of our highest aspirations, we must make choices to the best of our ability. Living life led by core principles helps us make the best choices we can. These keys will help you actively create the most meaningful life, in the time you have, here and now.

Key One: Think Big

Key Two: Set Goals

Key Three: Know Strength

Key Four: Know Time

Key Five: Practice

Key Six: Know and Accept Change

Key Seven: Persevere

Key Eight: Progress and Process, not Perfection

Key Nine: Work

Key Ten: Risk

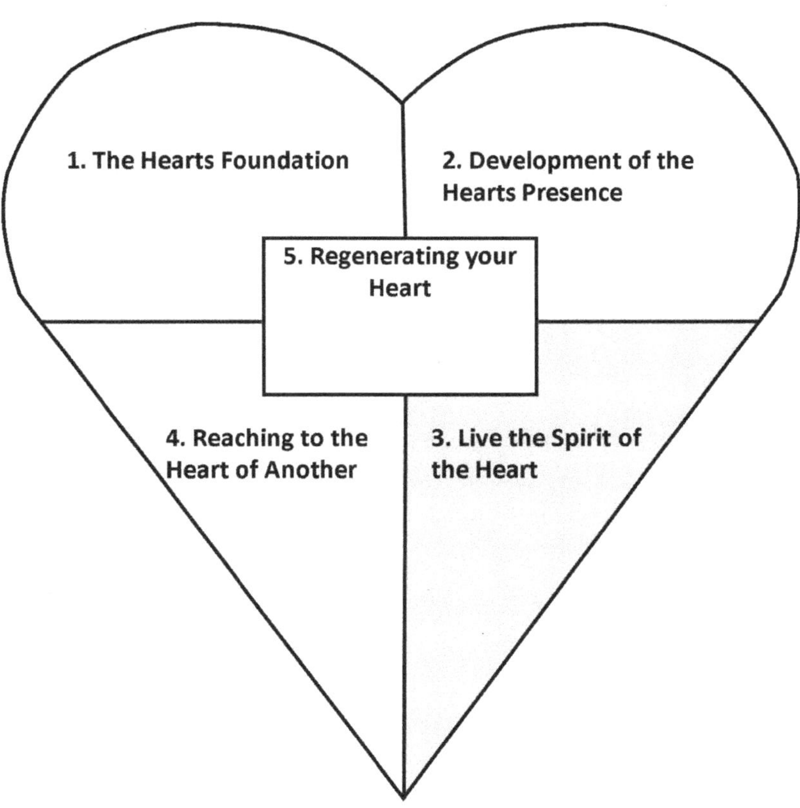
1. The Hearts Foundation
2. Development of the Hearts Presence
5. Regenerating your Heart
4. Reaching to the Heart of Another
3. Live the Spirit of the Heart

KEY 1

KEY ONE: THINK BIG

We do this when we're kids.

Somebody asks us what we want to be when we grow up, and we say we want to be a baseball player, or an astronaut, or a rock guitarist. We have no knowledge of limitations, restrictions, and discouragements. We have no awareness of peer pressure, disapproval, failure, or low self-esteem.

But we age. We face our peers. We do our best. We work on finding who we are, and standing strong in our unique identity.

And, for every one of us, doubt creeps in.

After that, we minimize our best selves, like our strengths, achievements, integrity, kindness, awareness, compassion, intelligence, perseverance, determination, hope, faith, optimism, and perception. And that's just the short list.

The qualities that allow us to dream, to visualize those dreams and think big are still there. We hold them close to us. They are never extinguished nor do they go away. They are still part of who we are even if we have forgotten. The voice of our childhood self, without hesitation, screams that they can be anything,that they can do everything, and all they need is the time to grow up and show you.

A Story from the Heart

About forty years ago, Big John was born prematurely to a young couple, both in their early twenties and still in school. Congenital deformities left John without much strength in his legs. He needed braces, and often required a wheelchair. His mother had become an attorney, and his father, a minister. They wanted to help John feel that, though his handicaps were challenges, his legs were a blessing. John told me "all that other stuff that I didn't believe for second. I thought of myself as limited, confined, and without much hope.

"But my father, he kept at me. He always told me to 'Think big,' to think past my perceptions of who I was, and what I felt I couldn't do. He was my biggest cheerleader. He encouraged me to stretch myself, to believe that anything and everything was possible."

John was a good student, though he said he "hated books. Every time I opened one, it was one more reminder that I couldn't go outside, I couldn't play with the other kids, and I couldn't fit in. I had more than enough time to brood, become sullen, and then finally just get into my studies. Eventually," he admitted, "I got through my work. I was thorough. And, if I'm honest, I got a great deal of satisfaction being a smart kid.

"And my father, he was so proud. He kept having me reach outside of who I saw I was. He kept setting that bar of accomplishment in front of me, not so much in what I needed to do every day, but what I needed to believe in. He set my vision for what was possible. Eventually, I believed in that vision, too."

When John was 16, he was one of the top students in his high school class. He started his senior year just before his seventeenth birthday. His teacher called a meeting with him, and suggested he apply to an Ivy League college.

"While I'm in her office, a kid comes in and hands her a note. She looks at the note, and the color runs out of her face. She looks back and me, and tears form in her eyes. 'John,' she says to me, 'your father has been in an accident.'

"By the time I got home, my mother and other members of my family were assembled in my living room. My father, a 39 year old man, was gone. Freak accident in the church basement. Something went wrong with a grounding wire and my father was electrocuted.

"I was stopped cold. My heart was numb. I couldn't think. For weeks after his funeral, I would hobble around the house, invariably finding myself in his bedroom, sitting on his side of the bed.

"One day, my academic advisor reminded me that I hadn't handed in any college applications. He was concerned about my emotional state, but was eager to get me moving toward the next level of my education.

"I told him that I wasn't going to college. I was convinced that, given my handicap and without my father, I didn't have the strength. I knew what it was like to be exposed to ridicule. Before my father's death, this hadn't been a problem. Now, moving into college would make it even more likely I'd fail. It was all I could do to finish high school.

"After meeting with my advisor, I found myself at home, alone with my crutches, my wheelchair, and my thoughts. And, as usual, I found myself sitting on my father's side of the bed.

"Well, this one afternoon, I saw a pair of shoes under his dressing table. I don't know how I hadn't noticed them before, but there they were. Black wingtips, size 12, almost calling to me. And at that moment, I thought of my Dad. And began to cry like my heart was going to break in two.

"I sat there just staring at those shoes. Then I slid off the side of the bed, crawled over to the shoes, picked them up, placed them on the side of the bed and put them on."

Big John had to stop. He wiped a tear from his eye, took a deep breath and said, "I grabbed one of my crutches, and stood up. I was wearing my father's shoes.

"My little feet, swimming in my father's shoes, and me standing up! There I was. Just standing there for the longest time. Then, as if a warm wind blew into the room, I was at peace. I just felt OK. It wasn't sudden, really, it was more like a feeling that started in my chest and radiated throughout my body.

"Right then," John said, pointing his finger to the ground, "I felt compelled to make a decision. I had to know what I was going to do. Biggest decision of my life. Should I stay home, help my Mom in her law firm, read books, and volunteer at the community center helping kids like me, or should I go on to college?

"So," John said, almost in a whisper, "I asked my Dad."

"I said, 'Dad, I'm standing in your shoes. I have to know what I should do now. I want to keep your vision within me. Please, please help me.' "

John smiled, nodded his head, and said, "And I knew almost immediately. I decided to go to college. This feeling came over me that I should go large or think big or however you want to put it. I knew, then, that college was the right decision.

"I didn't go Ivy League. I went to a college that I knew could accommodate my legs. But I went to college. And every time after that, when I had a big decision to make–usually one that made me face great deal of fear as I moved forward to another level–I stood up, put myself in my Dad's shoes, and thought.

"And every time, I ended up thinking bigger than myself. I have always moved forward into whatever challenge I was facing, everything from asking a girl out on a date to getting my PhD to starting up my private practice. I think big with every decision, by standing my father's shoes, looking at his vision, and making it my own."

At this writing, Big John is a psychologist in private practice. And a motivational speaker. And even on the road, he takes his father's shoes with him, wherever he goes.

How it Works

When you think big, you start by thinking of possibilities. You don't need to commit to doing anything right now. That will come, in time. But at this moment, you just need to think of what you want to do or be, that meets your highest good and brings good to others.

Then write it down and put it where you can see it, every day.

Here's what happens:

After a while, you begin to focus on the possibilities. You think of what it takes to make that dream happen.

OK, it might be a heck of a lot of school. Or learning a new skill. Or taking a really big risk.

Then, when you begin to think of what it takes to tackle your dream, write that down. Put some thought into the steps to get from where you are to where you want to be. Write down the money, the time, and the effort you will need to get from here to there.

Put that list in front of you.

Then do one thing that day, no matter how small, that will take you one step closer to your dream. Commit to that. One thing that will start you on your path.

Take that first step.

Maybe it's making a phone call to the local school to find out about a class. Maybe it's counting up the time it will take you to finish school, and figuring out how you could hold down a job and complete the coursework, online or in person.

Just do one thing.

Now.

Maybe it's talking yourself out of a bad day. Or repeating the mantra "I am a (fill in the blank with your dream)" over and over again.

This is how it happens. One day at a time, one step at a time. As Lao-Tzu says, "A journey of a thousand miles begins with a single step."[65] When you look back in a year, or two years or three, you'll have traveled that much farther down the path.

Don't let life pass you by without setting your course toward fulfilling your dreams. It will go by in a flash. It just does.

Think Big. One day at a time.

Now get to that list.

Why this is Important

Do not lead a mediocre life. There is no limit to what is possible in your life, so do not allow anyone, including yourself, to impose limits on your highest vision. Often barriers and statistics stop a person from truly thinking big. You must ask yourself, "Why be an average person? All the great achievements of history have been made by strong individuals who refused to consult statistics or to listen to those who could prove convincingly that what they wanted to do, and in fact ultimately did do, was completely impossible."[66] It is imperative that you set a high spiritual standard for your life, since your life is

[65] Laozi, , and Wing-tsit Chan. The Way of Lao Tzu (tao-Tê Ching). Indianapolis: Bobbs-Merrill, 1963. Print.

[66] Butterworth, Eric. Spiritual Economics: The Principles and Process of True Prosperity. Unity Village, MO: Unity Books, 2001. Print.

yours to create through your thoughts and actions. We are all living only a fraction of our true potential for love, creativity, and ability. Your mind, body, and heart have infinite potential.

Think big, create a big plan, and take big action. Remove negativity and doubt from your mind–"Act as if failure is impossible, and your success (as you define it) will be assured. Wipe out every thought of not achieving your objectives, whether they are material or spiritual. Be brave, set no limits on the workings of your imagination. Never be a prisoner of your past. Become the architect of your future. You will never be the same."[67]

Set your mind free from the limitations you have placed on yourself. Be free to dream, free to be brave, free to evolve and to grow. Truly, "believe it can be done. When you believe something can be done, your mind will find ways to do it. Believing in a solution paves the way to solution. Eliminate 'impossible,' 'won't work,' 'can't do,' 'no use trying' from your thinking and speaking vocabularies."[68] Words like these create a negative frequency of thought. Do not allow these limiting words to linger.

---

67 Sharma, Robin S. The Monk Who Sold His Ferrari: A Fable About Fulfilling Your Dreams and Reaching Your Destiny. San Francisco: HarperSanFrancisco, 1998. Print. pg 169

68 Schwartz, David J. The Magic of Thinking Big. New York: Simon & Schuster, 1987. Print. pg 124

KEY 2

KEY TWO: SET GOALS

Many of us are sick of the word Goal. Not because it's not important. It is. It's fundamental. If you have no goals, you have no target for your life's path. You would be spinning randomly in the wind, just moving day after day without much direction, or reason for your life.

It's just that the word goal seems so heavy, weighted with such potential. So large, so grand in scope, setting a goal can be cumbersome to many, even discouraging.

Let's try breaking this big step down a bit. Begin to take stock of our little goals, those steps that support and lay the foundation for the bigger goals down the line.

Setting a goal, every day and several times a day, is something we already do. Although we don't always see it that way, it becomes a way of life. A goal keeps us in motion. And recognizing the need for a goal is pretty straightforward. We have to have something to shoot for. It makes us who we are.

A goal does not have to be daunting. It is only a place that you reach for. It could be over the years, down the road, or across the room. A goal is nothing more than that. A destination that, when reached, gives us a sense of accomplishment, maybe a little peace. We have goals in every part of our lives. We have a million little goals, all day long, that we attain. Goals keep us engaged.

The goal is the place we want to be. Achieving big goals brings us to high places and helps us believe in ourselves. It tells us what we can do and sets the course for doing even more. It gives us definition and supports our identity. Achieving goals in life, no matter how small, tells us we're still alive.

A Story from the Heart

Jen is a social services administrator for children.

On her wall about her desk, a tapestry has the words, "Horizon."

I pointed this out and she said, "Well, it's not what you think. Let me explain a little of how that came into being."

Jen spoke about her background, before she started managing a 45-bed social service facility. "I spent a little over a year in the Peace Corps, and that changed my life. Because I spoke a little Spanish, I was sent to the slums of Costa Rica. One side of the island was built for tourists and what middle class still existed. The other was a mass of impoverished walls, roofs, streets and what infrastructure was left. My job was to organize the children from the streets, get them into our makeshift shelter, and offer them food, shelter, showers, and clothes."

"Now, once that was done, we scheduled school for every kid we could round up."

Jen talked about the conditions, and the demands that the poverty made upon their resources, and the sanitation but, most of all, she talked about her reason for joining this effort.

"I was there to make the kids feel better. And that's what I was determined to do."

"Well, one day, later in the afternoon, the children were leaving school, when the coordinator of the Costa Rican scholastic effort asked if he could speak to me."

"Miquel had been a liaison for this project with the Peace Corps. A man of about 60, he took interest in what he called my "commitment" to the children, but he had a concern."

"Jen," he said, "you seem so determined. What is your purpose? Why are you here?" And I told him I was here to help the children get some balance in their lives, and help them respond to their conditions. I mean," she said, shaking her head, "I didn't know how to answer the question. And I think he got that, because he said, 'Well, thank you for your effort, but what is your purpose, your goal in helping the children?' "

"And I had to stop and think. Did I have a 'goal' here? What was I supposed to be doing? I was told when I signed up that the project was to give them a place to eat, sleep and bathe, then set up a school for the kids to attend. And we're talking from about children from three to almost eighteen years old. Wasn't that enough of a reason to be here?"

"Again," she said, "he must have picked up my unease with my question, and a smile came to his face. And the next words out his mouth have affected me ever since."

"He said, 'Jen, look at these kids. They know, at least the older ones, that when you leave, many of them are going to be dealing with the same conditions that they left. They know that you offer a respite. And, they hope that others will come again, and bigger programs will take hold, maybe changes in our governmental policies.'

'But you speak of your goals as if they are acts of concrete measure, things that we achieve that then put aside. Those are only the results. To have a goal, you must have hope. And to have hope, you must have vision.'

Jen paused for a second, "And then he said, 'Jen, there is your vision,' and pointed to the horizon. The sun was beginning to set, and I asked him what he meant."

"Miquel said, 'Your see the horizon. Your hope is that you see it more closely. Your goal is to be closer when the sun goes down again.'

'Specifically,' Miquel said, 'the closer you get to your own potential, the closer you get to your goal.'

'Jen, it isn't that the goal is to give these kids the basic necessities. It's to make sure they have hope. It is to give them an example of what a better life can be. No, the goal is to not to provide the basics. The goal,' said Miquel, 'is to keep their focus on what can be.'

'They need that horizon, Jen, for without it, they focus on the ground. They will go nowhere. The horizon for each child may be different, and it's their own path that takes them there.' "

Jen smiled, "And with that, he shook my hand, got in his car, and I never saw him again."

"My life changed after that. From that point forward, I wanted to get to know the kids. I took many of them aside, and asked them what they liked, what they wanted to be, that kind of thing."

"And to a child, their hopes and dreams were like every other kid. Some wanted to be a doctor, some a teacher, some wanted to work on cars."

"My job, at that moment, was to give them hope and continue to offer services to their community to keep that hope alive. I had them focus on their goals. That was my job. To instill hope, to help them get clear on their goals, and to keep their focus on the horizon."

"Which, I should say," she added, "I literally did. Every Saturday night, I took a group of those kids up to a hill about a quarter mile outside of the camp. Together, we would watch the sunset, focus on that horizon, and talk about their dreams. 'Bring that horizon to you,' I'd say, 'Know the life that lives out there, and all your goals and dreams will come true.' We would talk about all their dreams and put together images in the sky of their goals and what life would be when all of them were met."

Jen opened a drawer. "Well, about a year ago, I got a package. In it was that tapestry you see on the wall. And with the package was a letter from Juan Cruz, one of the older boys I took up to that hill. Let me read this for you: 'Dear Miss Jen, I wanted to tell you that I am now the director of civic services in Costa Rica. I just completed medical school and specialize in childhood disorders. We here will never forget your kindness. Every day I take children up to that hill and let them know what they can be. We put their images in the sky, just like you did with us.'

'I wanted you to know that I kept my eyes on the horizon, and my goals were met. God Bless You, Juan Cruz, M.D.' "

Jen wiped the tears from her eyes. "So, I keep my eyes on the horizon. I keep my goals in my head and the horizon in my heart."

"That's how you make your goals happen, and turn your dreams into reality."

<u>How it Works</u>

You need to know two things right away about goals. First, most of them aren't of the "Climb Mount Everest" or "Learn to play Rachmaninoff" variety. Many of our goals are part of the normal routine of life. You don't have to think about all of them. These "Make sure you call your mother"-variety goals are of pressing importance, and achieving them sets the pace of our day. Secondly, our goals change. Big and small, there's turnover. That's normal. The goals of our youth may not be those of our adulthood. For that matter, the goals of last year may not be those of today.

Even if it seems unimportant or it changes, a goal concentrates your focus on the result out there on the horizon, the one that seems so unattainable right now. It keeps you going, moving, and putting your steps one after another. It sets your vision. It gives you motivation. It gives you drive. It gives you reason to be.

The goal is the thing that pulls us, pushes us, and inspires motion in life. A goal means that we want tomorrow to be better than today. It means that we want our yesterday to be a reference of where we were, and our tomorrow a vision of what we still can be. Goals make your life important.

Goals are things you will do. Not what you want to do. Decide your goals will happen. Your pace will quicken, and your head will keep up with the steps it takes to reach your outcome.

Break all goals, big and small, down into manageable parts. Reduce your goals to the steps leading up to the finish line. Writing down the goal "I will run a marathon" also means, for most of us, "I will walk a mile today." Each big goal should have a to-do list of smaller goals, breaking it down into smaller bites. You can certainly have goals like "I will lose twenty pounds" or "I will get my degree." But each goal contains a series of steps toward that end. Following your diet and doing your homework are the steps, and these daily activities move us along the path toward achievement.

Why this is Important

Goals are standards or achievements you set for yourself. Humans "are engineered as goal-seeking mechanisms. We are built that way. When we have no personal goal which we are interested in and which 'means something' to us, we are apt to 'go around in circles,' feel 'lost' and find life itself 'aimless,' and 'purposeless.' We are built to conquer environments, solve problems, achieve goals, and we find no real satisfaction or happiness in life without obstacles to conquer and goals to achieve. People who say that life is not worthwhile are really saying that they themselves have no personal goals which are worthwhile. Prescription: Get yourself a goal worth working for."[69] Having goals in life gives you something meaningful to work towards.

Sonja Lyubomirsky, in The How of Happiness, says "working toward a meaningful life goal is one of the most important strategies for becoming lastingly happier."[70] The key to this is setting meaningful goals. Meaningful goals must build toward the highest vision, or purpose, you have for yourself. David Deida, in The Way of the Superior Man, says "the core of your life is your purpose. Everything in your life, from your diet to your career, must be aligned with your purpose if you are to act with coherence and integrity in the world. If you know your purpose, your deepest desire, then the secret of success is to discipline your life so that you support your deepest purpose and minimize distraction and detours."[71] There is no one correct purpose in life; everyone is very different. As long as your purpose is emotionally significant to you and is neutral or helps other people, it is meaningful. Having this deep sense of purpose creates very compelling reasons why you must complete your goals. When the reasons to complete a goal are clear and strong, it is much easier to work towards them.

---

69 Maltz, Maxwell. Psycho-cybernetics. New York: Pocket Books, 1994. Print. pg 114

70 Lyubomirsky, Sonja. The How of Happiness: A Scientific Approach to Getting the Life You Want. New York: Penguin Press, 2008. Print. pg 206

71 Deida, David. The Way of the Superior Man: A Spiritual Guide to Mastering the Challenges of Women, Work, and Sexual Desire. Boulder, CO: Sounds True, 2004. Print. pg 37

KEY 3

KEY THREE: KNOW STRENGTH

To be a fuller person, it's important to know what you need to do. It is equally important to realize the capacity for strength lying behind that action. You must recognize and hold with both hands what strength means when it comes to matters of the heart.

But let us digress for a moment.

It has become assumed that to be "strong" translates into being in "control" or having "power." The general consensus of characteristics that define strength are those traits demonstrated by people we see as powerful: direct communication, unfailing confidence, absolute assurance in their knowledge and their decisions, and lapsing into impatience and anger when questioned. Think of your boss. Or a football coach. Or a drill sergeant. These are the images that come to mind most often when we think of what strength.

Control is also often identified with strength. Many feel that control means managing yourself and your environment. Life is a big to-do list, and our job is to get these tasks done. We organize our awareness and actions to respond to all obstacles in our path. Control is seen as paying attention to detail, handling tasks, getting things done, and moving on to the next challenge.

Power and control are often seen as fundamental to strength, but it couldn't be further from the truth. Power is temporary. Control is fleeting. There is no strength in coercion, in compulsion, in inconsideration, or in arrogance. Real strength has no association with self-centeredness, selfishness, egoism, or subordination.

A Story from the Heart

The pediatric orthopedic surgeon was waiting for me when I entered the front door of the Children's Hospital. The purpose of my visit was to talk to her about of the role strength plays in her life and her patients' lives.

"Come with me," she said, as she waved for me to follow her. On the way down the hall, children stopped what they were doing and came to see this physician. Children on crutches, in braces, on walkers, and in wheelchairs, some with missing limbs, all interrupted their activities to be with her.

She crouched, kneeled, or sat on the floor. Each boy and girl looked at the doctor and smiled as only a child can: open, loving, and so deeply grateful. Arms outstretched, even if steel appliances attached to their wrists, backs, and legs restricted their movement. Love overflowed as they met the doctor, and she offered the same in return.

We passed further down the hallway. Standing outside a small room, we heard the sounds of a young child inside, perhaps two or three years old. We heard the timbre of an adult voice giving instructions, and the applause and encouragement of another, maybe two other, adults, laughing and giggling.

In that room was a child with no arms and no legs. "Grace is going to be four years old next week," the doctor said.

It is hard to describe how Grace moved. She didn't exactly walk, or jump, or do anything like a child with legs would.

Grace's walk was more like a slide. Using the muscles that sustained her, Grace shuffled her limbless body across the rubber mat. With each movement, Grace's face showed a combination of joy and determination, discomfort and relief as she scooted to the left side, then came back to the right side, then . . .

. . . well, Grace fell flat on her face.

She had no hands, no arms to brace her fall. Grace hit her face straight and hard against the floor. We heard a loud "whap!"

The doctor, standing right next to me, put her hand on my elbow and whispered, "Watch this."

Then I saw the most amazing show of physical and emotional strength I have ever witnessed. This beautiful child, without limbs to support herself, got back up. She lifted herself back up, from face down on the mat to standing again, looking straight ahead, and ready to move across the mat. Straining, clutching, moving her torso up and sideways and back and forth, this child made it back, standing upright and focused.

I gushed to the doctor, "You're right. That is as great a demonstration of strength as I have ever seen. I mean, at the sight of this child . . ."

The doctor interrupted me and said, "That's not what I brought you here to see. Watch Grace again."

As I looked back at Grace, as she was straightening her torso and righting her place on the mat, she peered into the dark corner of the room, and smiled.

As I strained my eyes slightly to focus into the dark, the doctor again touched me on my arm and said, "This is what I wanted you to see."

In the corner were two adults, a man and a woman, sitting on the edge of their seats, smiling at Grace.

"That is Michael and Elisabeth," the doctor said. "They are Grace's parents."

Two adults. Beautiful smiles, no trace of sadness, just happy at their daughter's progress. "They never complain, never a negative word. Just positive things about their life, their feelings, and the beauty that is their daughter," said the doctor.

"To be that positive, to carry that spirit forward, in spite of the road ahead for themselves and especially for Grace? That's strength."

We walked over and shook hands with them. We talked about the wonder of Grace and let them both know how impressed we were with their care of this dear girl.

As we left, both Elisabeth and Michael thanked us, hugged the doctor, and continued watching Grace. The doctor walked us back to the lobby of the hospital.

"Grace shows you that strength is getting up, despite the odds or ability. But Grace's parents? The strength of spirit in watching their child struggle, to smile through the helplessness and anxiety, to calm their fears of the future and continue to feel blessed, fortunate and eternally grateful?"

"You know, I don't know about you," the doctor said, taking her glasses from her face, "but that's the embodiment of what strength is all about."

How it Works

Want to know strength? Strength is getting up and showing up. Every day. Strength is determination to think of somebody other than yourself in spite of all the responsibilities, the pain, and the fatigue you shoulder. Strength is deciding how you can make this world a better place; identify a burden you can share, a life you can improve, a condition you can make better despite your level of pain and adversity. Strength is bringing forward your best self. Smiling and treating every person with kindness, no matter your feelings. Being kind in the face of derision and being loving in the face of anger, prejudice, and fatigue.

Strength is inherently selfless. It is focused on your circumstances and the conditions around you. Strength never bullies and it is never angry. Strength is genuine, calm, and quietly confident. It is assuring, not assured. It is unfolding, not directive. It responds, it never reacts. Strength is mindful and deliberate. Confidence is brought forth from the spirit, never from the ego. Power is in faith, a calm knowing that everything you bring to the day will be good and helpful and present. It's knowing that you have the resources available, and can even learn new ones, to meet challenges. And it is being able to start again if you come up short. Strength gathers your energy with aplomb to meet the new day once more.

Strength stays steady, yet bends; it is firm but will compromise. Strength is fair. It is without a personal agenda. It is caring yet objective, guided by the head but rooted in the heart. Real strength comes from both compassion and empiricism, being able to use both in complementary ways.

Strength is patient. It leads by example. It teaches without pedantry or simplification. Strength is respectful and recognizes that you can use collaborative support.

Strength is persistence with a grin, determination with a smile, perseverance with humor. Real strength is participating in life with love.

Why this is Important

Strength is something you inwardly possess. To know strength is to know yourself. Strength is a deep trust in yourself, your capabilities, and the knowledge that you are strong enough to give selflessly to others.

Inner strength is the ability to persevere despite challenging circumstances because "Strength is the presence of abundant energy–a capacity and reserve to be a force in your world. It's inclusive of health and at the same time so much more; it's being healthy and flowing with energy, power and confidence."[72] Weakness is the opposite of strength; weakness is living a reactionary life based on fear, and it leads to selfishness. When people fear, they seek security above all else, risking very little to keep what they have, resulting in stagnation. They cut themselves off from the life's possibilities and live, as Chögyam Trungpa says, in an isolation of safety and comfort. Fear makes us "embed ourselves in a cocoon, in which we perpetuate our habitual patterns. When we are constantly recreating our basic patterns of habits and thought, we never have to leap into fresh air or onto fresh ground."[73] Being committed to living in comfort and safety forces a person to think selfishly; they are unable to act on their highest principles such as courage, faith, and selfless action.

To know strength is to break free from this cocoon. Cracking open the cocoon and living with strength begins with controlling your thoughts. Thoughts are not just fleeting words in your mind, they structure your reality, since "thoughts are just as much a part of the material world as the lake you swim on or the street you walk on. Weak minds lead to weak actions. A strong, disciplined mind, which anyone can cultivate through daily practice, can achieve miracles. If you want to live life to the fullest, care for your thoughts as you would your most prized possessions. Work hard to remove all inner turbulence. The rewards will be abundant."[74] Through the daily practice of maintaining a disciplined mind, we cultivate our strength. Only then can we live with a mind open to possibilities and the courage to take action.

---

[72] Phillips, Shawn, and Pete Williams. Strength for Life: The Fitness Plan for the Best of Your Life. New York: Ballantine Books, 2008. Print. pg 6

[73] Trungpa, Chögyam, and Carolyn R. Gimian. Shambhala: The Sacred Path of the Warrior. Boulder, Colo: Shambhala, 1984. Print. pg 51

[74] Sharma, Robin S. The Monk Who Sold His Ferrari: A Fable About Fulfilling Your Dreams and Reaching Your Destiny. San Francisco: HarperSanFrancisco, 1998. Print.

KEY 4

KEY FOUR: KNOW TIME

If we are to have a life that is fulfilled, centered, and balanced, if we are to experience a life that is fully engaged from a cognitive, spiritual, and emotional perspective, we have to know time.

This is more than just managing our time. Rather, it is recognizing that time is a presence that can support and teach us. Time sets the direction and outlines our course in any given moment and throughout any given day. Time does not make demands of us. It does not create pressure or stress–That is only our interpretation of time. time, rather, is how we measure our actions and, subsequently, our lives.

To pursue a life of heart-centered fulfillment, it's important to recognize how we use time. Do we measure our tasks in the time it takes us to complete them? If so, how do we value our time spent in work, thought, rest, and distraction? By what measure of time do we set our life goals? How much time is enough? Why does time drag when we are waiting for something but fly by while we're in the middle of an activity?

It is difficult not to speak in the abstract when considering time. A friend's favorite saying is also one of my favorite expressions about time: "Today is Thursday. A half an hour ago it was Monday morning." Time passes quickly when we are involved in action, and it passes so slowly while we wait for it.

We must regard time as an ally, a supportive tool. Its purpose is to tell us how much of the day remains to complete what we have set out to do and how much time we have in our lives to complete what we are here to accomplish.

A Story from the Heart

In the back of the Ranger Garage you'll always find Stan, a mechanic who has been the owner and operator of his town's only automobile repair shop, "since John Kennedy was elected President."

And to look at Stan, you'd think he had never laid hands on a tool. His uniform is pressed, his posture is straight as an arrow, and his hands are immaculate. Yet, at 81 years old, he still works on each car that enters the garage.

Each car is washed after it comes down from the rack. "I want every car to leave this place better than it came in," he says, with a baritone that you can hear from across the street.

Everything in this place is organized and clean. Everything is in precise working order. Well, almost everything.

On the back wall of the garage is a clock. On the face of the clock is an ad for a long out-of-production beer company.

When you look at the clock, you'll see something missing: the clock doesn't have any hands.

"That clock," Stan said, "was put there the year after I started this place," he said, "and I took the hands off of that clock about a year after that."

Stan and I sat down on a bench in the back of the garage. "The first year got busy kind of fast, being the only mechanic in town, so, I put an ad in the newspaper for a mechanic.

"Well," he said, pointing across the street, "about a hundred yards or so due north from here was a farm. And not a day after I put in the ad, I see this truck coming toward the garage. The truck came across the street, up into my driveway and stopped. Two men got out.

"Now, out of the passenger side was a young man. The driver looked to be about thirty years older. The younger man got out slowly, shut the door of the truck very carefully, and walked with slow steps toward the front of the truck. The older man came around the front of the truck and grabbed the younger man's arm, and they both walked into the garage.

"The older man shook my hand and said, 'Sir, this is my son Roy. He's the best mechanic I know. He's worked on all my equipment since he was a boy: tractors, trucks, combines and backhoes. He's torn down and replaced every bit of machinery on that place. Heck, this morning, he even fixed my toaster!' The older man laughed, and then he looked at the ground, got really quiet and said, 'Now, I need to tell you. Roy, here, well, he can't see too good. But that doesn't affect how good of a mechanic he is. He'll take anything you have and put it back, better than it was before.'

"Well, I stuck my hand out to Roy, and he didn't see it. His father instructed him to put his hand out for me to shake it, and he did just that. I took Roy's hand and saw that his eyes didn't focus. He couldn't see me. Roy, in fact, was blind.

"We agreed that Roy would start the next day. Well, when I got to the garage, Roy was already there. He was standing in front of the door, waiting for me. I asked him how long he'd been there, and he said he didn't know. 'A while, I think,' was all he was able to say.

"Roy would come at all hours of the day to start work. He said that his blindness kept him from sleeping a regular schedule. So, I put a key under the mat so he could get in. Then, I started putting the tools in order so he could find the ones he needed.

"Roy didn't know the difference between night or day, five o'clock or noon. So one day, while he stopped to have lunch, I asked him about if it mattered to him, the not knowing the time thing. He said, 'No sir, it doesn't matter. I only know time in respect to where I am, what I'm doing, and what I'm paying attention to. I cannot see you, but I can feel the energy of your presence. I can hear your voice, I can feel the sun and the cold.

'But for me, time tells me only what matters. I give my attention to that. And I draw my focus on the task, the sounds, the smells and the air.' " Stan stopped himself. I could see he was getting a little choked up. Stan took a breath and continued, "Then Roy said, 'Time surrounds us and it passes. But it's only measure, to me, is what I care about.'

"It was right then," said Stan, "that I looked at that clock and took off the hands. I did that for Roy. And for me, too, I guess."

Stan got up, straightened his back and said, "Time. It's there to be given to what matters. It's not something to be measured, it's something to be given to what means something to you."

"And," he smiled, "I've kept the time by listening, focusing, and caring about what matters. And, if I measure the time in my life by those things instead of the hours and minutes, well," he said, turning toward me, "I think I've used my time well. And my life has been one of time very well spent."

How it Works

To recognize time from an accessible, hands-on perspective, we need to see our time laid out in hours. The most basic tool of time management is to fill every hour with at least one activity. It requires a little writing and a little creativity at first, and you must be sure to include minutes for creativity, laughter, meditation, reflection, reading, exercise, conversation, and appreciation of your life.

The hour-by-hour system of time management is not a new one. People have been doing that for hundreds of years. We suggest, though, that you maintain a meaningful life by scheduling hours for meaningful activities. We are not suggesting you neglect your duties, but we are suggesting that you attend to your life. Take action! It can even be writing down plans on a calendar.

The limitations of time require that we put as much quality into each hour as possible. We must balance our priorities, and see time as passing, something to engage right now.

You must have priorities. Family comes first, but our school and work support our direction and offer engagement with life's meaning. In our lives, work takes up most of our time, and there's nothing wrong with that. As long as we do that job with our heart, and offer it our best, we are using our time well. And, as long as we take time for creativity, laughter, meditation, reflection, reading, exercise, conversation, and appreciation, we can sustain the energy of our life. The old saying, "it is not the hours in your life but the life in your hours" is appropriate here. Time requires us to add color to our routine, to honor the beat of our heart no matter the job we've chosen. Time will be our unfailing companion if we treat each minute as a possibility to express love, kindness, and gratitude for the life we have lived and the time of goodness ahead.

Why this is Important

The time in our life is a finite resource that we must understand and use efficiently. The Dalai Lama says "We are visitors on this planet. We are here for one hundred years at the very most. During that period we must try to do something good, something useful, with our lives. If you contribute to other people's happiness, you will find the true meaning of life."[75] In order to help make the most of the time we have, we must understand that there are two kinds of time: objective time and subjective time.

---

[75] Dalai Lama

Objective time can be measured in minutes, hours, and days. It allows you to plan and schedule events in the future. Eckhart Tolle, who uses the term "clock time" to describe objective time, says, "if you set yourself a goal and work toward it, you are using clock time. You are aware of where you want to go, but you honor and give your fullest attention to the step that you are taking at this moment."[76] Ideally, we use objective time the most often, to create a plan, and then return to living and appreciating the present moment.

Subjective time, though, cannot be measured. It is an emotional, affective perception of time. We create subjective time using mental formations and emotions based on dualities such as hope or fear and pleasure or pain. If we judge that the present moment is unpleasant and hope that the future will be better, we fall into what Eckhart Tolle calls psychological time: "if you then become excessively focused on the goal, perhaps because you are seeking happiness, fulfillment, or a more complete sense of self in it, the Now is no longer honored. It becomes reduced to a mere stepping stone to the future, with no intrinsic value. Clock time then turns into psychological time."[77] It is easy to think of the present as a tool to reach the future, but when you do, the present moment, to you, is lost.

To use your time here on Earth as best you can, create a vision of what you want for your life. Decide what is truly important to you and be creative, optimistic, and open-minded. Then decide why you have that vision or goal. The stronger and more compelling your reasons to do something are, the more likely you are to follow through. Create a plan, and then start taking action. Treat time as the finite resource that it is, and use it as effectively as possible.

---

76 Tolle, Eckhart. The Power of Now: A Guide to Spiritual Enlightenment. Novato, Calif: New World Library, 1999. Print. pg 40

77 Tolle, Eckhart. The Power of Now: A Guide to Spiritual Enlightenment. Novato, Calif: New World Library, 1999. Print. pg 40

KEY 5

KEY FIVE: PRACTICE

All the rest of that stuff that came before this key is theoretical. It won't matter a lick without practicing what you've read. You'll just be holding a big book of ideas. The spark that ignites the ideas is the practice of actions. Your actions set these theories into motion.

And, it's painful. Practice is uncomfortable. There is no way around it. Practicing what you've read up to this point initially brings up feelings. You begin to change into a new version of yourself, and the unfamiliarity can provoke discomfort, anxiety, and apprehension.

Practicing the Keys moves everything from mere theory to actual change–the change you were seeking when you picked up this book, the growth you've been promised if you've gotten this far.

Oh, and did we mention that practice, by definition, is repetition? It is doing something new over and over again until you see a demarcation between your old behavior and the new? Yeah, well, we thought we'd throw that in there, too.

But it is at this point that people lose it. They feel that getting through the discomfort of practicing is too hard. Yes, it's uncomfortable. People tell us a lot that practicing changing their behavior is only "making things worse." Most of you will say "Hey, pain brought me to this book in the first place, and you want me to do more, to feel more, to stretch myself into places I haven't before, and now you tell me this is going to be more painful?"

Well, for a short while, that's exactly what we're saying. Practice can be uncomfortable. It's not equivalent to severe pain. It is an increase, however momentary, in your discomfort level.

A good example is exercise–Any kind of exercise. Who likes exercise, raise your hand? Nobody! Well, that means you're all falling within the range of what we consider normal. And sane. But then, answer this one: Who among you knows that exercise is not only good for you, it is essential to your ongoing physical health, and you feel good after you've done it?

Seeing the point here?

Practice is, in this case, emotional exercise. Spiritual workouts. And, in the beginning stages of practice, you will find yourself knee deep in discomfort. This is where most people stop practicing to fix the things they want to change about themselves and stay stuck. They feel it's become too hard. Getting through the pain and discomfort practice brings forth isn't worth it anymore.

It gets better. You move toward your goal. The incremental steps you take are better, and take you further, than the life you lived before you made this commitment.

Trust us.

Just. Keep. Practicing.

A Story from the Heart

Kwa is a custodian at the office. He works late, generally starts around 6 and works until midnight. Most evenings, my last client leaves around 8pm. And if I see movement in the other offices, I know Kwa is working.

One of our first conversations started with a rather innocuous, throwaway line. He and I were still on the, "How are you? Nice day, isn't it?" level of dialogue, and I said something to him along the lines of, "Wow, Kwa, you truly keep this office beautiful." His response was very thoughtful, and very serious. His expression softened, and his eyes focused directly into mine. He raised his chin, folded his hands in front of his waist, and said, "It's because I practice." I was caught a little off guard. I fumbled for a response and said, "Well, um, yeah, I guess it takes a lot of practice to get things just the way you want them," and I thought to myself that I just said the dumbest thing that could have been expressed.

He said, "No. You're confusing repetition with practice. Let me show you. And I'll tell you a story."

Kwa bent down and reached into his cart. It was filled soaps, sponges, buckets, and brooms, the kind of thing that you'd expect to see in a custodian's arsenal. He reached up with a sponge in his hand, the kind you'd use in your kitchen sink. "This," he said, "is my instrument. I use this when I practice."

He was smiling but clearly serious. He bent down to show me a spot on the baseboard. Squatting next to the corner of the wall, he grabbed his sponge and said, "My father was a concert pianist in Vietnam. When the war came, we escaped in a boat. My father got very sick along the way." Beginning to scrub the baseboards, Kwa said, "We arrived at a camp in Los Angeles. My father was very weak. He would lie on his back for hours." Kwa looked at the baseboard, dunked his sponge in water, and said, "My father, to pass the time, would practice piano pieces on the blanket wrapped around his chest. Hour after hour, my father would literally play concertos on that blanket.

"I was nine years old. When I saw my father's fingers move across the blanket, I didn't ask him what he was doing; I already knew that. No, I asked him why he was making his fingers into chords.

"He said, 'Kwa, my hands know nothing except to practice. In my practice, not only my music becomes awakened, but my hands express my self. My hands tell you what I am feeling. When I play my music, my love for life is shown to you and to the world.'

"Now," Kwa said, working along the baseboard and moving up the wall, "I'd heard him say this before. But when he'd said this, he'd been playing the piano. So I said, 'Father, there is no piano here. You aren't playing anything. There is no sound.'

"He said 'You're right, Kwa. There is no sound. But that's not the point. My practice tells my hands how much I appreciate their skill. My practice awakens my heart and reminds it to cradle my music with love.' "

Kwa stopped his cleaning, stood up and looked at me. "My father then said, 'When I practice, I am now with the music, no matter if I can hear what I'm playing.'

"That is why I practice when I clean. I did not inherit my father's ability to play. I have no talent musically, at least none that I know of. But my father was an artist."

I asked if he was an artist, maybe in painting or sculpture, something along those lines.

"No. I clean office buildings. I just do it artistically." I asked, "So, where does the practice come in?" Kwa laughed a little, and said, "The practice comes when I do a good job. I know my hands have done the work lovingly, my results have shown care, not just efficiency. My cleaning reflects my heart. Just as my father played, my heart is in my cleaning, and my practice expresses my heart.

"You think," he said, "when you see a guy like me, there is no communication, no style, no giving of the heart in this act. Not true. My practice is my expression, my practice is my heart.

"And," he said, "This is what constitutes true practice. It is the act that improves you, that brings forth the strength in your spirit. No matter what you do," Kwa said, as he began his cleaning again, "Practice strengthens the music of your heart."

How it Works

Most people do the same thing when they read books like these: They read them, they like what they read, and they put them down.

And nothing happens.

They say "Oh, that's nice" or "I should do that" and leave the book on their bedside, then pick up something else, and life continues to tread along at the same pace it had when they picked the book up in the first place.

You have to do the things we ask you to do if you're going to change your life.

Here's what we suggest: Today, look through the table of contents in this book, and pick one thing that you could practice or even look at more closely. Whatever suits your fancy, pick it. "Be Present," for instance.

And this one thing, do it or bring it to your awareness for one minute an hour, engage in the thought or action. One minute this hour, therefore, you offer your focus to "Be Present," that's all we want you to do. That begins your practice.

We will then ask you, after a few days of this, to reach for two minutes. Then five. Then ten. It's up to you. But each day, you will challenge yourself to increase the time into increments that you feel are reasonable.

There is this caveat: you cannot stay on one period of time for more than two days. You have to increase it to two minutes, and so on.

This is the best way to change your life. You will see effects gradually, but the payoffs increase. As the changes take hold, and the level of satisfaction increases, you'll see yourself wanting to devote more time, and clearing more space in your calendar, for practice to truly become part of your life.

Why this is Important

Practice is a very common word, and we usually think about it in connection to sports or musical instruments. However, the definition according to the Oxford Dictionary is "the actual application or use of an idea, belief, or method as opposed to theories about such application or use."[78] The key point is applying the idea, belief, or method to your life. Just knowing something does not have an effect on your life. Ideas must be put into action consistently; even the best idea, belief, or method is nothing unless it is put into action presently and consistently in your life.

A practice is not something that is ever completed. Even at the level of mastery, "a practice (as a noun) can be anything you practice on a regular basis as an integral part of your life—not in order to gain something else, but for its own sake . . . For a master, the rewards gained along the way are fine, but they are not the main reason for the journey. Ultimately, the master and the master's path are one. And if the traveler is fortunate—that is, if the path is complex and profound enough—the destination is two miles farther away for every mile he or she travels."[79] Reading and agreeing with the principles stated in this book is a good start, but to have any effect on your life, you must actively practice them in your life. Do not just collect useful information that you feel will come in handy at some future time or may, through osmosis, change your life. Put the information into action. Practice!

---

[78] http://www.oxforddictionaries.com/us/definition/american_english/practice

[79] Leonard, George. Mastery: The Keys to Success and Long-Term Fulfillment. New York: Plume, 1992. Print. pg 74

KEY 6

KEY SIX: KNOW AND ACCEPT CHANGE

We are organisms that crave homeostasis, a comfortable state of equilibrium. We want things to be predictable, steady, and within our control. We look for ways to maintain the status quo, since it reinforces our sense of safety and calm. We want normal. We crave it. And we will do what we need to in order to keep the ship of life steady on its course, at least for today, and hopefully for tomorrow, too.

Yeah, well…

Life tends to drift off that course only about three hundred times a day. Every day. Almost on purpose, just to test your flexibility.

We are under this delusion we can control life. And that's pretty normal, actually. We just confuse ourselves with life and think that, since we are absolutely sure we are the center of the Universe, we can control everything and, in some measure, everybody, causing them to fall within the predictable measure of our expectation.

If that's not one sure sign of insanity, we're not too sure what is.

Life is not within our control. Not much of it is, anyway. We can only do that which is in front of us. We can get out of bed and reasonably expect our legs to carry us to the shower. We can get out of the shower and we can also expect that our hands can grip the towel and our arms can dry ourselves off.

And these expectations are generally and frequently fulfilled. We come, through the repeated pattern of their occurrence, to expect them to happen every day and in the similar fashion.

But what happens when our feet hit the floor and we turn an ankle? Or we get into the shower and the water doesn't come out of the faucet? These are two of the million or so things on a very long list from everything to losing your keys or getting a flat tire, to finding yourself without a job, a marriage, or your health.

Life is change. We don't have to walk around expecting that we will sprain our ankle, lose our keys, or believe that we will be fired at any minute. But we can adjust our focus to notice changes that inevitably occur, and keep ourselves stable and balanced even, if the rest of our life begins to unravel a little.

A Story from the Heart

On a snowy winter evening, I went into an elevator and got off at the 52nd floor of the John Hancock building in Chicago. There I met my friend Irv, a 72-year-old retired executive at a large insurance firm.

I had known Irv since I was a child. My father had trained him in business and he'd been over to the house a few times, mostly in the morning. He and my father would ride together into the city.

After my father's death, I'd gotten to know Irv pretty well. We corresponded for the last twenty years or so. When his own father died about eight years ago, Irv and I had extended conversations about how this one event "changed everything" about how he saw himself. "And," Irv said, "It changed how I treated people. I looked at everybody differently." Irv sat behind this huge mahogany desk. "Life changed for me the second I got the phone call letting me know he'd passed. Ninety two years old. Good, long life, you know?" Irv swiveled around in his large, black leather seat in front of a one-hundred-eighty degree view of the skyline. "But, I must tell you, that change was probably the best thing that could have happened to me. And," he said, leaning in toward his desk, "as I've told you before, it wasn't what I thought would happen."

Irv has told me this story a few times, but he likes to return to it when we get together. Before he starts, he always gets out his handkerchief. You'll know why in a second.

"So," says Irv, "I'm flying back to New York for my father's funeral. I get into the flight, I sit down, the plane takes off, and I start to cry. I haven't cried since I was in third grade. The feelings hit me like a wave. The stewardess even came over to see if there was anything she could do.

"Then," he says, "I start getting so pissed! Something almost jolted me out of my chair. I stopped crying and felt like I wanted to punch somebody. I'm a 70 year old man and if somebody looked at me sideways, I would've decked them." He put both hands on his desk, "Suffice it to say, I was a mess.

"I was so mad. But I didn't know what I was so angry about. I thought I'd be sad. Sad for my Mom, sad for my sisters. But nothing came out. I was just angry.

"I started to look out the window and the sun was just beginning to hide behind the horizon. I took a deep breath and thought of my father. And that's when things changed." He paused, then continued. "I always wanted to be like the guy. I thought if I could be just like him, I'd be as successful a businessman as he was." Irv put the handkerchief in his right hand. "I studied his moves, I listened to him on the phone, and I copied his walk. I even bought suits that were exactly like his.

"My career was great. I have no complaints. I rose to the top of my firm just like he rose to the top of his." Irv moved the handkerchief from one hand to another, and took a deep breath. "But you know what? It was all for him. All of it." The tears started running down his cheek. "And he never told me how proud he was of me. Never told me I was doing a good job. Never acknowledged me when I got promotion after promotion.

"And you know what else?" Irv said, now beginning to dab the tears from his eyes, "it wasn't until that moment on the airplane that I really knew how lousy I felt. All these years, I wanted his approval. All these years, day after day of feeling unsatisfied, of being resentful, angry and ready to snap at anybody who looked at me sideways."

Now the tears really started to pour. "Three divorces. A kid in rehab. Another one that doesn't speak to me. And for what? A good view? A big chair? I'm seventy years old at this point, and I'm just beside myself in anger, the same anger that I've lived with all my life!"

Another deep breath, another few tears, and Irv said, "And right at that time, as I saw the sunset outside the plane window, I felt something change. I don't know what it was. But something inside of me let go. Maybe it was removed from me, I'm not sure. But I felt myself literally change in that moment. My anger was gone. In its place, as close as I can figure, was a deep understanding and forgiveness for my father."

Now the tears really came on strong.

"The first thing I did was call my son from the plane and apologize for having been such an angry father, and I told him I wanted to hear all the things I'd done that had hurt him, so I could work on changing them. Then I called my daughter, and told her the same thing. And neither one of them hung up on me! It was a miracle. Then, I called all three of my ex-wives and asked them to do the same thing. And they didn't hang up on me either! Another miracle." Irv went on to say how he apologized to his staff, his company, and even his board for his behavior, his attitudes, and the way he spoke to people. "Change was upon me, and I needed to meet it. By releasing all the anger and rage that had been stored within me for years, I let go of the person I was. Not easy, you know," he said, wiping his eyes, "but sometimes we have to go with the changes that come to us.

"My changes came through my amends and my ability to forgive my father. Then I asked for forgiveness from those I hurt.

Come to find out," he said, now smiling a little, "that any change, all change, comes from this decision in your life. You begin to be honest with yourself. You become the person you were supposed to be all along."

We talked for another hour, then it was time for me to go. "My friend," Irv said as he stuck out his hand, "Changes in business, in money, in trends were never any problem. The biggest change I embraced was within myself, through letting go of my anger and accepting kindness as a way to live. Since that moment, I have welcomed all change as a way to become a better person."

How it Works

Change kind of jumps out at you from behind the sofa. It's nothing huge. Most of the changes we encounter are of the "misplaced car keys" variety.

But some of it is the death of a family member. Or a loss of income. Or terrible news in health.

You are to deal with both kinds in the same way: With knowing, acceptance, and faith.

Knowing change is a part of daily life doesn't make the adjustment any less painful, but it does make it something you're ready for, at least in part. Change will surprise you, but it will surprise you far less if you know that, at some point, it's coming. You can be aware of its arrival, but you don't have to put it into the crosshairs. You just know. And then you can put it on the back burner. When it shows up, you're ready.

Accepting change will be an adjustment, but acceptance means you can roll with the severity of change far better than if you resisted it or, even worse, expected that it wouldn't last. Acceptance means your expectations are a little lower than they would ordinarily be, and that's good. The more we expect that things will return to normal right away, the less we can accept the change when they don't. But, the more we accept change in our life, no matter how severe, the better we are able to move easily with that change.

If we have faith that we will transcend whatever change befalls us, knowing that we have adjusted and moved past other changes in our lives, we will strengthen our resilience and our flexibility. Our faith will result in a belief that better times are ahead.

Change is. But you can handle it. You already have. You'll handle it again.

Why this is Important

To know change is to understand that nothing is permanent in life, not even you. Everything changes, either evolving into something more complex or deteriorating away. Understand that, as Pema Chödrön says, "nothing is static or fixed, that all is fleeting and impermanent, is the first mark of existence. It is the ordinary state of affairs. Everything is in process. Everything—every tree, every blade of grass, all the animals, insects, human beings, buildings, the animate and inanimate—is always changing, moment to moment. We don't have to be mystics or physicists to know this. Yet at the level of personal experience, we resist this basic fact. It means that life isn't always going to go our way. It means there's loss as well as gain. And we don't like that." [80] Internal resistance to change increases suffering. Because change is an inevitable, we must accept it as part of life and have empowering attitudes and strategies to handle change. Change must not be viewed as a problem; it must be viewed as a challenge.

In Reflections on the Art of Living Joseph Campbell says,

---

[80] Chödrön, Pema. The Places That Scare You: A Guide to Fearlessness in Difficult Times. Boston: Shambhala, 2001. Print. (2nd page of chapter 3)

> "The psyche knows how to heal, but it hurts. Sometimes the healing hurts more than the injury, but if you can survive it, you'll be stronger because you've found a larger base. Nietzsche was the one who did the job for me. At a certain moment in his life, the idea came to him of what he called 'the love of your fate.' Whatever your fate is, whatever the hell happens, you say, 'This is what I need.' It may look like a wreck, but go at it as though it were an opportunity, a challenge. If you bring love to that moment—not discouragement—you will find the strength is there. Any disaster that you can survive is an improvement in your character, your stature, and your life. What a privilege! This is when the spontaneity of your own nature will have a chance to flow. Then, when looking back at your life, you will see that the moments which seemed to be great failures followed by wreckage were the incidents that shaped the life you have now. You'll see that this is really true. Nothing can happen to you that is not positive. Even though it looks and feels at the moment like a negative crisis, it is not. The crisis throws you back, and when you are required to exhibit strength, it comes."[81]

Everything in life is useful. What seems like a tragedy in the moment opens the door for something new. It may allow you to help someone in the future who is going through a similar situation. It may teach you a valuable life lesson. It may build in the inner strength you will need later in life. Reframe negative change into a positive potential. Fearing change or resisting change uses mental energy, and takes you out of the present moment. Life's randomness will get in the way of even the best made plans. Accept that, and handle change as it arises with as little mental resistance as possible.

---

[81] Campbell, Joseph, and Diane K. Osbon. A Joseph Campbell Companion: Reflections on the Art of Living. New York, NY: HarperCollins, 1991. Print.

KEY 7

KEY SEVEN: PERSEVERE

Perseverance means we go forward in spite of pain. No matter the discomfort, its origin or its depth, its nature or its severity, we move forward. No matter how long the pain has endured or is expected to remain, we persist. We continue to move in the direction of our goals, assignments, duties, and desires. Despite feelings of discouragement or doubt, we believe. No matter how small or routine, each step forward is a statement of commitment to the ideals we set for ourselves and the accomplishments we see as critical, to fulfilling our life's direction.

Throughout our lives, it feels unnatural to step into discomfort. We have no enthusiasm to invite pain. Yet, it is from pain we learn, and from pain we achieve. This is not an endorsement of masochism. We started stretching out from our comfort zone naturally, beginning with our transition from crawling to our first steps. Each step we took brought us closer to everything that was within our reach. Pain helped the universe unfold into our grasp.

Sometime, somewhere along the line, we confront the desire to stop. At some point we all reach the place when we tell ourselves the pain is too great, the road is too long, the goal too elusive. Some of us remain forever at that stopping point. Some of us may take a few steps more. But for so many of us, we rationalize our remaining steps and live in a place that falls far short of our original goal. We rationalize further that not only have we achieved what we now feel as appropriate, we actually see it as supporting our sense of happiness and contentment. We make do with what we have. We resign ourselves to a life of asking "what if?" and "I wonder if I could have been . . ."

Perseverance re-engages our ability to become resourceful and believe in the beauty and strength of our goals. Perseverance refuels our faith in ourselves and our ability to achieve and attain all that we believe in.

In short, to persevere means to keep trying, despite the odds, failures, near misses, periods of doubt, discouragements, or the urge to give up. When we persevere, we honor the inner voice inside of us that tells us that we can do what we believe we can do. And we go forward.

A Story from the Heart

My friend Elaine is a physical therapist. Coffee with Elaine is always a treat, largely because she always buys the coffee and I have the honor of listening to her stories of hope and persistence.

She told me that she'd had a client come who'd been experiencing deep depression and hopelessness. "I've been at this for almost thirty years," Elaine said, "and this woman was close to the edge."

This client, we'll call her Anna, had come into therapy following a stroke. She'd had a year of physical therapy and was able to stand. But she'd lost the dexterity in her right hand, had minimal feeling in some of her fingers on that hand, and experienced difficulty controlling her right arm. "Her depression had gotten so bad, I was afraid she might get worse. That happens, you know," said Elaine, putting down her coffee cup, "people give up hope. It isn't the pain, even the lack of mobility. So often, it's feeling that you'll never get back what you once had.

"See, Anna was an artist. Her work had been displayed in New York, London, Paris, all over the world. And since this stroke, she couldn't hold a brush, couldn't manipulate a pencil, nothing. Every time she tried, she'd drop whatever she was holding in her hands. She wouldn't bother trying to pick it up. She leave it on the ground, and stare out into space.

"No matter how hard I tried, I couldn't get her to work toward getting better dexterity in her hands. For months, she came to the center. Every day, she'd try, and every day she'd never get that pencil or brush or whatever she was holding firm enough in her hand to make any kind of stroke on her pallet with anything close to the skill she'd had before.

"Well, Anna comes in and says, 'Elaine, I've going to give it one more try. Today is going to be my last stab at this. If I don't get better today, you'll never see me again.' And I knew she meant it. For a second, I felt sorry for her, but I knew how frustrated she was.

"I was at my wits' end," Elaine said, shaking her head, "so I took a walk down the hallway. I was going to speak to the director of the therapy center. He'd always had some good suggestions in the past, and I thought that he could help me. So I asked him if he had any ideas and he said, 'Well, I would've had her come in for art therapy, but since she lost so much dexterity in her hand, that wouldn't make much sense. And besides, the art therapy instructor had to quit yesterday. Moved away suddenly.'

"Now," Elaine said, "this gave me an idea. I asked my Director if he'd cancelled the class for art therapy and he said he hadn't. He said, "Well, no, I was going to go in there and help them with their lessons that our last teacher had planned. But I have interviews scheduled for a replacement this afternoon."

Elaine sat straight up in her chair. "I said, 'Hold on. I think I have found you an instructor.'

"I ran back to the physical therapy center, and I bolted through the doors, and I grabbed the back of Anna's wheelchair. And Anna, bless her heart, just about had a heart attack to add to her stroke." Elaine laughed out loud, flung her head back, and said, "you should've seen her face, poor thing. She didn't know what to think.

"I said, 'Anna, I need a favor. You're going to teach an art course. Might be just for today, but let's see how this goes.'

"I rolled her into the room where about fifteen people, all in wheelchairs, were ready for their art lesson."

Elaine paused for a second, sipped her coffee and looked down at the table. "I wheeled Anna in, and had her face the class. And the woman right in front of Anna, dead center of that class, was a quadriplegic. Her hands lay stiff on the arms of her wheelchair. But around her head was a harness, kind of like a helmet.

"And out of that harness," Elaine said, "was a paintbrush. It was positioned in front of her mouth." Elaine stopped and took a deep breath. "That woman painted with the brush in her teeth.

"Right then, Anna stopped, looked over at a table full of brushes and pencils, picked up a brush with her left hand, looked at where the art lesson had left off, and began teaching the class.

"And I just stopped and watched her. Her face lit up, I mean literally came to life. She wasn't evaluating what she was doing, she wasn't self-conscious. She did what she could with what she had. And, for those people in front of her, she kept going.

"You know," she said, putting her index finger against her cheekbone, "I think she's been at for over a year now. And, man, has she gotten good!"

She got up and asked me to come with her over to her car. In the back seat was a large rectangle covered with a blanket. "I need you to look at this."

She took off the blanket and showed me a painting. It was a portrait of her. "Anna did this. Pretty good, don't you think? Hated sitting that long for her to paint me, but she said she wanted me to have it."

I looked over at the painting. The likeness of Elaine was remarkable. "She took about four days to finish this. Almost thirty hours of her working on this. And left handed, too. She kept at it, though, I have to give that to her. She never gave up. Still teaches that class, too. Isn't that something?" Elaine said, "I'd never seen such determination. Once she was given that challenge, she just kept on. Never missed a class, always showed up early and stayed late to help anybody that needed extra attention."

Elaine then bent back over, picked up the portrait and, showing it to me again, said "And she made an old woman like me look pretty good on canvas, don't you think?"

How it Works

Perseverance engages three tools: time, compartmentalization, and a list of tasks. You have to give yourself a set amount of time in which to persevere. That is, if I'm going to practice the piano, I am going to set myself an arbitrary length of time in which to practice. It could be an hour or it could be three hours. A set amount of time, a period to devote focused energy and effort, gives you the framework for perseverance to take place. Research shows it is better to set aside a small amount of time every day rather than a large amount of time once a week.

That framework becomes your operating space. When you compartmentalize the tasks and how they are prioritized, you become efficient. Within this framework, you begin to recognize your strengths and your weaknesses, and modify your framework accordingly.

Once you have a framework in mind, you can now begin to use what is commonly referred to as the list. This powerful tool is your guide for your continued perseverance. When we set forth to achieve our goals, we start with a list of the necessary steps, and cross them off when completed. This is a symbol of progress. As mundane, and worn out as the list can be, it works miracles in setting the course of your perseverance.

Perseverance is minute by minute, day by day. Everyone has doubt and we all have periods of great frustration, discouragement, and even depression. We thoroughly endorse the idea of taking an hour off here and there. We absolutely recognize that people sometimes need a little vacation from their to-do list. Just remember to get back to it. Keep the effort alive. Your perseverance will pay off.

Why this is Important

Former American president Calvin Coolidge says "Nothing in the world can take the place of persistence. Talent will not; nothing is more common than unsuccessful men with talent. Genius will not; unrewarded genius is almost a proverb. Education will not; the world is full of educated derelicts. Persistence and determination are omnipotent. The slogan 'press on' has solved and always will solve the problems of the human race." [82] All successful people have had significant obstacles along their way to greatness. Instead of becoming discouraged by obstacles, they refused to quit. Life is challenging, and obstacles will arise. To persevere is to let nothing stand in the way of the outcome you are committed to.

To persevere with resilience, know without a doubt what your desired outcome is, and have compelling reasons why you must attain that outcome.

Mountaineer WH Murray says, "Until one is committed, there is hesitancy, the chance to draw back, always ineffectiveness. Concerning all acts of initiative and creation, there is one elementary truth, the ignorance of which kills countless ideas and splendid plans; that the moment one definitely commits oneself, then providence moves too. All sorts of things occur to help one that would never otherwise have occurred. A whole stream of events issues from the decision raising in one's favor all manner of unforeseen events,

[82] Coolidge, Calvin

meetings and material assistance which no one could have dreamed would have come their way. I have learned a deep respect for one of Goethe's couplets: 'Whatever you can do or dream you can, begin it. Boldness has genius, power, and magic in it. Begin it now!' "[83]

It is easier to stay comfortable and maintain homeostasis. When the effort required becomes too much, people give up. This path at best leads to comfortable mediocrity filled with statements such as could have, what if, and if only. A proactive lifestyle exceeds expectations.

---

[83] Murray, W H. The Scottish Himalayan Expedition. London: Dent, 1951. Print.

KEY 8

KEY EIGHT: PROGRESS AND PROCESS, NOT PERFECTION

We aren't perfect. Your friends aren't perfect. People who think they're perfect really aren't perfect. We aren't either. We are all so far away from our definition of perfect, it's barely worth mentioning. But we have to.

You will, at first, go sailing into every part of this book with enthusiasm. And, maybe after day two or three, you'll get distracted, and you'll settle back into your routine, and the book might be used for a doorstop or a toy for the dog.

Most of the books we use to make ourselves better, to get more out of our lives, end up in the bookshelf and, when you move, the local used bookstore. Even worse, you suggest the book to somebody else and let them know they can "take all the time they want" with it. In short, self-improvement efforts tend not to last. We change, our priorities are shuffled, and we focus on other things.

We eventually get back to needing that little boost, though. We don't want to abandon our journey altogether. We just want to make it easier. We don't want it to be so much work. And we'd like to have it fit into our schedule right now, as opposed to our having to rearrange what we need to do and when we need to do it. Just let me do a few things and I'll be on my way, thanks very much.

We have been at exactly the same place you are now. We have felt the discouragement at doing one more thing, sacrificing one more minute, in order to make our lives better. And we didn't get it right the first or second or seventh or fifteenth or forty second time we did it, either.

We want to make sure that you keep at it.

A Story from the Heart

Luis is a psychology professor at a local university. He is one of the hardest working people I've ever known. I spoke to him about the importance of progress and his thoughts on perfection. It was that last one–perfection–that drew me to Luis in the first place.

Luis keeps going. He does things well. He's really accomplished. Even his car still smells new and it's about eight years old. I'm not kidding.

The thing with Luis, and I'm not just the only one that will tell you this, is that I've never seen him withdraw. He just keeps forging ahead. Even when he is at rest, he has a book in his hands. And it's not science fiction or light reading. Luis studies new research on anxiety treatments, different ways to approach a hostage situation, and the novels of the ancient Greeks.

If you haven't picked this up yet, Luis is a really smart guy. But he's more than that. He's always busy. I have yet to see him do anything that isn't organized and structured.

"Well," he says, as we both sit down in his office chairs, "you haven't been paying attention. I'm really not that perfect. In fact, I tend to withdraw, sometimes just let things happen."

"Seriously?" I said.

He put his pipe in the ashtray next to his chair. "Yes, I give myself a little breather now and then. I learned at a young age to just keep going forward, without focusing too much on the results. I'm just aware of what I'm doing. I got my perspective from my uncle."

"Your uncle?"

Luis told me that his uncle was a first generation immigrant from Tijuana. "He was one of the first Mexicans to operate an avocado orchard. He built the processing plant himself.

"I should know," Luis said, putting his pipe back in his mouth, "I helped him put the whole production together."

I sat silently while Luis lit his pipe. "I was ten years old. I went to school, but as soon as I got home I'd quickly do my homework and walk the mile or so out to my uncle's farm. There, he would be on a ladder, picking the avocados. The trees looked so monstrous to me. The closer I came to each one, the more imposing its presence. 'This is your tree, Luis,' he'd say, 'Let's see how many you can pick today.'

"Do you know how many avocados a ten year old boy can pick in an afternoon? At first, not many. But I watched my uncle.

"Everything he did seemed to have purpose. First, I saw him count the avocados as he picked them from the tree. Secondly, I saw him arrange the avocados in the basket, to fit the most in each one. And lastly, I saw him smile as he would drop one of the avocados on the ground, watching it smash against the dirt."

Luis stopped himself for a second, and inched forward in his chair.

"My uncle always measured his work. He saw how much he was doing, and always seemed happy with the results of the efforts, no matter if they were a little short. The quantity didn't always affect him. His work, and his persistence toward completing his task, was how he measured his success.

"One day, I dropped an avocado. It slipped out of my hands and crashed against the ground. I was mortified. I could feel my eyes grow into the size of saucers. My mouth was open, and I was just about to say, 'I'm sorry' to my uncle when he said, 'Luis, it's OK. Come with me.'

"We got off our ladders and he put his arm around my shoulder. He said, 'Luis, we can't be perfect. We try to go through a whole day without dropping an avocado. But you know what? I have never gone more than a week without at least dropping one.'

" 'I saw you pick so well. Every day, you picked a little more. Every day, you put more in your baskets. And you know what? I saw that you haven't dropped a single avocado in almost a month.'

"Then my uncle said, 'But, Luis, I need you to do me a favor. Every now and then, give yourself permission to let go and drop one. It's OK. In fact, Luis, it helps me out a little bit.'

"I had no idea what he was talking about. He must have seen that in my face, because he smiled as we were walking into the barn where he stored the avocados. He pointed to the refrigerator across the barn. We walked to it, he opened the door, and there on the shelf was an enormous bowl. 'This is why it's OK to drop an avocado, Luis.' The bowl was full of guacamole.

"From that point, I saw that his work was toward progress, not perfection. Even his mistakes, his dropped avocados, were examples of progress."

Luis got up from his chair and waved me into his office. "I'm not perfect by any means. Here, let me show you an example."

His office was a mess. Papers everywhere, books opened on his desk, folders in stacks on the floor.

"It's progress, my friend." Smiling, he put his hand on my shoulder and said, "Let's just call this room my big bowl of guacamole."

How it Works

As we suggested in Key Five–Practice, you take one Key at a time, anywhere in the book, for about a week, and bring it to your awareness for one minute an hour.

Or take a more relaxed approach and choose three. And these can be any Keys you like. Take, Be Present, Know Yourself, and Dance. That's as good a combination as any. And it's also easy to manage.

Just be aware of a few things at a time. Nothing more than that. Once you have a handle on a couple, move around a little bit.

The book offers reliable variety and the freedom to do it your way, in little bites. You can take this at your own pace, at your leisure, and have some variety in the process. Don't look at these as your marching orders, starting from beginning to end and then doing it all over again but, rather, choose the sections spontaneously to suit your needs.

You may have a day when you absolutely need to wrap your head around "Patience" or you might just go off on somebody. In that case, just flip right to that point and dive right in. It's OK by us.

Your progress doesn't depend on looking at each point in the book. It depends on you making this book a part of your daily life. You will grow in places you hadn't thought of before.

We do not expect miracles from what we have here, but we've seen them happen. After reading this book, yours may be one of those miracles, too, if you move forward in life with this book as a roadmap for your heart.

You will see change. You will see growth. You will progress. And who knows? You may feel absolutely perfect as a result.

Why this is Important

Meaning in life is found in the progress and process, not in the end result. Our achievements do not define our worth. Our worth is determined by the path we take. We can control our ability to take action, but we cannot control the results; therefore, we must consistently continue to improve. Someone "who is attached to the outcome suffers if he does not get the outcome he wants, whereas the happy, peaceful person prefers the outcome he wants but is not attached to it. If he gets a different outcome, he remains just as happy and peaceful as he was to begin with. His happiness comes from within, and does not depend on what goes on around him."[84] A person set on a singular outcome limits the infinite possibilities that can emerge. Enjoy the process with an open mind, allowing what arises.

Perfection is an unrealistic expectation. Tal Ben-Shahar in his book The Pursuit of Perfect uses the term Optimalist to describe a person who, instead of focusing on perfection, uses optimism to make the most of their life. The life "the Perfectionist expects is one of a constant high; the Optimalist expects his life to include emotional ups, emotional downs, and everything in between. The Perfectionist rejects painful emotions that do not meet his expectation of an unwavering flow of positive emotions; the Optimalist permits himself to experience the full range of human emotions."[85] The Perfectionist aims for a perfect life, and anything that does not meet this standard is viewed as a problem. Nothing in life works out as planned, and having a standard of flawless ideal vision will cause suffering. This creates a very narrow existence, with limited risk and growth because, when a person steps out of their comfort zone, they will make mistakes. We must be free to experiment, to think big, to take risks. Mistakes will happen, and when they do, you will handle them. Continue to make progress while enjoying the process.

[84] Harris, Bill. Thresholds of the Mind: How Holosync Audio Technology Can Transform Your Life. Beaverton: Centerpointe Press, 2002. Print. pg 127

[85] Ben-Shahar, Tal. The Pursuit of Perfect: How to Stop Chasing Perfection and Start Living a Richer, Happier Life. New York: McGraw-Hill, 2009. Print. pg 40

KEY 9

KEY NINE: WORK

Work does more than support your financial life and professional identity. It is often an expression of you.

In other words, we are often identified with, and derive meaning from, what we do. We say we are a teacher, a cashier at the grocery store, a healthcare worker, a bus driver, a landscaper, or a thousand other different jobs. Each requires us to develop and commit to memory dozens of tasks. Work is what we wake up prepared to do every day. It offers us stress and satisfaction, reward and disappointment. It tests our patience.

Our jobs define who we are. Our actions on the job give the world an impression of what we're about.

Our parents, siblings, partners, children and friends may not recognize this side of us, and it's too bad. Our jobs require that we are at our most consistent, most contained, and most cordial. We act in such a measured fashion that if we treated those we love with the same kind of respect we treat those in our work environment, our lives would be much calmer and probably a good bit happier.

In addition to bringing forth our better selves, work can make us empathetic. But, in this context, empathy is a little sideways. We want to be recognized for how hard we work, so we recognize others for their efforts. We appreciate the kinds of strain they endure to do their job. Our empathy comes forward from knowing how hard people work and how they struggle every day, just we you do. Work helps us understand another. We see life through their eyes. We see others as we want to be seen.

Work gives us the motivation to get up in the morning. Work may only be a way to pay the bills, to put food on the table. And yet, even in this form, work gives us a purpose–to provide for and support the lives of those we love. We discover and exhibit our greatest strengths of character through our work: persistence, drive, analysis, forethought, consideration, stamina, patience, and humor.

We need work for this reference. It requires us to bring forward a different, sometimes better, part of ourselves. Work keeps us from being bored and isolated. So many of our social contacts begin at work. It helps us balance our lives, to deal with disappointment and accomplishment with the same kind of aplomb we often abandon at home.

A Story from the Heart

Velma is ninety. When I was putting this book together, she and I had just met two weeks before.

A friend who worked at a rehabilitation facility steered me towards her after Velma had broken her hip.

I met her while she was rehabbing her leg. She had been out of her wheelchair and on crutches a mere two weeks after her hip was replaced. She was walking into the hallway with a cane when she agreed to sit down with me and talk.

We talked about work. Velma has a job at the nursing facility in the kitchen, preparing meals for the residents. She has worked there for the past twenty two years. She was hired when she was sixty eight years old and has held on to the job ever since.

When I asked her why she'd been working so hard, she said that she wasn't any different than anybody else. "I got my first job, if you can call it that, when I was six years old. My job was to tend to the squirrels."

"Squirrels?" I said, not exactly sure if I heard her correctly. She nodded her head. "It was my job to help set the traps, catch them, put them in cages, feed them, and then get them out so my father could kill them, skin them, and eat them." She said, fidgeting with her cane. "We ate squirrel meat. My father was raised on it. He was terribly poor, raised way in the country in Missouri. He and my grandfather farmed, but when times were bad, you had to eat whatever you could get your hands on. Bread was about all they had, and if they wanted any meat, well, they had to trap squirrels.

"My father got to like the taste of squirrel meat, so he had them in traps and cages ever since I can remember." Velma adjusted herself in her chair. "Now, it was my job to tend to them. My father taught me this. See, once you caught a squirrel in a trap, you'd put them in a cage, and you'd have to calm them down. Well, that was my job. Give the squirrels attention. Feed them, let them know you were there. They'd eat more if they were calm, so I'd feed them and talk to them.

"Now mind you, I was six. And there wasn't much to do around my house. My Mom took in wash from the neighbors, and my father worked the fields and did handyman work around town. So, when I had time – and when you're six years old, that's about all you have–I went out and played with the squirrels. I'd feed them, I'd talk to them but most of all I'd just watch them."

Velma smiled, "The thing that fascinated me about them was the way they just kept in motion. They'd pile up the sticks and grass we put in their cages. Then they'd take all of it and move it to the other side of the cage. Then I'd see them groom themselves and sometimes the other squirrels in there with them. They never stopped.

"My daddy said I could have a couple of squirrels for pets. That was my joy. And I just kept watching. Back then, we didn't have a TV and half the time our radio didn't work. But I had the squirrels.

"Now," she said, putting her chin in her hand, "what I learned from them is that motion is a beautiful thing. I saw them move, move,

move. I just loved that. It was almost like dancing, what they did. I couldn't get enough of it.

"But," she said, looking at me, "you asked me about the meaning of work. Well, son, the meaning of work to me is just motion. You were not given this body to sit. This thing we have right here is made to be moving." Velma twisted her backside in the chair as if she was dancing, and the both of us started laughing. "And I don't buy into this whole thing about daily exercise. Work should cover that. I don't blame people for sitting in a chair and working their brain. That's work, too. I did that for years. But, you see, it was those squirrels. Their purpose was motion. They just kept going. And I loved that. That movement, that energythat was their work. And, so," Velma took a deep breath, "that became the example for my life.

"And don't misunderstand me," she said, "movement and motion, whether it physical or mental, was my purpose. It is what we are here for, and those squirrels taught me the beauty of work, that ease of their motion." She sat back in her chair. "So, whether it was school, work around the house, or a job in the community, I never stopped. I had to do something, I needed to. Those squirrels, although frantic, taught me a good lesson about life, and it's this: Do something and keep at it. And, to me, that something was always work. It started with the squirrels, took me through school, put me teaching in the classroom, but also kept me after my garden, my yard, my reading, my friendships, all the things I do.

"Young man, you have to do life. And it has always been work, in some fashion, for me. Work has been my life, in some way or another." She looked straight ahead, "Now, if you'll excuse me, I need to get moving. This hip isn't going to heal any faster by my sitting on it. It needs work."

She stood up and leaned on her cane. Looking up at me, she said, "Thank goodness for those squirrels. Today, they're going to help me work on this hip!"

How it Works

Work is a result of a need, generally the need to survive. Without work, we have no money and . . . well, you know the rest.

So many of us, when we're young, get a job. Any job. A job that will pay an inexperienced kid to do something most of the folks with experience won't do.

We may find that the first job we get is good enough, or later find another one that suits our temperament a little better. From there, we begin to formulate what we see as important for us as a career or, at least, another job. And the criteria for choosing a job may change. Often, we discover that we can take a job for its pay or hours or even location as opposed to the level of income or personal fulfillment it offers. Some jobs require more education, and we may go back to school.

Once we find a professional groove, we begin to discover a different part of ourselves. We see the need to get along with people, to respect the boss, and work in an organized and thorough fashion. We see the cause and effect beginning with our work performance and turning into our level of satisfaction (and our paycheck). We change on the job, and our preferences may change too. We change jobs. We meet new challenges. And we grow. In the context and variety that work offers, we find the value of engagement. It is from this engagement we are kept interested, active and alive. It keeps the heart beating. And it sets the pace of life. Our heart remains engaged. We find meaning. And our identity is formed, defined, and strengthened. We become a little more of that identity, and our lives align with that work, that occupation, that routine. Work becomes us. And a truly good, strong part of our heart beats on.

Why this is Important

Modern civilization is a result of hundreds of thousands of years of collaborative work. From hunting and gathering to our modern information age, we are all part of an evolving collective society. Individuals work, which adds to humanity collective strength.

Externally, there are many reasons people work; it can be for money, it can be from the desire to contribute to family, to the community, or even the world.

Internally, people's work can be an expression of their deepest gifts. As Rumi says, "everyone has been made for some particular work, and the desire for that work has been put in every heart."[86] Every person possesses skills distinct to them, based on life experience, personality type, and type of intelligence. Find the work you are meant to do, work that is fulfilling. American philosopher John Dewey says, "to find out what one is fitted to do, and to secure an opportunity to do it, is the key to happiness."[87] Psychologically, fulfilling one's purpose and making a difference gives the individual significance. Carl Rogers says that finding and doing what one is put on earth to do is "the urge which is evident in all organic and human life – to expand, extend, become autonomous, develop, mature – the tendency to express and activate all the capacities of the organism."[88] We work to actualize our potential in the world.

---

[86] Rumi

[87] Dewey, John. Democracy and Education: An Introduction to the Philosophy of Education. New York: The Free Press, 1966. Print. pg 360

[88] Rogers, Carl R. On Becoming a Person: A Therapist's View of Psychotherapy. Boston: Houghton Mifflin Company, 1961. Print. pg 35

KEY 10

KEY TEN: RISK

The biggest challenge of strong, heart centered-energy and awareness is actually being brave enough to use it. This heightened emotional focus involves risk.

If we aren't willing to put ourselves out there, if we can't steady ourselves to step out of our emotional comfort zone, we will delay so much of the good that is waiting for us.

Risk is what moves us outside of what we see as safe. But the operative phrase is "what we see." Our experiences can give us a narrow idea of safety, creating false limits based on fear or misunderstanding. We fall into routines that suit this concept of safety. Our default mode is to seek predictability and safety. And you awake one morning and see your routine offers you nothing other than what you're used to, what is predictable. This is particularly the case in finding love. We are all afraid, all hesitant, all afraid that our efforts will be met with rejection. Many of us have tried and given up. We decide to risk less. Many of us feel, "What if we put ourselves out there and we don't find love and happiness?"

Our response to this legitimate, but fear-based, question is: "What if you do?"

Risk lets us stretch, to reach, to dream outside of our past experiences. Risk takes us past who we've been and into who we can be. Risk must be repeated until we can say we've given our best. After taking these risks of the heart, you will find that your best is, by far, better than you've ever imagined.

If we're honest, though, we need to consider two other things. First, a risk that falls short can hurt like no other pain imaginable. And, secondly, this pain will fade each time you venture out of your comfort zone. The pain lessens, and quickly. You begin to take less and less personally, and the scale of risk becomes more manageable. You gain a balanced perspective. You adopt an attitude of "oh, well, I guess it wasn't meant to be. I'll keep trying tomorrow," which is as healthy as you can get. The hard part is to keep taking risks, not giving up when things get hard. It often hurts less and less as you keep trying, keep expressing, and continue to reach for all of life's goodness.

Resolve to push yourself. Ask her out. Take that trip. Go to that class. Make that call. Cry when you're sad. Laugh loudly when you're happy. Hug when the urge comes over you. Let somebody know how much you love them. And risk when you stand up for yourself, too. Take the risk of speaking on your behalf. Risk blowing your own horn. Risk, in particular, staring down injustice and unkindness. Risk saying "No" when it comes to your wellbeing or the wellbeing of someone you love.

Stretch your heart. Move your feelings upward and outward. Speak your inner truth. And stand in the faith of the beauty and goodness that is your inherent nature. Moving into a place of peace and faith will take away your fear of risk, turning it into an emotional adventure.

A Story from the Heart

My friend Charles has cancer. He's sixty one years old. He has been sick for five months.

Charles would describe himself as a "very successful entrepreneur." He had started two businesses, both doing very well.

In speaking to him about risk, he said "taking a risk in business was never that big of a deal. You never were quite sure whether or not the venture would take off, but there are always a variety of things to keep from losing your money. You might not make any money, but you can retrieve what you lose or just not lose any." He shook off the idea of losing money in business ventures by saying that he was "always conservative, and I never invested my time or money in something I didn't diligently study and consult on. And even then, I made sure I had an exit plan if my investment was compromised.

"No," he said, "I'll tell you about risk. You pay attention, OK? Sometimes this treatment makes my thoughts a little foggy."

I sat at the edge of his recliner. Getting up was hard for Charles. His IV treatment had begun. A bag hung from a metal hook on a makeshift hat rack in his home. His wife Kathy excused herself.

"I was nineteen," He said. "Kathy was a girl I met in college. We were really close friends. We'd known each other since the first year we were in the dorms. And I'm not sure how we met or spent time together, but being with her was easy.

"I didn't know anything about romance or sex. I didn't really ever have a girlfriend. I tried to catch up with a couple of girls, but I wanted to find one that not only liked me, but that I liked, too. And it never seemed to work that way.

"So, I thought, maybe if I could be somebody's friend, I could be with them long enough for romance to be introduced, even broached a little. I mean, I heard that a romance built on a friendship first was a great way to build a solid relationship. And, if it didn't work, I'd still have that friendship.

"Well, Kathy was my friend. And, she and I had been pretty close. One day, she said she was moving. She was leaving for another state, I'm not sure where. I wasn't sure that I'd ever see her again. I'd moved back home from college for the summer, but we'd been friends for a while. I'd always loved her company. We'd sit and drink tea and talk. I loved listening to her, too. Her voice would always make the hairs on the back of my neck stand up. I remember I made her laugh. And I know she made me feel relaxed, that it was OK to be myself.

"I'd thought to myself, 'this is what I want from partner for life. If I could feel this good with somebody, I'd be able to be a good person, and a good and solid partner.' So, we set a time to hang out, and have that one last cup of tea and talk for a while. I was pretty sure that, at the time, I figured we'd stay in touch, that we'd see one another again.

"Well, I went to her apartment. I really loved Kathy, but I didn't know how she felt about me, I mean in the way that I wanted to be loved. And, I thought, if I told her, maybe she'd reconsider her feelings, or at least think about it for a while.

"So, I got there and we had tea, and talked literally all night. The hours passed so quickly. We talked about where she was heading, who she would be with, and what her plans were. She asked me about where I thought my life was heading, and what I felt would be the next move I'd make.

"My feelings grew stronger. I knew she was going to be the one. I could trust that the person I really wanted to be–the confident, easygoing, contented person I knew was inside of me–would come out throughout my whole life with her. We went to a diner, I can't remember where, and ate something. I think it was about four in the morning. We went back to her place, and talked some more.

"But, you know," he said, adjusting in his chair, "I couldn't. I just couldn't tell her how I really felt. And the feelings were right there, I mean right in my throat. And they just didn't come out.

"Then I left. I hugged her, and I left. I never told her how I felt.

"I threw myself into business, got pretty lucky, made a good living, and never looked back. But," he said, "you want to talk about risk? Try this one on for size, my friend."

Charles took a deep breath, "I have cancer, and I'm going to die.

"And the cancer is nothing compared to the regret I have for not telling that woman I loved her and wanted to try our hands at romance. I can never get that moment back. Yes, I was young. But I wish I'd had taken that risk.

"Risk in business? Nothing. Risk in love? Everything. And now it's too late."

Charles started to cry, and we were interrupted. Kathy, his wife, came in and adjusted his IV, kissed Charles, on the forehead, and left us alone.

I said, "Wait. Kathy . . . ?"

"Different Kathy." he said, interrupting my question. "She doesn't know. It would hurt her too much."

Charles took a deep breath and said, "Your biggest risk in this life will be to share your feelings with someone. Teach this to your kids when they're young so that they don't feel this regret when they're my age. Teach them to be fearless with expressing their feelings.

"And, my friend," he said, looking over at me, "tell everybody you know. Risk in expressing your feelings, no matter where you are or whom you're with. Your life will change in ways you can only dream of."

Charles died three weeks later. Kathy, whomever she is, will never know about his feelings for her.

How it Works

Understanding risk is the emotional equivalent of making sure the coast is clear, before moving forward. We can do three specific things nearly instantaneously to allow ourselves to express the emotions that we once suppressed, bundled inaccessibly inside of us.

The first is to know that we're a little outside of what we would normally do, and it is perfectly OK to feel the uncomfortable sensation tugging at our guts. This tells you that, yes, you're taking your first step into a new direction.

Secondly, you'll instinctively take a breath, usually a deep breath, as an automatic physiological attempt to calm down. It works. When you feel it, stay with that breath; take that breath as a signal that you're right there, and you're about to move into a little personal growth.

Finally, you're going to take the risk, and it is going to feel odd. Here's the warning. You have the ability to stop right here, and we are going to urge you to move, move, move. When you take that deep breath, all you need to do is breathe out. That's it. That's how risks works. You feel your gut, breathe in deeply, and let that breath out.

Risking our heart isn't really that scary. There are one hundred times more successes than failures. People are in the same boat. All of us want to have friends, to be loved, to be listened to, and to have some company and conversation.

Risk allows all of this to happen. Risk replaces fear with faith. Risk moves us forward into a more fulfilling life.

Why this is Important

The ability to act despite risk allows a person to develop. We aren't talking about the unjustified risk of a degenerate gambler; we are talking about pushing your comfort zone to achieve and grow. This type of risk requires faith in yourself, as well as an acceptance of failure, because "ultimately, fear of failure generates a vicious circle that creates what is most feared. To break this cycle, you need to make peace with failure. It isn't enough to merely tolerate it; you need to appreciate the failure and use it."[89] Fear paralyzes us and stops progress. Fear of negative results stops many people from following their heart in life. Failure happens; things do not always go as planned.

To increase your ability to take risks, accept failure. Reframe how you think of failure. Value growth, value trying, and value stepping up to a challenge. Understand that the lessons of failure may serve you later in life. Even the most successful people fail and fail often; Michael Jordan said, "I've missed more than nine thousand shots in my career. I've lost almost 300 games. 26 times I've been trusted to take the winning shot and missed. I've failed over and over again in my life. And that is why I succeed."[90] If you focus on doubt and the fear of failure, you cannot grow.

Put yourself in the position to win or lose, but try not to become attached to either outcome. Instead, value your decision to stretch and grow. Dare to step into the unknown. There are many smart or athletic people, but the ability to take risks allows people to reach their potential.

---

89 Millman, Dan, and Dan Millman. Body Mind Mastery: Creating Success in Sport and Life. Novato, Calif: New World Library, 1999. Print. 48

90 Goldman, Robert, and Stephen Papson. Nike Culture: The Sign of the Swoosh. London: Sage Publications, 2004. Print. pg 49

CHAPTER 4

REACHING TO THE HEART OF ANOTHER

To reach another's heart is one of the true gifts in life. Humans are all interconnected. Nobody is self-sufficient; we have all relied on another person in our life. We must value and nurture our relationships with others. A meaningful life does not come from material possessions, it comes from relationships with others, a true heart connection. To make a difference in another's life, to stop focusing on yourself. Connecting with another transcends our isolation. These keys will help you reach the heart of another.

Key One: Follow the Golden Rule

Key Two: Cultivate Friendships

Key Three: Be Honest

Key Four: Listen

Key Five: Empathy

Key Six: Giving

Key Seven: Ask for Help

Key Eight: Be Clear

Key Nine: Say No

Key Ten: Apologize

Key Eleven: Hug

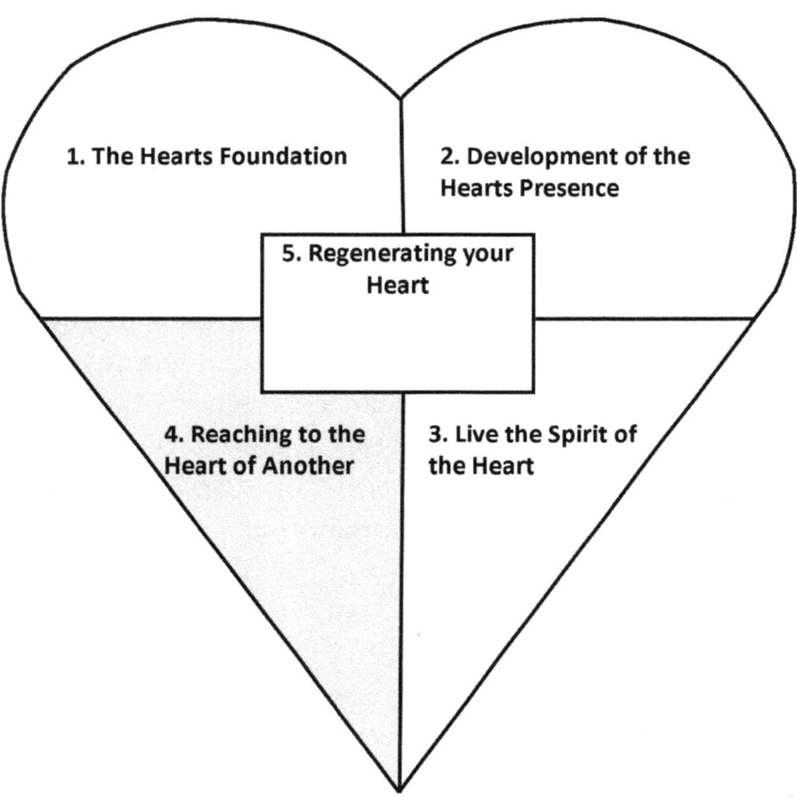

KEY 1

KEY ONE: FOLLOW THE GOLDEN RULE

The Golden Rule, "Do unto others as you would have done unto you," is the foundation, the spiritual and moral reference point, for hundreds of millions of people.

It is the energetic connection between your heart and another's.

Empathy lives here in this connection. So do understanding, kindness, patience, and love. If you know you'd like to be treated with all of these, you must first treat others this way. You don't have to know the nuances of another's personality to address them in this fashion. Embracing the very basic tenet of The Golden Rule and knowing these universal virtues sends you down the path to bring your heart to another.

This is the bottom line. The blueprint. The first step on the path.

Adhering to this premise puts your life on the fast track to emotional growth, spiritual awareness, and a life of balance, purpose, and meaning.

We cannot stress this enough: Recognizing the value of this rule and applying it on your journey to connect your heart with another is not just the first step on this journey, it is every single step. It is the breath within your words, the spirit behind your meaning, the emphasis of your message, and the understanding and acceptance of their response.

This is it.

<u>A Story from the Heart</u>

My office was less than a mile from the largest Alcoholics Anonymous meeting in the county. It was large for three big reasons: the location was remote but accessible from public transportation, there were a lot of "old timers" with twenty years or more of recovery, and they accepted everybody: felons, ex-cons, people with anger issues, co-dependency issues, and anything else they brought to the table. At this meeting, everybody was accepted.

Now, my friend Marv fell under the first three categories: He was a felon, he was an ex-con who had served time in prison, and he had significant anger issues.

I'd first spoken with Marv several years ago. Since then, Marv was working at a drug rehabilitation center.

He ran anger management classes.

I sat in the back of one of his classes, and I heard him tell this story.

"I had been released from prison on an assault charge. In that twelve-month sentence, I had become sober and discovered a spiritual path that helped calm my anger.

"Not two days after I was released, I went to an A.A. meeting. I had been a year sober, having had all that time in prison to attend meetings and work the steps.

"They tell you in recovery to be aware of your anger and resentment. I thought I had a handle on it. Well, as on any morning in any given week, I went to the 7 a.m. meeting. I'm sitting down, and there's about one hundred of us at this meeting, so it's hard to get to know everybody. I sat down as the meeting began, and then I saw a guy I recognized, but I couldn't place his face. I didn't remember where I'd seen him before, but I had the sense that I knew him. HE sat down a couple of rows ahead, and I'm just getting annoyed, trying to figure out where I might have met this man, and it was giving me a headache.

"Then it hit me. My trial. I remember this guy from the trial. It was so long ago, I wasn't sure, but all of a sudden, I remembered, and it almost floored me. This was the guy that said he witnessed me commit the crime. I mean, there he was, right in front of me, attending the same meeting. I couldn't believe it. I knew he still lived around here but I didn't know that he was an alcoholic. And I absolutely didn't know he was going to meetings, let alone this very one.

"The rage began to rise within me. I mean, it had been a year since I'd experienced this kind of anger, and I did not expect how quickly and strongly these feelings arrived."

Marv started to pace in front of the chalkboard. "We stood up in a circle, held hands, and said The Lord's Prayer to end the meeting and this guy, the guy that fingered me in front of a judge, stood next to me and held my hand!

"Now, you see this?" Marv held up a hand large enough to palm the head of a Holstein. "I wanted to squeeze this man's hand so hard his fingers would snap in two. My anger began to come through my arm, into my hand, and I could feel my muscles tense as I wrapped my hand around his.

"Right about now, the group got to the part in the prayer that said, 'and forgive us our trespasses, as we forgive those who trespass against us,' and this man looked up at me. He looked right into my eyes.

"And as I could feel my hand holding hard onto his–squeezing his hand more tightly, with more force–his eyes widened. He held his mouth open for just a second, and the eyebrows on his head arched in pain. His stare deepened into my eyes, and his lips made the words, 'Please . . . stop.'

Marv bent down from the waist. He put his hands on his hips and, facing the class, said, "At that moment, I hurt for him so much. My breath escaped my lungs. My legs felt so weak, I could hardly stand. I was struck with a pain that shot through my body unlike any I've ever felt before.

"I backed off. I let go of his hand. I stood there, I remember, and I put both of my hands over my mouth. I said, 'I'm so sorry, I . . .' and I couldn't speak any more.

"I cried. Man . . . " he stopped, again bent at the waist. Standing back up, he said, "Whew. I mean, I start to talk about this, and those same emotions come forward. Those same feelings come through me and the same sadness and shame puts tears in my eyes."

Pacing slowly in front of the class, Marv said, "I knew something right there. At that moment, I knew I couldn't hurt another person in anger. And it's not for the reason you think. It's not because I hurt him, but that's part of it.

"It's because, at that moment, I learned what 'Do unto others as you would have done unto you' means. I couldn't stand the pain of what I was doing to this man, because the pain I was experiencing as a result was too great. The shame was too corrosive. The angst was too deep.

"The Golden Rule happened to me in that moment. I was that man. And that man was me.

"His fear was mine, the pain coursing through his body was mine. His pleas for the pain to stop were my words, coming through my mouth. In that instant, I had 'embarked on a journey of revenge' and, as Confucius said, I was about to 'dig two graves.'

"If you are to know anything about managing your feelings, know this: We are all one. What you do to another, you do to yourself. It is an inescapable tenet of life. We are each other. What we do to another will, in that moment or at another time, return to us and within us.

"The Golden Rule guides us in fairness and compassion. I learned it that day. It brings us all together and guides us into our best selves." Marv put his hands behind his back, stood in front of the class and said, "Let it begin to guide your spirit now."

And as he walked a few steps, the students became quiet. He looked at the clock, smiled and said, "Take that with you, today and every day. Class dismissed."

How it Works

The Golden Rule is like your spiritual GPS. It gives your heart direction. If you're at a loss about how to treat somebody else, or if you can't figure out how to connect or engage another person, The Golden Rule leads you outside of yourself to bring you back to the basics. It is both the how to of emotional expression and the you are here of spirituality.

In short, it puts you in touch with another. You don't have to think too hard. By considering another person's feelings, you express the universal principle: love.

Why this is Important

The Golden Rule takes the guesswork out of what constitutes right action. It is hard to argue with an idea that crosses so many cultures. Beyond that, The Golden Rule makes innate sense. You, as a human, have the same psychology and physiology as another human. Although each person's mind is different, everyone wants to avoid pain and maximize pleasure. As American president and philosopher Thomas Jefferson said in the Declaration of Independence, all humans are entitled to "Life, Liberty and the pursuit of Happiness." The Golden Rule is a philosophical foundation for the interaction and treatment of other human beings, and it guides us into consideration and empathy. We see it in the fundamental structure of every major religion and spiritual teaching in the world:

> Aristotle: "As the virtuous man is to himself, he is to his friend also, for his friend is another self" (Nicomachean Ethics 9:9).
>
> Buddhism: "There is nothing dearer to man than himself; therefore, as it is the same thing that is dear to you and to others, hurt not others with what pains yourself" (Dhammapada, Northern Canon, 5:18).
>
> Christianity: "Do unto others as you would have them do unto you" (Matthew 7:12).
>
> Confucianism: "Surely it is the maxim of loving-kindness: Do not unto others that you would not have them do unto you" (Analects 15,23).
>
> Hinduism: "One who regards all creatures as his own self, and behaves towards them as towards his own self attains happiness. One should never do to another what one regards as hurtful to one's own self. This, in brief, is the rule of righteousness. In happiness and misery, in the agreeable and the disagreeable, one should judge effects as if they came to one's own self" (Mahabharata bk. 13: Anusasana Parva, §113).
>
> Islam: "Woe to those who cheat: they demand a fair measure from others but they do not give it themselves" (83:1-3).
>
> Taoism: "Regard your neighbor's gains as your own gain and your neighbor's loss as your loss" (T'ai Shang Kan Ying P'ien).

The philosophy that we will treat all people as we want them to treat us is fundamental to living a life from the heart. We will only live life from our heart if we are willing to consider, through our most basic values of kindness, compassion, and love, the emotional and spiritual desires of another. We may fall off course in our daily lives, but it is simple to correct our course. To live a life of love, follow the Golden Rule.

KEY 2

KEY TWO: CULTIVATE FRIENDSHIPS

Friendship is earth underneath our hearts, the emotional granite and ground, the stuff that keeps us standing. Friendship is where your heart practices. Friends are the mirrors of your emotional effort and reservoirs of love and care. They know the road you've travelled. You know their travels, too.

Friendship give us the knowledge that we're human, that we have our highs and lows, our faults and our frustrations, and lets us know that we're OK anyway. Friends see our humanness, and like us in spite of our flaws. Mind you, a friendship is also about sharing of joy. I don't know a lot of friends that don't, at least sometimes, laugh and then laugh some more. Friends, by nature, don't take one another too seriously. Friendship gives love its lift. From the ground underneath you, you stand on its fellowship. And from the joy that is only shared when two or more friends are together, you are elevated by its love.

Friendship is the action of the heart. Between two people, friendship is what helps you deepen and experience the value and pure goodness of all that is within us.

But it is a reminder, too. Friendship makes the engagements of the heart easy. It is within this arena that we need to stay attentive to the feelings of another other person. Friendship centers us on the other, which brings forth our loving self, the most attentive and responsive side of our nature.

A Story from the Heart

I have always had a soft spot in my heart for those folks that have been ignored, left alone, and often forgotten. These people are often called seniors.

Bonnie, a social worker of extraordinary patience, kindness, and compassion, worked as the activities director of a nursing home or, "retirement center" in a small town about 100 miles outside of Chicago. The center had about twenty-five residents.

The criteria for admission was that these folks could care for themselves, for the most part. Specifically, they were ambulatory, had few or no signs of dementia, could feed and bathe themselves, and had no chronic health problem that required intensive medical support.

Now, the problem wasn't with the seniors, it was with the location. 100 miles outside of Chicago is a long way out. A good two hour drive. Bonnie said it was a rural community. "Even the staff have nearly an hour's drive to and from the facility," she said

"People get depressed," Bonnie said, "and it's a hard time for all of them. Visitors are few. It's a long drive. I suspect that many of these families put their parents or older relatives here, in part, because of the distance. It's cruel.

"And," Bonnie continued, "the place is kind of small. There's not a lot of room to do many things. The TV is on, but people tend to stay in their rooms. Most folks get ready in the morning, have their breakfast, read the paper, and nap. And they do the same things throughout the day. "Nobody calls. People have cell phones but only a few know how to use them. And I don't see anyone talking on the phone. It's so sad sometimes."

One day, Bonnie found out that the administrator's father had passed away. One of the residents got wind of this, and got the other residents together to memorialize the administrator's father. They sent a small basket of pink azaleas. An older woman who lived at the facility had raised pink azaleas' in her yard many years ago, and always made a point of sending them for weddings, funerals, baptisms, and births.

A week later, without any warning, five members of the Administrator's family made a special trip to thank each of the residents in person. The family catered a dinner and dined with the residents on smoked salmon, barbecued ribs, and roast turkey. The residents were beside themselves.

The next day, the mood of the facility had changed, as Bonnie put it, "from January to June." And it gave Bonnie an idea.

Following the lead of the woman who raised the pink azaleas, Bonnie got out the newspaper. She saw that in their town that week, two people had died and one little girl had been born.

She ran down the hallway and spoke to the Administrator. It turned out that sending a small basket of pink azaleas, plus shipping, was fifteen dollars. Bonnie asked if there was a fund that could cover the forty five dollars to send the family of the deceased and the new parents some azaleas.

The Administrator, who was still so appreciative of the gesture to his family, looked at Bonnie and said, "No, but let's start one. I'll pitch in the first fifty dollars."

With that, the pink azaleas were sent.

Not three days later, a thank you note came in the mail from the family of one of the deceased. In the card was a story of the person's life and a check for fifty dollars, made out to the retirement home.

A week after that, the parents of the newborn made the drive to the facility to show the residents the new baby!

Bonnie said, "The residents, they knew they were on to something. Now, when they got up, the first thing they did before coffee, breakfast, or anything else was to open the paper to the obituaries and birth notices."

After a while, according to Bonnie, people started showing up at the center. Families of loved ones, parents of babies, all came to share their appreciation. Most stayed for dinner, but all of them met the residents and thanked them for their generosity.

A few months into this process, the grandson of one of the residents graduated college. Azaleas were shipped immediately. Now, according to Bonnie, "the residents started looking at the obituaries, the birth notice, the local events, the society pages. They even found out that a famous string quartet from Chicago was coming down to play in the next town over."

"Don't you know it," Bonnie said, "they sent that quartet a basket of azaleas and not two days later, we had a string quartet playing at our Sunday night dinner!"

We cultivate friendships by giving. Random acts from strangers and anonymous overtures of love keep friendships blossoming.

When I last spoke to Bonnie, she couldn't talk long. She said, "It's Sunday. The parking lot is full. I have to get out there before people run into each other!"

Caring develops friendships. One gift can result in a lifetime of love.

How it Works

To be a friend is to focus on another. You're interested in them, you care about their welfare. You feel safe enough to share part of yourself with another person, but the prerequisite of that sharing is the trust between two people. This supportive relationship cultivates gratitude. In turn, gratitude develops the appreciation, care and love that breathes life and continuity into friendship. Friendship, if you're doing it right, is all about what you feel for the other person.

The first thing you notice about friendship is how much you care. That applied caring–through calls, texts, letters, and email–that sustains the spirit between two people. Friendship is attention, and you can't be attentive to yourself and to a friend at the same time. If a friendship is to be, the other person is the object of your attention. This attention is sustained through caring, so the cycle of friendship continues. Empathy takes hold, and the attentive caring becomes a reflexive connection, a sense of presence that you take for granted.

Mind you, your friends also pay attention to you. Friendship has reciprocity; when you first care and show interest in a friend, that caring comes back to you. What you give, you will receive. All you need to do is give. Give your attention, give of your genuine nature to another person through trust, interest, and kindness; this love is returned. It is the nature of friendship: inherently shared, inherently reciprocal.

And a word about acquaintances: the people we see at work, in the store, in our neighborhood, or in our offices. These are just friendships waiting to happen. When we speak to someone as they pass, we cultivate this relationship. When we stand and talk to them, a conversation begins the process of knowing one another, and we become familiar and easy in sharing ourselves.

Context can be limiting, since the contact we have with people is restricted to the spaces we inhabit. Certain protocols, given the roles people play, limit our disclosure. But the potential for friendship can extend past context and away from our roles. An acquaintance can become a friend when, given time, the boundaries of our context begin to widen, and our attention becomes more focused and free.

We absolutely believe this: Every person can be our friend. Do not give up your pursuit of friendship, regardless of what outer limitations may exist. We all have a heart that longs for loving kindness from another. Begin by saying "Hello" and asking about their day. Start a new friendship just by being present and attentive in whatever fashion you choose. The possibilities of friendships are endless; each one holds its own unique energy. Our hearts are the same; we all require love to live.

Friendships are the reservoir of love in our lives.

Why this is Important

Friends make life better. As Vincent van Gogh says, "Close friends are truly life's treasures. Sometimes they know us better than we know ourselves. With gentle honesty, they are there to guide and support us, to share our laughter and our tears. Their presence reminds us that we are never really alone."[91] Friends offer us a different perspective on the world. They can teach us things. They can act as a sounding board for ideas.

Friends help us through challenging times. As Aristotle says, "In poverty and other misfortunes of life, true friends are a sure refuge. They keep the young out of mischief; they comfort and aid the old in their weakness, and they incite those in the prime of life to noble deeds."[92] But friendship is not just important when things go wrong. Friends inspire us to be better people. Friends motivate us; they act as a resource. The sense of belonging, and not being alone in the world is powerful. Abraham Maslow says that friends provide inner strength, since "the ones who have loved and been well loved, and who have had many deep friendships . . . can hold out against hatred, rejection or persecution."[93] Friends provide us with the sense that we are accepted, giving us the ability to act from our heart.

---

[91] Vincent van Gogh

[92] Aristotle

[93] Maslow, Abraham H. A Theory of Human Motivation. , 2013. Print.

KEY 3

KEY THREE: BE HONEST

You would think it goes without saying for all of us to be honest. Yet this fundamental tenet of human relationships and intrapersonal health is so often overlooked. I mean, we all think we're honest, right? At least we think that, if we put in order our more important personal characteristics, honesty would be right at the top.

Well, in fact, it turns out that when people think about and number their virtues, honesty doesn't make the top ten. Intelligent, Hard-working, Friendly, and Attractive, are almost always in the top five. When honesty does make the top ten, it's usually around ninth.

Honesty means you speak truth through your actions and your beliefs. Think about that for a minute. You don't sugar coat things. You don't say things just to be tactful. You don't omit information just to avoid conflict. You're straightforward. You do not exaggerate in order to sound more intelligent or interesting. You say things that are truthful. Period.

Honesty means you're not going to be strategic in how you express your sentiments, your feelings, or your observations. You don't think about whether you should say the truth or not. In short, you don't lie. You commit to being truthful in all of your encounters. You neither lie by commission, meaning directly telling a lie, nor omission, meaning leaving out some aspects of the truth. Everything you say and do is an honest expression. Although you give thought to the words you speak, your communication is honest. And honesty is your priority.

That's what being honest means. Tall order, huh?

A Story from the Heart

Bill is a self-described "former thief, hustler, alcoholic, and professional liar."

"Everything I did was based on deceptions. Half-truths, omissions . . . my life was a blur of a thousand different stories and lies I'd have to keep in my head. I could've taught a Graduate School seminar on 'Keeping your lies organized enough to sound somewhat plausible and avoid serious trouble.' "

He said he had an insight when, "I was in a bit of a jam. I had been arrested and I was about to be arraigned for bail. But I knew the judge wouldn't grant it. My attorney was not encouraging. He said I was looking at jail time.

"I had a wife and we just had our first child. I needed to take care of them. And, since I was a nearly obsessive liar, my wife never knew the extent of my legal issues.

"I took a review of my life. I had responsibilities that I needed to take care of. I needed to be an honest man. So I did the thing that I felt would take care of everything I needed to correct. I made a decision on the spot –

"I packed up the family and left town. In short, I jumped bail."

I asked him to repeat that.

"Yeah," he said, shaking his head, "I know. But there was a bigger decision. Right then, I decided I would be rigorously honest in everything I did. I decided I would stop lying. I would tell the truth, even if it meant I would have to face consequences for my actions.

"Right then, as I saw the lights of the town fade in my rear view mirror as I headed west, I became an honest man."

Bill went on to tell me that, over the next eighteen years, he established himself in his own business, became a fixture in church meetings around the county, offered assistance to several men through those meetings, and became a good husband and father.

"I took an oath: If I couldn't tell the truth about what I was about to do, I didn't do it. That was the code I lived by. If I couldn't tell my wife and my son everything about my life, then there were parts of my life I had to change."

One day, Bill said he received a certified letter. "You know that bail I jumped eighteen years ago? Well, the court asked that I appear to explain my actions.

"And you know what? I wasn't scared. Well, that's not altogether true. I was, but it was fleeting. I knew I needed to do the most honest thing, and that was to go back to that courthouse, face the judge, tell him what I did, the reasons behind my decision, and explain to him everything I'd done.

"But the first thing I needed to do was to tell my wife and son."

Bill said he'd prepared a speech. "I was all ready to sit them down and explain to them what happened. But before I started, my wife said that she'd read the letter, she figured all along that I'd jumped bail, and she understood completely that I had to go back and face the charges. She reassured me that she was behind me and whatever happened, she'd be right there beside me to give me love and support, as would my son."

Bill reached into his pocket for his handkerchief and wiped his eyes. "That still makes me cry. You can imagine how much I cried when they first told me."

Bill went back to court. He said he "sat in the back of the courtroom and waited for my name to be called. Hours went by.

Everybody went in front of me. Some charges were dismissed, some were sentenced. But my name still wasn't called.

"Then, nothing. The judge just sat on the bench, and said nothing. He was fiddling with some papers, looked down at the DA, and waved for him to come forward.

"The bailiff joined him. The three of them, as well as the court reporter, stood in front of the bench. I was in the back, alone. For the first time throughout this whole process, I was getting nervous. I took a deep breath, looked down at the floor and said a prayer. I promised God that I would play whatever hand was dealt. I'd been a good man up to this point, and I would accept the consequences.

"The DA went back to his table, and the judge finally called me forward. He asked me if I had representation and I told him I didn't. He said, 'No matter.'

"Then he said four words that I didn't see coming: 'Your case is dismissed.' He must have seen the shock on my face, and he asked, 'Would you like to know why I'm dismissing two felony counts?' I nodded, because I wasn't sure I could speak.

"The judge said, 'I have in front of me a dozen or so letters from your community. They arrived at my desk in the last week. I've read them all, and I was impressed. But that's not why I'm dismissing the charges. Would you like to know why?'

"My head was spinning. I was afraid to interrupt him. So I just stood there. And I couldn't believe what he said next. He leaned over the bench and said, and I swear to god, the four words that made me cry in front of total strangers: 'Because you were honest.'

"He went on to explain how in his thirty something years on the bench, no one had ever shown for a bench warrant older than a year. He even said I'd set some kind of record. He said he called every one of my reference letters and he said that they referred others for him to call. In all,' he said, 'I must have spoken to about fifty people, all speaking so highly of your integrity.'

"He stretched out his arm and shook my hand. As did the bailiff. And the D.A. And the court reporter. I wiped the tears from my eyes and left."

Bill put his hands on his knees. "I never expected such a thing to happen. But, regardless, I was going to stay true to myself. Being honest has saved me. But, it always has, and not just from prison. It's saved me from disappointing the ones I've loved, saved me from having to look away when I see the reflection of a liar and a cheat in the mirror every day.

"I'm an honest man. And there isn't a better thing I could say about myself than that."

How it Works

Honesty can be gentle. We often associate the word "brutal" with honesty. It doesn't have to be that way. You can be easier with your honesty; it requires a little calm and a little thought. The temptation of being a little dishonest is with us all the time. In fact, if you try to be completely honest for just twenty four hours, chances are you can't do it. It's not because you're not trying. It's just that we exaggerate, practice tact, and defend ourselves against situations that activate fear. We say things to make us look a little bigger, we hold back from hurting anybody's feelings, and we generally say, "No, that wasn't me" when we think we're going to get into trouble.

Here's a common example. Let's say you're confronted with the age old question, "Do I look fat it this?" The honest answer may not always be the first one that you feel should be expressed. "Yes, you do," is the honest answer, but usually, "No, you don't" comes out of your mouth without even thinking. Tact and conflict avoidance is our autopilot setting. That's just how we're wired. It doesn't mean we're all a big pack of liars. Rather, it means that we're trying to be nice and, if we have to bend the truth a little, we don't think it's such a big deal.

And, therefore, this gives us permission to lie. A lot, actually. We are all under the general assumption that we're good people and our intentions are good. So, if we lie, so what? We're not trying to hurt anybody. Hurting somebody is far worse than lying, right?

Well, no. And this is why we talk about being calm and thoughtful. In order to tell the truth, you must phrase your words in the most honest way possible, and that takes a moment's pause. Your first thought is to be kind, but choosing your words is important. Therefore, it might take a second to express things succinctly without being dishonest, but letting the person know that, for instance, they may look a little plump but they're still a good person (which, now that we're reading this, is being honest but the line could use a little work if you don't want them to fall into a fit of uncontrollable sobbing. Another, better phrase would be, "Well, a little, but I still really like you." That one's not much better. We didn't say it would be easy.).

Practicing honesty also requires a little fearlessness. We do get a little apprehensive. We are at least slightly wary of the other person's response. Honesty is not an attempt to make someone angry, rather an opportunity for us to be straight and clear with our opinions and feelings. The object is to be open, not hurtful.

This may take a little adjustment from the people you're with, but do your best to cushion your opinions and feelings so they are soft on their ears. A well placed sympathetic adjective or saying "I'm sorry" at the right time can do a great deal to shelter your honesty, giving you freedom to speak with both clarity and consideration. In short, honesty may take a little practice–not in spirit, but in delivery. Tact, grace, and fearlessness must underscore all honest communication.

Why this is Important

Being honest both with yourself and others is a cornerstone of living a life of meaning. Being honest with yourself sounds simple, however, you must objectively assess every part of your life. Life is a finite resource; we must, in our short time here on Earth, align our life with the values that lead towards our life's purpose. Through the lens of your values and life purpose, view the activities and people in your life, and the way you spend your time. The first step to becoming the person you want to be is being honest with yourself, and clearly establishing your values and life's purpose. The second, more challenging step is breaking habits and routines that don't align with who you really want to be. True honesty starts and ends with yourself.

Honesty is the foundation of any true relationship, and it usually comes to mind when speaking to other people. But honesty starts with your relationship with yourself. An honest person has a clear understanding of their values and code of conduct; they live life according to these standards. As Mahatma Gandhi says, "to believe in something, and not to live it, is dishonest."[94] Inner honesty inspires trust in yourself, and allows a person to live and act with strength of character. Being honest raises self-esteem, while lying decreases self-esteem.

Once you are honest with yourself and live in a way that is true to your values and life purpose, your energy is focused where it needs to be. Energy spent on indecision, guilt, or maintaining a persona to create an impression on others fades, giving you the freedom, as Dr. Seuss so eloquently says, to "be who you are and say what you feel because those who mind don't matter and those who matter don't mind."[95] Guilt and embarrassment are rooted in a person's desire to be something other than what they are.

---

94 Gandhi, Mahatma

95 Dr. Seuss

Honesty and trust are essential to all relationships. Communicate with openness. Do not withhold parts of yourself; if you are truly living in accordance with your values and life's purpose, you have nothing to hide. Admitting faults, mistakes, or being wrong, however challenging, is how you take responsibility for your actions. Over time, being honest in these situations will reward you with a better relationship with yourself and others. A person who is able to admit the truth with conviction inspires trust. Fear arises from the unknown. By behaving honestly in all actions, you make people feel safe. Their fear of your unknown potential actions disappears.

Being honest reduces stress. Both lying and holding in secrets takes mental energy – energy that can be used in more positive places. To lie requires much more effort than to tell the truth. Lies are rarely individual; usually a single lie becomes a tangled web of lies. In the act of lying, a person must think of what to say and, in the future, they have to keep track of who they told what to. After lying a person then fears that the lie will be found out eventually. An honest person does not have any of these worries. Even if you manage to achieve a goal by lying, that achievement is tainted.

KEY 4

KEY FOUR: LISTEN

Everybody thinks they know how to do this. Everybody. We all think that we have learned, at least by young adulthood, how to listen. And we think we do it effectively. I mean, think about it: every time we have a conversation, we are engaged in listening. Every time we have followed a direction at school–for that matter, every time we have followed a direction since we arrived on the planet–we have listened. We focused our attention on words and their meaning.

As a result of this, we think we know how to listen. Unfortunately, what we just described is hearing. When we recognize sounds and their meanings, we hear the words and have a cognitive understanding of them. We recognize their applications in our life. We can carry out actions from how we understand their meaning. But that's still not listening.

Listening is an emotional exercise. It is hearing with feeling, that then reaches meaning. We can hear the facts that support intellectual understanding. We can hear what teachers tell us. We can register principles and postulates and regurgitate them back when it's time for a test. But when we listen, there is meaning associated with our attention. Listening means absorbing words on a visceral level.

Listening is hearing when it matters. It is absorbing the feelings behind the words. Listening activates empathy. Listening is the first step of caring. Listening is hearing with your heart.

A Story from the Heart

Sheila is an emergency room nurse. When she was in college, studying nursing, she would take care of a blind man named Stanley before and after she went to class. It helped pay for her books and tuition.

Now before you stop reading because you already get the concept that blind people listen well, keep reading. Because, as Sheila put it, "it's not that he listened well; instead, it's what he listened to."

Sheila told me that when Stanley interviewed her for the job, "He asked me the standard questions: Where I'm from, what I studied in school, did I have any favorite subjects, that sort of thing.

"Well, when I told him I was from St. Louis, he said, 'oh, you had a tough childhood?' My immediate response was, 'Uh, no, it was fine,' when, in fact, it was tough. My father was alcoholic and my mother worked two jobs. But I didn't think it was appropriate for me to go into that. I mean, it was a brief job interview and I thought so much disclosure would turn him off. But I'm thinking this guy is psychic, or something. Anyway, He nodded his head and just said, 'Hmmm. Well, tell me about your favorite classes. So I told him the one that I liked the best was English Literature. And before I could tell him about my other classes, he said, 'Oh, but that Literature. Your last grade or paper . . . a little disappointed in your grade?'

"I was stunned. 'How did you know that?' I said. And I was really taken aback. At that moment, I wasn't sure if I really wanted to take the job.

"He said, 'You know, it was the way you said, LIT-ER-AT-ture. You dropped that last syllable like it was a hot rock.'

"I twisted my head to the left, and must have scrunched up my face or something. 'Yeah,' he said, 'I'd look that way too.' And I'm thinking, 'What, wait . . . is this guy really blind?'

"And then, he answered that question. The question I had in my head!

" 'Honey,' he said, 'I'm blind, yes I am. I know how you looked because I just listen. I listen with my ears, sure. Anybody can do that. But I listen with everything.

" 'Look,' he said. 'I can't see, but I can feel the wind change on my skin. I can hear things that, because I am short one of my senses, you may not pick up. Now, when you did that little thing with your face, I could hear your head move. And, from the change of the air in the room, I could figure your head was moving to your left, like this.' And he showed me, with his head, exactly the position my head was in when I had that 'What the . . .' moment.

" 'Not bad, huh?' he said, and he got this big grin on his face.

" 'You listen with your feelings. We are trained to believe that we listen with our ears. No, we hear with our ears. You just take in what's around you.

" 'You know, when I asked you where you were from, and you said, St. Louis, you know what you did?'

" 'No,' I said, 'but I'd love to find out what you felt.'

" 'I'll tell you,' he said, putting his finger in the air, 'you held your breath. You breathed in, and held it, just a split second before you said St. Louis, almost as if you were preparing yourself to tell me bad news.

" 'I'll tell you something else, Sheila,' he said. 'Listening is observational. But when I could see, I didn't allow my eyes to help me listen. I could see, but I didn't really look. My ears could hear, but not listen.

" 'Being blind made me rely on everything else around me to really tell me what was going on. And that's when you really listen. You see things with your ears, you hear things with your fingertips. It's paying attention, sure, but it's more than that. Listening is being right there, trusting your senses, and relying on the ones you ordinarily take for granted. Shelia, one day, listening will save somebody's life. You'll begin to hear something, but you'll feel something else. You'll know the words they say, but their meaning will be entirely different.

" 'The air. Listen to the change in the air. Their breath will do that. It's subtle, but you'll get it. And that's just a start. Feel them shift in their chair. Get close enough to hear their words through their chest, not just through their vocal chords.' "

Sheila smiled and said, "The wisdom that came out of this man's mouth was something I'd never experienced. And, what surprised me, was that he was so matter of fact about it. Then Stan said, 'Now if you'll excuse me, I have to get the mail. It comes at 2:00 sharp every day.'

"I asked him how he knew the time since he couldn't see clock and he didn't wear a watch.

" 'I can feel that, too. The pace of the traffic, the change in the air, the number of people I hear walking along the street.' And just then, the postman came up to the door and put the mail through the slot in the bottom.

" 'See?' Stan said, 'two o'clock, on the button.' Then he leaned in, and took my hand as if he could see exactly where to put his hand on mine. He said, 'Sheila, listening is attention, but it's also trusting in what you feel. If you just start that process a little at a time, you'll experience your world so much differently. I had to lose my sight to be a better listener. You don't have to lose yours. Just use all you have to listen to this life. You'll become a different, and certainly more aware, person. That's a promise.' "

<u>How it Works</u>

When we listen, we have to want to understand what is being said, and really want to feel that understanding. Listening involves depth; it's more than just being interested in what someone is saying. If you're interested in what somebody's telling you, you can remember it for a while, and you can exchange that data with somebody else. You can converse intellectually about facts and principles. But if you're truly listening, particularly in a conversation with someone or something that you care about, you'll hold the words more deeply and for longer, because of their significance.

Since you liked your favorite course in school, you probably retained much of the information from it. For everything from poetry to biology, depending on your interests, the feeling of love you had for that subject helped you to attain a level of proficiency, not just because you remembered what you were told, but because what you were told mattered. Scientists, college professors, physicians, and other professions are required to remember a great deal of information. Because they assign meaning to this information, listening is far easier.

It is the same with the people in your life. The words of your friends, your family, and your peers evoke a deeper meaning than someone you have a conversation with while pumping your gas. When you listen to your mother speak, you remember her words. When you listen to a spouse or child, it's the same experience. When you listen to their words, whether good or bad, the feeling is distinct. This is how you know you have listened appropriately. There's accuracy in your recall. But there's a feeling in the memory, too.

It is the same when you pay attention to your environment. You hear the sounds of the traffic, the wind, the birds, even the shuffling of papers on your desk. But when you raise your level of attention, and assign even the slightest meaning to the sounds, listening makes the sounds matter. When you assign meaning to the way the wind begins to rise and fall, the halting measure of birds song, and the scattered shuffling of the papers passing off your desk, listening holds the action close.

We challenge you to offer your attention, through your heart, to the words of another. Make their words matter. It's easy to begin this by listening to someone you love. Their words already matter. Listening brought their words into your heart.

Why this is Important

When true listening takes place, it creates a new dimension of the world that the philosopher Ken Wilber calls "the Miracle of We." This space is truly a miracle because, to truly listen is the practice of letting go and moving beyond our filters of opinions, beliefs, and desires. Listening this way takes practice, attention, and skill. One must understand "our capacity for listening deeply and skillfully is affected by many things: our momentary energy level, emotional makeup, personal preferences, needs, and biases, as well as our developmental conditioning and the defenses we erect to protect us against the pain of the losses we've suffered."[96] True listening is deeper than listening with your head, it is listening with your heart and being fully present in the moment, aware and responsive.

The listener must have the wholehearted intention of giving attention, validation, and love, not the intention of getting attention, validation, and love. A listener truly hears the other person, hearing not just their words, but the true meaning and emotion conveyed. The greatest gift we can give another is our complete, unfettered, compassionate attention. Listening deeply and skillfully nourishes others, it alleviates pain, and it cures loneliness.

To practice listening, "our perspective shifts from 'I' to 'You,' and suddenly, we emerge into another world. When we discover our commonalities there, the gap between 'I' and 'You' closes, and we become 'We.' From then on, it is a dance of sameness and difference between us. The sameness gives us cohesion; we recognize each other

[96] Brady, Mark. The Wisdom of Listening. Boston: Wisdom Publications, 2003. Print. pg 25

and feel we belong. The difference gives our relationships vitality, heft, and occasionally, as you know, good problems."[97] All the meaning and joy in life takes place in this dimension of We. True heart listening is like watering a thirsty plant, growing this We dimension all around you wherever you go. By giving the gift of listening to others, you create this connection.

---

97 Hamilton, Diane M. Everything Is Workable: A Zen Approach to Conflict Resolution. , 2013. Print. Pg 85

KEY 5

KEY FIVE: PRACTICE EMPATHY

To be empathetic is to understand the feelings of another. To do this, we must refine our sense of ourselves and others. To be empathetic, we have to live a life from the heart, and we need to know how to deeply engage our heart with another.

In using empathy, we put ourselves in another person's shoes. We put ourselves in their place. We visualize our life as theirs, and feel what it is like experiencing life from their eyes, from their perspective, and from their feelings.

Empathy is different than sympathy. Sympathy recognizes and acknowledges. Empathy feels and acts. Empathy means placing yourself in another's situation and, as your thought process evolves from this empathetic place, you decide on the next steps.

Empathy is learned from our references of pain. It is remembered from our feelings of injustice. It is activated from our memories of what we have understood as being unfair, hurtful, and wrong.

Empathy is often best when we remember times that we were hurt, misunderstood, or ignored. Empathy is forged from incidents of being slighted, diminished, discarded, and put down. Empathy within our spirit comes from the seeds of our pain. When we see someone is in pain, we use our past experiences of pain to understand what they are feeling now, and even feel it ourselves. And as we evolve, if we allow our heart to be warmed by the light of understanding, we will immediately know how another is feeling and what we can say or do to quell their pain. Empathy is knowing another's plight by feeling what they feel. Our interpersonal references can be extremely useful in recognizing this, but just placing ourselves into another person's shoes is the first step toward an empathetic exchange.

A Story from the Heart

Henry is with the United States Border Patrol in California. He has been a Border Patrol agent for over twenty years. Prior to that, he served in Iraq and Afghanistan for the U.S. Army.

"We are trained to look at the enemy as–how do I put this–a little less than human." Henry paused for a moment, and said, "In Vietnam, we called the enemy 'Charlie.' I'm not supposed to repeat what we called the enemy in the desert."

Henry sat on the edge of his desk. "Now I come back to the States, get back to my job with the border patrol, and confront a new enemy: Illegal Aliens. I recognize, and certainly maintain and reinforce, the need for safety and reinforcement of the laws at the border. And it is my job to maintain compliance of those laws with vigor and, if necessary, force.

"But," said Henry, "We represent the spirit and goodness of the United States. We are the first faces so many of the people see when they engage with our people. We must–absolutely must–show everyone in this world that we are good, fair, and faithful to the tenets of peace and equity reflected in the spirit of our Constitution.

"As a Border Patrol Agent, I am serving the public. Protecting the Border, sure. But I am providing a public service. And, in order to do that, I had to change my perspective on whom I was providing that public service toward."

Henry poured us both another cup of coffee, leaned back on his desk again, and said, "In order to perform my duties to the utmost effectiveness–which includes reducing and eliminating conflict, managing tension, and offering the best service possible–I had to know the people I was serving.

"So I moved to Tijuana for six weeks."

"You what?" I said, nearly spitting out my coffee.

"You heard me correctly."

Staring at Henry in utter disbelief, I said, "Couldn't you have attended a few seminars? Gone to a cultural awareness lecture?"

Henry opened a drawer, pulled out a piece of paper, and said, "Let me share with you this quote by Mark Twain: 'Travel is fatal to prejudice, bigotry, and narrow-mindedness, and many of our people need it sorely on these accounts.'

"I had to," said Henry, "I had to know these people, as best I could, in order to serve both sides of the border more effectively."

Henry described his six weeks as "life changing," but he also said it was "more than that."

I stopped him right there. "How can something be more than life changing?" He laughed and said, "I see your point. Here's what I mean: Something can change your life in how you respond to it. Life-changing circumstances will alter your perspective, your actions, and your thoughts.

"But being in Tijuana, living among those families, seeing what they saw and living the life they endured, every single day, changes who you are, and changes fundamentally how you see yourself. That person in the mirror changes. You're not the same."

"But you went to war. Twice." I said.

"In war, you engage the enemy from a distance. You're protected. In this move, I lived with this so called 'enemy.' I was in their living rooms. And the only protection I had was my character, my experience, and my ability to understand their lives. Something that changes your life, yeah that's life changing. But when you learn to truly understand the heart of another, that's when your decision about your own life change.

"In Mexico, I learned to empathize. I was removed of my preexisting prejudices. I hope that I became a more empathetic and understanding person. And I hope it's made me better in my job." Henry described the events and activities he participated in while he was there. "I was welcomed into their homes. I was invited to their festivities. I slept on their couches. I ate with them, prayed with them, and worked with them.

"You do that," Henry said, "and something within you changes, that's for sure."

"Now trust me on this: I'm a United States Border Patrol Officer. This is my priority and my duty. However . . ." he said, and paused for a moment. "How do I explain this so you understand?"

"I think I have it." I said.

"I want to make sure," said Henry, "this is important."

"Sun Tzu says, 'Know thy enemy.' But the Bible says, 'Love thy neighbor.' These are our neighbors. And to truly serve them to the best of my ability, I had to understand who they were.

"My empathy was my love. This is the essence of empathy. What Mark Twain said was true, inasmuch as we see other people, not with our eyes, but our spirits. It is within this sight, the eyes of our heart, that we begin to know that we are so similar to one another. We are the same people, with the same concerns about food, shelter, clothing, and the health of our children. We want the best for ourselves and our loved ones. We experience pain, grief, joy and happiness. We strive to be better. We set an example for those we care about.

"And by being with these people, We is redefined by empathy.

"Empathy is the travel of the heart."

How it Works

Empathy is nothing without action. Otherwise it would just be Sympathy, and you're not going to find that on our lists. Sympathy is for people who want to think they care by thinking about the person or thing they care about. Empathy actually does something about the problem.

Empathy is being able to say, "I've been there. I'll help you. I am here." You may not be able to stop someone from hurting, but you will walk with them through the process. Sympathy is saying, "If you need anything, just call." Empathy is picking up the phone and calling. Sympathy is saying, "Oh, I'm so sorry your girlfriend broke up with you. That's must be really hard." Empathy is showing up at the door with pizza and beer.

Empathy is when you extend yourself to another because you know their pain, you can put yourself into your friend's place, and you act in the way that you'd like to be treated.

Empathy is often more reasonably afforded to our family, our friends, our coworkers, and acquaintances. We are more apt to engage in immediate actions for those we care about or have some shared relationship with. It is easy to have an immediate empathetic response to people who we see often and we already care about. But empathy is not limited to this context. Empathy is also demonstrated by trying to end to hunger, poor sanitation, polluted water, and substandard housing for communities around the world. We may not be able to share in their intimate understanding of what it's like to live in those conditions but, using empathy, we consider the discomfort we have felt, and engage that pain to heal another.

We are empathetic when we have recognized the value of our heart and are able to set into motion its healing energies of care and assistance to another's pain. Empathy connects our most human and vulnerable selves with that place in the heart of another. Empathy knows. Empathy cares. And Empathy does something. Empathy is the energy behind each gift we offer and every overture of kindness we extend.

Why this is Important

Your capacity for empathy is born from the pain and struggles of your own life. Empathy requires you to step outside of your skin-bound self and outside of your thoughts and feelings. You must pay attention with your heart to both verbal and nonverbal cues, learn what another person is feeling, and compassionately identify with their emotional state.

Although human nature is complex, humans share the same emotional framework. That is because, as Albert Einstein says, "a human being is part of the whole, called by us 'Universe'; a part limited in time and space. He experiences himself, his thoughts and feelings as something separated from the rest—a kind of optical delusion of his consciousness. This delusion is a kind of prison for us, restricting us to our personal desires and to affection for a few persons nearest us. Our task must be to free ourselves from this prison."[98] Empathy is a heart connection between you and another person or group; instead of separateness, there is a bond. Conversely, "self-absorption in all its forms kills empathy, let alone compassion. When we focus on ourselves, our world contracts as our problems and preoccupations loom large. But when we focus on others, our world expands, our own problems drift to the periphery of the mind and so seem smaller, and we increase our capacity for connection - or compassionate action."[99] With empathy, we create a positive effect on the world by making heart connections with others.

---

[98] Einstein, Albert

[99] Goleman, Daniel. Social Intelligence: The New Science of Human Relationships. New York: Bantam Books, 2006. Print. pg 54

KEY 6

KEY SIX: PRACTICE GIVING

Of the concepts outlined in this book, it can be argued that giving may be the most misunderstood. The interpersonal, social, even political implications of giving bring forth a variety of images and feelings. In some cases, giving can be seen almost as a negative act, enabling dependence on the one hand, on the other a self-serving gesture to satisfy the ego.

And we understand this. Life is made up of countless acts to serve the self. Therefore, it can be argued that our focus and energy is, as a matter of speaking, "self-centered." In following this definition, the act of giving may feel somewhat counterintuitive.

Yet, any time you're with another person, you are giving of yourself. Whether it is conversation, time, attention, or just your mere presence, you are engaging in the act of giving. Any communication, no matter its tone or content, is an act of giving. Any intention, no matter the direction or merit, is an act of giving. And any thought- yes, even the mere thought- of another person, incident, circumstance, or process is an act of giving, any way you measure it. Giving is an offering of ourselves.

Giving is a very difficult thing to define because it's so large. It incorporates so much energy. As we are putting this book together, we are giving you our thoughts and assistance. As you are reading these words, you are giving back to us your time and interest. No matter how you break it down, life is a moment-by-moment process of giving.

We most often associate giving with acts of kindness and generosity. It incorporates thoughtfulness and time. When we think about giving to one another, we usually think of trying to make another person happy. Birthdays and holidays bring forth the most distinct and familiar form of giving; they hold the spirit of kindness that giving, as we most commonly see it, is all about.

A Story from the Heart

Near my home is a lake that, during the winter and spring, provides shelter to mud hens and Canadian geese.

In the mornings, when I have time, I take a few slices of bread and feed the birds that congregate. I throw some bread their way, and spend the time looking at the lake and taking in the peace.

I do this about a dozen times a year, and have for the past ten years or so.

And every time I've been up there, I've seen the same man sitting on a bench, doing the same thing.

When I see this man, I tend to move away from him, to avoid interrupting him while he feeds the birds and enjoys the scenery.

I'm usually there for about thirty minutes. And when I leave, I always pass this man on the way to the car. Every time I pass him, I say something like, "Nice day," "Good Morning," or some other salutation.

And every time, he says nothing. No response. Looks straight down at the ground, no eye contact, no acknowledgement.

One morning, as the weather was changing, I knew that this was going to be one of the last times I'd be coming to the lake. The birds move a little further north as the air gets warmer, and I'd already seen a thinning of their ranks.

So, this particular morning, I thought I'd double my efforts to be solicitous to my friend on the bench.

"Looks like the birds are starting their way back home," I said. "Might be gone in a couple of weeks."

Nothing.

"So, do you come up here every day?" Again, nothing. So I repeated the line. "So, um, do you come up here . . . ?"

And before I could complete the sentence, he said, "You know, I don't like you."

"I'm sorry?" I said, making sure I heard him correctly.

"You heard me. I don't like you. Now leave me alone." Dumbstruck, I stood there looking at this guy, wondering what I did to offend him so much. He looked over at me and said, "You're still here? I thought I told you to leave me alone."

"I'm . . . I'm sorry," I said, stammering from the shock of his tone, "but I didn't mean to . . . " And before I could complete my thought, he sighed heavily and said, "Look. Shut up. Come here. And bring your bread."

I reached down and grabbed what was left of my bread. "Sit down," he said, "I'm going to show you something."

He reached down into his bread bag and said, "Watch what I do."

He held a piece of bread in two fingers, the rest of the scraps in his palm. While extending his arm, the birds came forward. They gathered around him, each bird taking turns to peck at the bread, and the man rotated his palm, offering the bread to the rest of the birds. He then leaned forward and allowed the birds in the back of the throng a chance at his scraps, lightly brushing aside the birds that have already had their share.

Then he put his hand back into his bag, and repeated the process.

I was impressed not only with the gracefulness of his gesture but with the ease and order with which the birds came in, got their scraps, and left. No bird seemed too aggressive. There was a pattern of approach, and it appeared that every bird got their share.

"You see what I'm doing?" he said, turning his head to look at me.

"Yes. It is quite impressive."

"See? I figured you say something like that. You're missing the point. It's not in the order. It's in the act of giving.

"You give," he continued, "like you could care less. You don't give with any thought. You come up here with the idea that you're going to 'feed the birds,' as if bringing them bread, taking handfuls and scattering it on the ground has anything to do with giving.

"Wonder what you're like at somebody's birthday. Or a wedding. God forbid anybody would want to be around you at Christmas."

I started to laugh a little. He caught me off guard. And when he saw me laugh, he smiled.

"Look, you give from one place, right here," pointing to the middle of his chest. "It has to have meaning, thought, and care. You don't throw a present at somebody. You don't invite somebody at your house and scatter their meal all over your dining room table in hopes they'll fight over it.

"Giving is a caring act. And it is universal. Every gift has to have meaning. If you're spending time with somebody, make sure you listen attentively. If you're offering service, make sure it's fulfilling a need. And if you're giving a gift, make sure it's something they like.

"Offer your gifts with care. It starts here with the birds, and it carries into every gesture of giving you have."

The man stood up, brushed the crumbs in his palm back into his bag, and said, "If you're going to give, make it mean something. Put yourself into it. Let everybody, including these little creatures here, see your heart.

"Make your giving matter. Give from right here."

He went to the parking lot, got in his car, and left.

So I sat down, got my bread, put some in my palm, and waited for the birds to come.

Three birds bit me immediately, a duck chewed on my finger, and one mud hen pecked me so hard he broke the skin.

I made a mental note: I need to begin to giving from the heart, if for no other reason than to save the skin on my hands . . .

How it Works

It's important we recognize that everything we do is an act of giving. If you get right down to it, breathing is offering carbon dioxide to the atmosphere. So the first part of knowing and understanding giving is recognizing where giving lives. And, in understanding this concept, giving becomes more accessible.

Specifically, as we focus on every action, calmly observing our behaviors, thoughts, and intentions, we become giving. Our life is an act of giving. We then direct our focus into how giving is received, and how energy is directed. Giving now underscores the connection between yourself and another person.

It is at this point, giving means you also have a responsibility to the receiver. I'm now aware my gift is going to affect the person to whom I am giving. It will affect the person with whom I am exchanging energy. Therefore, my awareness of the quality, depth, and meaning behind the gift is mine to control.

This spirit of awareness should guide your giving. When you give your attention to somebody, is that attention supported with anger and upset, or love and kindness? When you are giving of your time, is it colored with resentment and annoyance, or willingness and peace? We have to ask ourselves these questions as we focus on the feelings behind our spirit of giving.

Every morning, when we awaken, we set forth on a path of giving to this world. Giving is all of what life really is. Therefore, we owe it to those around us to make our life's purpose giving our best selves. Every act of life is a gift. Every point of attention to this gift is an act of deliberate intent.

Why this is Important

Giving is an important practice, not just for the people who receive a gift, but for the giver's self-development. Giving teaches selflessness by taking the focus off of yourself and placing it on another's needs. When a person starts thinking about the needs of others, this builds empathy. With empathy, a person breaks the pattern of I thoughts: thoughts about yourself, your life story, your needs, your pains, your hopes. Giving improves your daily interactions with people because your focus is external instead of on yourself; this allows you to connect more with other people.

The opposite of giving is selfishness. The desire to keep things for yourself. With a focus on greed and attainment, a person is consumed by desire. This desire causes the person to look for happiness somewhere else, possibly in material items, relationships, or even in the future. The selfish person loses the joy of the present moment. Suffering is rooted in selfishness, but "it is not outer things that entangle us; it is inner clinging and fixation that entangles us."[100] It is the inner attachment of the ego. Because the ego feels in its deepest core that it is incomplete, it has huge trouble parting with anything it feels adds value to itself. The ego feels that the more it has, the bigger it becomes. The bigger the self becomes, the more permanent it is, the more real it is, and the more eternal it is.

The antidote to this suffering is giving. To give is the practice of letting go. Having the ability to not hold onto things reduces selfishness. "Practice giving things away, not just things you don't care about, but things you do like. Remember, it is not the size of a gift, it is its quality and the amount of mental attachment you overcome that count. So don't bankrupt yourself on a momentary positive impulse, only to regret it later. Give thought to giving. Give small things, carefully, and observe the mental processes going along with the act of releasing the little thing you liked."[101] Although this will be a struggle, it will help untangle the knot of selfishness. As a result, your ability to give will open your heart, sharing your life and your spirit with another.

To give to another is the action of the heart.

---

[100] Surya, Das. Natural Radiance: Awakening to Your Great Perfection. Boulder, CO: Sounds True, 2005. Print. pg 72

[101] Karma-glin-pa, , Sambhava Padma, and Robert A. F. Thurman. The Tibetan Book of the Dead, As Popularly Known in the West: Known in Tibet As the Great Book of Natural Liberation Through Understanding in the between. New York: Bantam Books, 1994. Print. pg 53

KEY 7

KEY SEVEN: ASK FOR HELP

In the grand scheme of life, most of what we do is a pretty individual. We take the steps necessary to make ourselves happy. We put in the time. We do the work. We see life as a series of causes and effects. In other words, we are the cause of our behaviors. What we do is how we live.

We eat and drink to activate our bodies, we learn to activate our minds. We seek out the company of others to stimulate our hearts, to develop trust, friendship and love. Our actions produce results. Our decisions support growth and progress in our lives.

Life is a continuous flow of stimulus and response. It is an ever-connected stream of existence, each piece intricately affecting every other. With each step we take on our path through life, a thousand different events and activities are interacting with us, details of light and sand and wind that affect everything we do, from this second to the next. How we choose our words in any conversation will affect the other person's response. The messages we give to ourselves direct our decisions. Every action produces a reaction. And we are the ones that generate that action.

And yet . . .

We do not walk through this life as a solitary entity. We are not without family, siblings, friends, partners, and spouses. We humans are an interactive species. We sustain life as a result of these connections. Mothers, fathers, brothers, sisters, friends, spouses, and children are all examples of the range of roles other people have in our lives.

They are resources. They are guides that we have referenced along our path. We have seen them as examples of behavior. We have learned from them. They have shown us, in allowing us a glimpse of their lives, how to make better decisions and achieve better results.

Now, if you hadn't noticed, the journey of life is not without a detour or two. This could be by a big boulder in the middle of your path, or just a dead end. The bridge is out. The road is closed. The vultures are circling. The cliff is a four hundred foot drop. And you don't know how to fly. Confusion, bewilderment, immobilization or abject fear has sat down beside you. It just stopped you dead in your tracks. Your walk through life has come to a rather lengthy pause. You don't know your backside from buttermilk. And you're not sure what to do next.

It is in times like these that you ask for help. A call for assistance, a request for clarity, a path out of the woods. The answer, the direction, the reason, the perspective. You ask for help.

A Story from the Heart

Three and a half years ago, Malcolm lost his job. It was his career, his identity and his purpose. "Part of my job was helping people put their lives back together. Now," he said, sitting in his new, but very small, office, "I was the one in need of major reconstruction.

"I had bills. I had a mortgage, and I had been supporting two of my children as best I could. I had given all I had to my ex-wife in a divorce, but I thought I could be OK making it on my own, sustaining my career. But, now that my career was over, I could see the funds dwindle. I got a job, but I was too anxious about losing my twenty-five year career. It was hard for me to concentrate, to learn new things. I was let go after four months.

"I found myself, in a matter of a few months, going from being on the top of my profession, respected by my peers and colleagues, to facing debt, bankruptcy, and homelessness.

"For some reason, one Tuesday I was driving around the industrial section of town, seeing what there was to do, maybe figuring that I could get a job. I don't remember, but I do remember getting lost. It's not familiar territory, so I was taking left turns into dead ends, and finally I ended up at a restaurant. A breakfast and lunch place, right between a motorcycle repair store and a tire shop. Beautiful little place, kind of a throwback, and it served the best variety of comfort food I'd ever seen. And 'comfort' is exactly what I was looking for. So, I sat down, ordered breakfast, and the woman that waited on me turned out to be my old friend, Lisa. She said she'd bought the restaurant a few years ago, after having worked there as a waitress for over twenty years.

"She said she was going to close in an hour, and asked if I could hang around and have a cup of coffee to catch up. She said she wanted to know how life had been treating me, but I said I'd much rather know how life had been treating her, given my state of affairs.

"When she chided me into talking about my life, I told her my career was over. I gave her the details of my loss, including the most recent job that didn't last very long. And then she interrupted me.

"She said, 'Do you need a job?' I said that I did, that I was looking for jobs in my field, but given the circumstances behind my fall, not very many people were willing to hire me.

"Then she said, 'I have an opening here. You can clean the tables and pour coffee, and ask people what they want to drink when they sit down. It pays minimum wage, and I can give it to you part time.' I was dumbfounded. I was a licensed professional, and the only kind of work I could find was waiting tables. But then she added, 'Oh, and I'll feed you breakfast and lunch.'

"Lisa's a sweet woman, and I know she was trying to help, but my first response was 'No.' I said that I was going to continue to look, see if I something better came along, particularly something in my field. I mean, I didn't want to be a waiter. I'd never waited on a table in my life, not even as a teenager.

"Well, nothing better ever arrived, and one day I was in that same part of town, and I rolled into Lisa's place. As she was pouring me a cup of coffee, she could see I was pretty down.

" 'Hey,' she said, 'the job offer still stands.'

"I told her thanks, but no, I would find something. 'Look, Malcolm,' she said, 'you and I go back a long way. I've always considered you my friend. But I need to tell you something. You're really lousy at taking any help.' I leaned back on my chair and said, 'Excuse me?'

"Lisa said, 'You and I have been friends, off and on, for a while. I consider you a part of my life, and when I see people struggling, I try to help. But,' she said, kind of abruptly, 'you have to be able to put your ego and your pride aside and let me.' "

Malcolm smiled a little and said, "My expression right then had to have shown displeasure, because before I could say anything, Lisa sat down across the table and said, 'You've been a big fish, a guy that could do a lot of things for a lot of people. Well, for whatever reason, you're at a new beginning. You don't know what to do or where to go. I'm not saying that this is a job forever. I'm saying that you need a hand, and I'm giving you one. Might not be the one you've expected and I know it may not meet all your needs. OK, you'll adjust. But, you've got to become more humble, more centered on what's happening around you right now, and take your worries off what tomorrow will bring. And,' Lisa said, 'right now, you've got a job offer. It's a start. And it looks like you could use both a job and a new start.' "

Malcolm said, "Well, right then, I knew she was right. I had to accept a little help. I had to readjust my sense of pride, humility, and my perspective about myself and my future. I had to let somebody hold my hand for a while. And, the hardest part, was that I had to let her. I needed to be guided through this next part of my life, and she appeared.

"Maybe it was fate, but from that day, my life changed." Malcolm said that he was able to hold on to a few clients, and got some more opportunities teaching a little. It's about one-fourth of what he made before, "But I can still work at the restaurant once or twice a week."

Malcolm said his friendship with Lisa continued to thrive. "She taught me how to stay in the moment, to be guided by your faith but continue to put your shoulder to the wheel, and to allow others–in my case, her–to offer support and comfort when it's recognized, and to be humble and grateful when receiving this help.

"I'm nowhere near where I want to be, but I have faith that this chapter of my life will be better than any other. A friend and I have written a book, I've got a social media buzz around it, and we're just getting started. I maintained a weekly essay at a local radio station every week, and I've met a new and wonderful friends.

"All because Lisa showed me the value of asking and receiving help when you need it, my life has grown in directions I'd never anticipated." As I left his office, I shook his hand and went to my car. Just as I was about to get in, I hear Malcolm's voice from his office door.

"Oh, I forgot to tell you one thing.

"Me and Lisa? We're getting married next spring!"

How it Works

You realize, at first, that you can't do whatever you were hoping to do. In short, what you've done hasn't brought you the results you were hoping for. Or maybe you're learning something for the first time. Or you just didn't understand the task at hand and got in a little over your head. Whatever the reason, you've gotten stuck, lost, misdirected, confused, discouraged, frustrated, or bewildered. You ain't moving. You're stopped.

And you require a little help.

There is a specific way to ask for help. It's a two part process, and the men who are reading this book need to pay particular attention.

The first part is: Realizing you need help will solve your problem faster. This realization generally comes a little later for men, because men are often not in touch with their limitations. Men tend to push through a problem, generally making it worse, before they ask for help. If they stepped back and saw that wasn't a failure of character to ask for assistance, they would solve problems faster. But they don't.

Nevertheless, realizing that you're stuck, and that your further efforts will not improve matters, is your first step.

The second step is to ask somebody for help. That comes with a small adjustment in attitude: You must yield to the teacher and be willing to accept their assistance. In short, you are saying, "I am lost. Please guide me. I'll follow you for a while." It requires a little humility and a little trust.

Once you ask, define the problem as clearly and succinctly as you can. Then listen for their counsel.

Asking for help can be difficult for so many of us. It's hard to get out of our own way. It can be a little smack to the ego. We want to be independent and self-directed. However, getting a little lost now and again is just part of life, no matter how skilled we might be. Life throws us a curve ball now and again.

Being able to ask for help, without any ego or pretense, is one of the most effective interpersonal skills you can learn.

<u>Why this is Important</u>

Asking for help is essential to a healthy psyche. People do not want to ask for help for a number of reasons, like they do not want to be a burden on others, they do not want to look weak, or they do not want others to know they are in need. No one can do everything alone. Realize that everyone needs help at one time or another.

If you are a person who seems like they have everything together, you may not be used to asking for help. Bottling things up to appear successful and trying to handle everything on your own is a long-term strategy that will fall apart during the toughest times of your life. Maintaining this false persona creates more stress for you by forcing you to live up to an unrealistic reality.

Many people who are willing to help others are unwilling to ask for help. Give your friends and family the opportunity to help you just as you strive to help them. Asking for help allows others to show how much they care for you, and also shows that you value their insight and assistance.

KEY 8

KEY EIGHT: BE CLEAR

Take a moment to digress, if just for this one step, into a critical behavioral technique to grow and deepen your heart.

You need to be clear.

This can be a challenge when you are dealing with difficult concepts that can be hard to express. It is almost impossible to be precise when articulating your feelings.

Which is kind of why we titled this chapter, "Be Clear" because "Be Precise" is . . . well, impossible.

To be clear is pretty easy, and it's integral to truly expressing yourself. But you need to know what we mean by clear.

If I am to explain something, I choose words that are as descriptive as possible. I'm going to be looking at a lot of adjectives. And I have to know that, adjectives might fall short of truly describing my feelings

To clearly describe your feelings, you need to clearly understand them. And you'll most often reach to the words that are most familiar to you as you try to describe what is important.

We think we are being clear when we use words like "sadness" or "fear," to describe our negative emotions or, on the other end of the spectrum, words like "happiness" or "joy." As hard as we may try to achieve that clarity, we often fall a little short. Think about it: if you hear, "I'm happy" those words can mean 100 different things to 100 different people. Consider this when you try to express your emotions: The effort, on your part, is merely to be clear. And you're dealing with terms that have, by definition, vague and often elusive meanings.

A Story from the Heart

Ernie teaches social science at a local high school. A gentle, smiling man, Ernie and I had become friends over the past few years. I'd spoken at his class, and we went to lunch in the cafeteria. We talked about his life, how he came to teaching, and what he felt was most important for the kids to learn from his class.

Ernie thought for a moment and, putting both hand into his lap, said, "To be clear. So many thoughts come in and out of a kid's head these days. Distractions are everywhere. It clouds our feelings and misdirects our intentions. But," Ernie said, "more than anything else, these distractions keep a young person from really getting a handle on who they are.

"To me, there is nothing more important than that a child know his good and bad, strengths and weaknesses and, at the very least, have a clear sense of who they are and who they might want to be."

I asked him to explain that to me. "Well, let me tell you how I arrived at this sense. I tell this story to my classes at some point throughout the year, so I'll share this with you.

"I came from a big family. Nine kids. Yelling was our favorite form of communication.

"My father was an angry man. And in my family, everything revolved around my father."

"It was akin to living in a dictatorship. If my father said something, and he was trying to be funny, I laughed regardless of how unfunny it was. If my father asked a question, I knew to be quiet. If I was wrong, my father would make fun of me.

"Now, of the nine of us, I had an older brother named Chris. Chris was a force of nature. Brilliant student, but always in trouble. A brawler with straight As. And Chris was the only one who stood up to my father." Ernie smiled. "He was fearless. He had big fights with my father, but my father seemed to treat Chris with a little more deference. He didn't talk to Chris much, and they gave each other a great deal of space.

"Now, of the nine kids, Chris was the first to bring music into the house. Albums of a variety of sound and style were always tucked under Chris' arms, ready to be played. Rock, jazz, blues, gospel, and folk music were in constant reach. His music was his passion. He learned to play the guitar, started a band, and played around the city at big and small clubs.

"One weekend afternoon, I think I was about 9 years old, Chris saw me playing off to himself in the backyard.

" 'Ernie, come here a second. There's something I want you to hear.' Chris really loved me. He took me under his wing. He taught me how to play the guitar, was always really patient with me."

" 'I ran into one of your teachers on the way home from work,' Chris said, 'and she said you needed to get your work done. Anything wrong?'

" 'No, I said. 'I'm just not…' then I quieted down.

" 'Not what?' Chris said, with a certain bravado in his voice.

"Now, Chris never minced words, but he had a temper, too. And when he wanted to get to the bottom of things, he was very direct.

"So, I said, 'I'm . . . I'm not smart. I don't want to say anything in class. I'll get the answer wrong.'

"Now, to that, Chris didn't say anything, which was unusual. Chris always had an opinion.

"Finally, Chris said, 'Yeah, that's what your teacher told me. The kids laugh at you. And you don't try in school anymore.'

" 'But, do me a favor. Don't ever say you're not smart. You are. You just don't know how to be clear in your thoughts about who you really are.'

"Mind you, I was nine. I didn't know what he meant by that, and Chris could tell. Chris stood up and said, 'Just come with me. I'll show you what I mean.' He took me to his room, next to the stereo, and said, 'You're going to listen to two guitar players. Your head sounds like the first one. Kinda fast, a little confused, not really sure what's going on up there. You want to sound like the second one.'

" 'Who am I going to be listening to?' I said.

" 'The first guitarist, the guy who's playing sounds all over the place, I'm not sure. The second? Sam Houston Andrew the third. Guitar player with Big Brother and The Holding Company.

"Chris said, 'Sit down. Listen to this,' and I sat and listened to Piece of my Heart sung by Janis Joplin.

"The guitar break came, and it sounded like a rock guitar player. Lots of notes, played fast, seemed like hundreds of pieces of music were thrown into the air.

"Then Chris stopped the record.

" 'You hear that? That's you, Ernie. Lots of notes all jammed into that little bit of time. That's how you're thinking. You want to avoid Dad, make the kids at school laugh, stay out of trouble, always wondering what to do to make everybody else happy and avoid conflict. It keeps you from being clear about who you are.'

"I was quiet. Chris had described me with exact measure. Then Chris put the needle back on the record. 'OK, now listen to this part.' Waiting for the first part of the song to finish, Chris pointed at the record, turned it up and said, 'Right . . . here.'

"Seven notes. Sam Houston Andrew the third played seven notes.

"Then Chris lifted the arm of the record.

" 'Did you hear that? Did you hear how clean that was? How clearly he played those notes?' I didn't say anything, just stared back at him. 'That's what you want to be, Ernie. You want to be that clear.'

"I wasn't sure what Chris meant, and he could tell. 'Ernie, look at it like this. Everything you say has to be you. And it has to come from your voice, your sound, the person that you really are, in there.' And he pointed at my chest.

" 'Make your words as clear as Sam's notes. Each one, make it have meaning. Each word, each thought you say, make it be heard. It's not an accident that this song is called Piece of my Heart. Because, I'll tell you what, when ol' Sam plays those notes, it's as if he's sharing a piece of his heart with us.'

"Chris took the needle off the record. 'Ernie, you don't have to do a lot. Do a little bit. Think just a second before you make another kid laugh at you. Take a deep breath before you try to say something to please Dad. And focus for just a moment while you're taking on another math problem or writing another sentence. Be as clear in your mind and your words as the notes on Sam Houston Andrew's guitar, Ernie. It will keep your mind at peace.' Then Chris rustled the top of my hair and went to his room to read.

"Now, with my class, I do the same thing: I play that song to let these kids know how clear I want them to be, and how much it matters to have their voices heard.

"Come on," Ernie said to me, "Come back to the classroom."

And Ernie, for the next few minutes, got out his old record player, turned it on, put the needle down on the record, and the two of us listened to those seven notes by Sam Houston Andrew the third.

How it Works

Any time you're trying to express your feelings, know going in that it's going to be tough. You know how you feel. There isn't any doubt about that. But letting someone else know how you feel is no small feat. You have to grasp this as you speak, or the conversation can get frustrating at the very least. Maybe "frustrating" is a little vague. Let us be a little more clear: "maddening" is a little closer to the mark.

When you're trying to express yourself emotionally and with clarity, do it slowly. Deliberately. Almost as if you're saying one word at a time. Soften your voice. Take a deep breath (yeah, there's that "deep breath" thingy again. We use that a lot in this book.). Then take a couple more. This is particularly helpful when dealing with emotions driven by fear. If you are in the throes of anxiety, for instance, you want to settle yourself the best you can before choosing a word. This will help you keep any strong emotions you are carrying from interfering with your clarity.

If you are trying to describe events or circumstances that provoke feelings, specificity adds to clarity. It helps describe a cause-and-effect relationship between the circumstance and the subsequent feeling. It also helps you focus on the interaction, or the effect circumstances may have on your feelings.

Recognize, too, that feelings may arise from a thought. You may be going along just fine and the thought of somebody doing something unkind to you may come into your head, bringing with it and fear, sadness, or anger that feels like it comes out of nowhere. When you try to express that, go to the thought first. Identify the cause of the feelings and your explanation becomes clearer. It has a reference point.

Why this is Important

Being clear with yourself and with others is essential to achieve goals and live with meaning. Life often gives us the opportunity to become more clear. Conan O'Brien says "the beauty is that through disappointment you can gain clarity, and with clarity comes conviction and true originality."[102] Change must begin with a clear view of the present reality.

Being clear with yourself is essential because you must know your values and purpose in life. Being completely clear about how you will conduct yourself limits your potential regrets and fears. Being completely clear about your goals or purpose, and knowing what effect you wish to have in the world, allows you to take decisive action. Acting without a clear purpose is like an archer trying to hit a target with an arrow, blindfolded and spinning. Clarity of values are the archer's skills, and clarity of purpose is his aim at the target.

A major theme of this book has been living in the present moment. Acting with clarity is being in the present moment while acting with purpose. You must be able to live your truth, with clarity, in all aspects of life: in speech, motivation, and action. Live your truth. Speak your truth. Be clear.

---

102 O'Brien, Conan

KEY 9

KEY NINE: SAY NO

When we first put this in the list we took a little flack. Although it made perfect sense to us, we were told that to point out the importance of saying so in a book where you are allegedly drawing forth the heart rings as a little contrary, even contradictory.

We took that into consideration. Here's what we came up with: Saying no is essential, if not fundamental, to living a life with meaning. Without the ability to say no, you're like a kite with nothing to tie you down.

We understand that it's not always pleasant to say no. And it isn't really meant to be. "No" is as much of a warning as anything else, and it certainly morphs into disapproval as we age. We associate all kinds of negative and unhappy memories with it. Nobody really welcomes hearing the word no. We think it's safe to say that, in general, it's a pretty unwelcome sentiment.

Saying no draws a line on what you can and can't be to other people, and it's important to know where that limit is. When you don't know how to create limits, they will be created for you. Without the ability to say no, you lose power over your feelings. You fatigue. Your energy drops. And you draw back your heart.

When you live a life that is heart centered, you can get pretty emotional. Sentiment and emotion can begin to rule, instead of just influencing, your decisions.

Saying no makes the limits clear. It gives you a sense of management and control over your heart. It doesn't mean you're inviting anger, nor does it give you permission to be unkind.

Instead, it gives you choice. Living a life from the heart can be challenging. The advantage, however, is that you become open all that is good within this world. And that is a lovely feeling. But saying no offers you some predictability, even some structure. It helps set your agenda. It gives your feelings organization.

Saying no helps you relax a little and keeps you from responding to your impulses. It sets you on your own path, offering clarity and direction for your heart.

A Story from the Heart

There's a donut shop outside of my office. J.P. is a fixture of this place. Tall, lean and dignified, his bespectacled face shines from underneath his weathered Cubs cap. Every day, I see him whiz by my office window. On the days I think I may be deficient in my daily allotment of sugar and fat, I take a walk there, get my donut, and ask J.P. how he's doing.

One morning, my friend who owns the donut store didn't come up to serve us right away, so I had a chance to hear a little more about J.P. After I offered the perfunctory "How are you?" J.P. got a little quiet. He took a bite from his donut, looked out the window, and said, "Well, Ed, if I was honest with you, things could be a little better, but it will work out."

Right then, I sat down. I sat diagonally across from J.P., since he didn't seem to want direct eye contact, but I knew he wanted to talk. I asked "What kind of things, J.P.?"

"My kids, see, they don't talk to me," he said. "I had my kids young. I'm not using this as an excuse, but when you're young and you begin to do something that you don't know much about, you tend to look toward somebody that's had experience in that thing you're about to do. For instance, if you're learning how to fix a car, you're going to look for a mechanic. You're learning how to become a teacher, you're going to find somebody you know can teach.

"But when you parent," he said, "for some reason, you believe you know what you need to know. It's such an odd thing. In any other capacity, we'd reach out for help.

"And that was me. I never reached out, never asked questions, never really knew what to ask. But then," he said, taking a bite of his donut, "I never had anybody to ask in the first place. Never had a good example of what a parent was supposed to do.

"So, I fell back on my experience, which was zero, and then figured I'd copy the person that was the most convenient example. That would've been my father.

"Well," he said, "the word copy wouldn't be the right one. Is there a word for making sure I didn't copy anything he did, and therefore set myself in the exact opposite direction? Well, maybe that word doesn't exist, but that's what I tried to do.

"Unfortunately, I was my father's son. And, not to belabor the point, I was just like him. When I was stressed, I got angry. If something didn't go the way I wanted it to, I got angry.

"And my kids . . . well, they got out of my way. And now," he said, looking at the floor, "they've stayed that way."

I ate half of my donut, sipped my coffee, and the silence lengthened. I was uncomfortable, but I wanted to stay with the conversation since I could tell that he wanted to talk. I asked him, "J.P., is there anything that you would have done differently?"

He was quick with an answer. "I always took the easy path. I gave into my anger, my impulses. I let my resentment and feelings of nervousness direct my actions. I always allowed my emotions to lead the way, to direct my behavior."I always said no to what was hard, what was right, and what would've been the best choice for myself, my children, and their feelings.

"And now," he said, "my children say no to me."

We were both quiet.

"There was this quote by Emerson. I read this after my youngest left home after he and I got in a terrible fight. It read, 'Do not go where the path leads, go instead where there is on path and create a trail.' I cried when I read that. Cried so hard . . ."

J.P. teared up. He wiped his eyes and took a deep breath. "That path, you know, it calls to you. It wants you to find it. It's there, right there, in front of you. It's yearning for you to follow its direction.

"But you're afraid. You see the other path. You know all the people that have gone through the standard steps, giving into their impulses, scrambling to get money, squeezing out time for their family, and building up resentments throughout the process.

"I didn't follow the path to my heart. Had I done that, I would've been a better father.

"I never said no to my fear. And now here I am, wishing my kids would call."

J.P. became quiet again. Breaking the silence, he said, "I never denied my first instinct, and I should have. I learned the value of gentleness far too late. My kids were gone by then. And there's too much distance between us for them to know how I've changed, for me to know the people they've become."

J.P. looked at me and said, "Living as your best self means to say no to some things. You need that word, my friend. It brings out your good side, keeps away the laziness, the anger, and the fear.

"Best word in the English language, if you ask me. Wish I would've learned a lot sooner the true meaning of the word."

How it Works

You can say no directly, as part of an apology, or with warmth. It can draw people in or keep them at a distance. It can be offered in kindness or anger, friendship or conflict.

We recommend that you be as easy as you can with this word. Use it sparingly, judiciously. For so many of us, the word no has the impact of a sledgehammer, falling generally between "What were you thinking?" to "I don't like you." Other interpretations range from "I'd-rather-you-not-do-that" to "this-wouldn't-be-a-good-time." Therefore, you need to take a minute before you say no. And you want to breathe and feel before delivery. Anger and upset need never to be associated with no. Remember, the effort is only to set a limit, to point out a boundary.

This takes practice. Even if you've gotten the hang of it, you want to incorporate the big breath before delivery. It's important that you take in a five-second inhale and exhale before you say no. This helps ensure there is no anger in your delivery.

Here's the trick, though. The signals of a crossed line or compromised boundary are often fatigue, impatience, or discomfort. This, naturally, can give rise to annoyance. Anger, then, is a half-step away from that, ready to do battle.

This deep breath keeps anger on its heels.

We're suggesting you deliver the word no in a mindful, attentive fashion. And it just takes a half second to gather your focus.

We want you to practice this in the mirror. About three times in the morning–which will take all of thirty seconds–breathe and say "No." Watch your expression and listen to your inflection. Get it down, so you have it ready when you need it. Whether it is counterintuitive for you, in the case of those who sometimes fall into people-pleasing, or whether you have the word no ready for any situation, be aware of the person who is hearing the no and the boundary you're trying to set. Be deliberate and thoughtful. Practicing saying no helps you deliver it mindfully.

Why this is Important

You must know what actions, thoughts, relationships, and other aspects of life should be kept or dismissed. Like taking care of a garden, you must say "yes" to the fruit trees and the flowers and say "no" to the weeds. The weeds of your life must be pulled.

Earlier in this book, there was a chapter about acceptance. Saying no and acceptance seem to be in opposition, however they often happen together. Acceptance is seeing reality for what it is, and taking action. Often this action is setting boundaries in your life. Setting boundaries is not a bad thing. There is a conception of the spiritual, benevolent, or enlightened person simply accepting everything. In the relative sense, this is true. But in the absolute sense, people of this level of development must be a beacon of positive change in the world. There are many examples of the enlightened saying no: Jesus flipping the tables of the temple vendors, or the nonviolent protests of Martin Luther King Jr., Nelson Mandela, or Mahatma Gandhi. A no, said for the right reasons, is often the spark that starts the fire of positive change in the world. It begins with you. Keep that word close to you and be gentle, but firm, in its use.

KEY 10

KEY TEN: APOLOGIZE

An apology is taking responsibility for something, either done or said, that hurts another's feelings.

A good apology clears the way to another person's heart. It removes the hurt and resentment that was caused by your action. It is a beginning toward healing.

Let us make this clear: an apology is only necessary because your actions or your words injured another. And let us make something else clear: It is not the person's interpretation of your words that caused the injury alone. If you had not done or said something in an angry or insensitive way, you would have no need for an apology. We need to point this out, because time after time, we find these words appearing in an apology: "I'm sorry that your feelings were hurt." That is not an apology. There is no place for the word "your" after the words "I'm sorry." An apology goes like this: "I'm sorry that I hurt your feelings."

Then you take a little deeper. "I'm sorry that my actions or words were anything except kind and thoughtful. They should have been brought forth in the spirit of peace and friendship. I ask for your forgiveness."

Ladies and gentlemen, that's an apology. If you hear or read anything else, you're not reading an apology. You're reading a rationalization.

Another wrong way to apologize is "I'm really sorry I was so angry, but you shouldn't have . . ." This puts the blame for your reaction on someone else's action. "I'm sorry I got angry but had you not been such an annoyance, I never would have lost my temper." That's not only not an apology, it just confirms that you're a jerk.

An apology is when you take responsibility for your actions. Period. Of course you didn't want to hurt somebody's feelings intentionally. That's not the point. You hurt their feelings without intention, without forethought, and without the presence of mind to choose your words and deeds to avoid harm. And had you been a little more thoughtful, their feelings wouldn't have been hurt.

An apology is an important tool to have at the ready, but you have to know how to use it.

A Story from the Heart

John Robinson was the custodian at Central Valley High School for fifty years. He had seen teachers and children come and go, remembering names, faces, events, and celebrations, as well as all the times he spent cleaning the classrooms and sweeping the hallways. I sat down with John in a warm September afternoon, just as he finished his work on the first day of his fifty first year at Central.

"My greatest memory," John said, "was the time Ms. Hazelton received an award when she retired. It was a few years ago, but I have never seen how a person could do what she did. It was remarkable."

John sat down, put a little tobacco in his pipe, and said, "Central Valley High has always been a small school, with no more than one hundred kids ever graduating from the high school class at any time. Most families knew one another, and most of the kids grew up together and often stayed in the vicinity of the surrounding town.

"Over the years at Central Valley, many of the parents and their children were taught by the same faculty members: Mr. Norris taught Algebra, Mrs. Copley taught Biology, and so on. You could often hear any number of teachers using the phrase, 'You know, when your mother (or father) was in my class . . .' throughout a person's tenure in that school.

"Of all the teachers, over all the years, the one who stood out as the toughest, most critical, most disapproving, and just plain meanest teacher of all was Ms. Hazelton. Ms. Hazelton was the chemistry teacher. And there wasn't a student alive in the forty two years of her tenure at Central Valley who could stand being in her class." John tapped his pipe on his knee and said, "Some of the unhappiest kids I'd ever seen were the ones leaving her class at the end of the day.

"The whole town would mimic her phrases. 'I'm sick, sick, sick of this imprecision! Eyes on your experiment, all of you!' And, their favorite, 'Measurements are to be exact. Sloppiness will not be tolerated!' She'd been around for so long that those phrases became legendary.

"So, this past spring, when Ms. Hazelton announced that she was retiring at the end of the school year, it came as no surprise. Forty two years at Central Valley as their one and only chemistry teacher, and Ms. Hazelton was ready to call it quits.

"The reaction through the town was swift. Kids cheered on the schoolyard, parents high-fived each other in line at the grocery store. Someone even put up a 'Countdown to Hazelton's Retirement' poster in the back of the local bar. Nobody liked this woman, and they couldn't wait to see her go.

"Now, against the advice of a few teachers, the principal and the school board had gotten together and decided that Ms. Hazelton deserved a proper send-off. She was going to receive an award for her service at a school assembly two weeks before the end of school. It wasn't that the teachers didn't want Ms. Hazelton to get an award. The teachers felt that, if Hazelton got this award at an assembly, there might be a riot.

"Well, the time finally came. On June 1st, a little more than two weeks before summer vacation, the assembly took place. Students and their parents gathered to see her stand before them to receive her award. You couldn't find a seat anywhere. People crowded in, stood in the back, and they all waited until she came forward to face the crowd. Mutterings of 'Good riddance' and 'I hope she takes her award and gets out' were circulating through the masses, their anger increasing as each minute passed. And when the principal read the plaque, and presented her to the audience in the school, you could actually hear people booing. I couldn't believe how angry this crowd was getting.

"Then," John said, "what I saw next, I couldn't believe. When Ms. Hazelton accepted the award, she brought with her a ledger book, one of those big, cloth covered books from way back. Hundreds of pages in that thing. And when she got to the lectern, she opened it up and said, 'Many of you have been through my class and, from what I can hear, not many of you have been terribly happy with me.' And you could hear the muffled voices, breathing insults under their breath.

" 'But,' she said. 'I have been happy with you. It just took me until now to find the right time to tell you what you've meant to me. I have been blessed to have every one of you in my class and I've taken notice of all the things you've done well and those that caused you struggle. In short, you mattered to me. All of you.

" 'In this book is an accounting of those things I've noticed about all of you, over the years.' And then Ms. Hazelton opened the book. She went right to the first page, ran her finger toward what seemed to be the first entry and said, 'Is Joseph Williams here?'

"And," John said, "a fifty year old man raised his hand, from high in the back of the auditorium.

"Ms. Hazelton said, 'Joseph, when you were a sophomore in high school, I had you second semester. All year long you got nothing better than a C+ but on the final, you got a B. I remember the smile on your face when I gave you that paper. I saw how proud you were. Joseph, I was proud of you, too. And I apologize for never letting you know.' The hush that came over that auditorium was, as they say, deafening. Then she looked back down at her ledger book and called out another name. 'Ann Marie Thompson? In your senior year, you discovered it was my birthday and put a card on my desk in my office. I was touched beyond measure by your kindness, and I never thanked you for such consideration and thoughtfulness. I apologize for my withholding my gratitude and appreciation from you.' "

John shook his head. "You could've heard a pin drop. All that conversation stopped, stopped dead right there," he said, pointing at me with his pipe, "and Ms. Hazelton kept going. She went down the list, covered about four other people, then paused. She took off her glasses and reached for her handkerchief. She wiped tears from her eyes, put on her glasses and, softly into the microphone, she said, 'You all have meant more to me than I have let on, and I apologize for every time you felt unnoticed, for every word of unkind criticism, and for every thought of despair you felt in any of my classes." 'You all have a place in this book. Every one of you. Many of you have moved, and a few have passed away. But for those who are still here, as part of my apology, please feel free to meet with me between now and the end of the school year. I will be happy to share with you what I wrote in the book, and apologize to you in person.'

"And with that," John said, "Ms. Hazelton closed her book and started to leave the gym. But," John said, "that's not where the story ends.

"As Ms. Hazelton left, people started to clap. Slowly at first, but then it came together. Got real loud. Then they started standing up. These people, these folks that came there to bid, good riddance to old Ms. Hazelton, they gave her a standing ovation.

"People were crying. Ms. Hazelton started to cry. I even started to cry," he said, giggling a bit.

John sat up, paused for a second and said, "An honest apology is a beautiful thing sometimes. It seems no matter what happened, or how long ago it took place, if you apologize from your heart, it does so much to ease someone's pain.

"Took a lot of guts for that woman," John said, "and those apologies changed a lot of lives."

How it Works

A good apology, as we've just explained, recognizes what you've done and asks for the other person's forgiveness. We must view other person's interpretation of the event as valid, and listen to their response. Nevertheless, we also see the need to maintain integrity and personal responsibility for the harm that resulted, in whole or in part, from our actions.

Now, a great apology takes responsibility, recognizes the hurt, asks for forgiveness, and vows to never act in that fashion again. An apology is followed by a commitment to change your behavior. This is why so many people feel that apologies are gratuitous or, at least, short lived. I'm sure you have all heard that "an apology is just words," and that is correct. An apology is just words. Good words, mind you, particularly at the time when angry words are also conveyed. But they are worth nothing if not followed by a sustained effort toward kindness, thoughtfulness, and calm.

An apology, therefore, should be used in the rare incident that you absolutely lose it, and it should be at the ready when you do. And it should signal the need for immediate personal change.

Unkindness can truly damage a person's sense of trust and friendship. Chronic anger will keep people away or cause them to leave you all together. An apology can immediately draw back your words and replace them with consideration. Further commitment to speak and behave only with love and care will make apologies obsolete.

Why this is Important

Apologizing benefits both the person who has been harmed and the person apologizing. The person harmed is able to regain lost dignity and emotionally heal more effectively when the wrongdoer acknowledges the wrongdoing. This, in turn, lets them forgive the wrongdoer. The threat that the wrongdoer once posed now seems less likely to happen again.

An apology gives the wrongdoer the chance to make up for the wrong. The guilt or shame associated with a negative act can harm the wrongdoer both physically and emotionally. Apologizing relieves this guilt or shame.

Apologizing creates an emotional connection between the both the person apologizing and the person being apologized to. Removing the negative energy of the event opens the door to deepen, or even renew, the relationship.

Apologizing requires humility and makes a person less prideful because it requires admitting a wrong. Pride makes someone work hard to create the image of perfection. Some may fear that apologizing makes them look weak. But a person who can readily admit faults and wrongdoings demonstrates true self confidence instead of a prideful facade. Stephen R. Covey says, "It takes a great deal of character strength to apologize quickly out of one's heart rather than out of pity. A person must possess himself and have a deep sense of security in fundamental principles and values in order to genuinely apologize."[103] The ability to apologize shows strength of character, as well as care for the emotional well being of others.

---

[103] Covey, Stephen R. The 7 Habits of Highly Effective People: Powerful Lessons in Personal Change. , 2013. Print. pg 207

KEY 11

KEY ELEVEN: HUG

Physical embrace is absolutely fundamental to the engagement and expression of the heart.

The embrace is our first and most basic physical form of affection. It is also our first form of comfort. It is the embrace that takes us from the womb into the arms of our mother. And it is her embrace that begins our journey into life. The hug offers us safety and assurance, love and togetherness. Hugging validates you. It is the physical reminder of life. It brings us back to the beginning of ourselves, reacquainting us with our first touch, our first support, our first experience of love. Hugging reminds us that we are human and that we matter.

When we hug another person, we share that humanness with them. In drawing them close, we exchange the same, fundamental feeling that all of mankind can relate to. Each one of us has experienced this gift from the very beginning.

When we hug one another, we become one again with Love. We connect on the most visceral level of life, giving rise to immediate congeniality. Hugging brings us together.

Hugging breaks down the walls of pretense and ego. It integrates the spirits. It is a joint experience to show affection, offer reassurance, exchange comforts, and let somebody know how important and meaningful they are. Hugging heals.

The hug is the fastest connection to the heart. It is the physical expression of "I love you." It is expressed appreciation and gratitude.

Hugging is natural as walking. Think of your feeling when you have your arms around somebody you love. Think of the effortlessness, the natural glow of your spirit when you are holding a baby. Watch your mood change when you put your arms around your pet. This is an extension of your heart, a reaching for the heart of another. Hugging is human and natural.

A Story from the Heart

Donald was the son of a Lieutenant Colonel in the Marine Corps.

"Look," he said, "It's not like my father was The Great Santini, OK? He was a really good man, and he never lost his temper with us. He showed us what it meant to be a good father and a really good, kind person.

"But my father didn't hug us. Not once. Not ever. But when he finally did . . . well, let me start at the beginning."

Donald and I met at a wonderful restaurant about thirty miles south of Camp Pendleton, a large Marine base just outside San Diego. Over tea, Donald told me about the life of his father, a man who had seen two wars, trained infantry to serve in two more, and taught basic training to young men throughout his career. "My father was a decorated Marine, and he served his country with pride and valor. I am blessed to be his son, and I want to make sure I turned out to be at least half the man he was. But," Donald interjected, "with one exception: Unlike my Dad, I wanted to be affectionate to my wife and children.

"I always looked to him as an example. I copied his every move. I would wear his outfits when I was a kid. On Halloween I always dressed as a Marine. I went through ROTC in high school. And, even though I studied education and became a teacher, he encouraged me every step of the way. I just loved the guy." Donald paused, and looked out the window, "And yet, he was probably the most emotionally distant man I'd ever met in my life.

"My Mom tried, bless her heart, but it wasn't the same. She was a very proper woman, showed very little affection to me. I knew she loved me but, between the two of them, I felt like I lived in this 'no touch' vacuum of existence most of my life.

"So," Donald said, "I had to learn on my own. I was lucky enough to meet and eventually marry a wonderful woman who was patient with me. Truth be told, she taught me what I needed to know in the hugging department. My wife could be a professional hugger. As for me, I never learned this skill in my family.

"Well, many years passed, I got a job, started a family, and my father retired. He stayed active, always involved himself with the Marines in some capacity. And one day, just days before my father's 70th birthday, my father found a lump in his side. He went to the doctor and said he had colon cancer.

"When they did an MRI, they found it had metastasized. The next day, I went to my father's house. He seemed calm, but was busying himself. When I arrived, he was cleaning the mirror on the mantle, rearranging some of my childhood pictures, and making a grocery list. He was speaking to my mother about what she wanted for dinner, and was asking her if the thermostat in the refrigerator was a little too high.

"My father is told, for all intents and purposes, that he's got weeks to live, and he's acting as if nothing's changed.

"For the first time in my life," Donald said, "when I looked into my father's eyes, it was as if he wasn't there. His focus was off. He looked like his thoughts were far away. And when I tried to catch his glance while he scurried through the house, I called his name: 'Dad. Dad. Dad!' Just like that, three times.

"Finally, on the third time, he looked at me. He saw me stand there, waiting for me to say something. 'Dad,' I said, 'are you OK?'

" 'Yes, son,' he said, 'I'm fine.'

"So," Donald said, "I focused on his eyes as hard as I could. And seeing his face, I became really frustrated. I was so anxious to get his attention that I just blurted out the words, 'Dad, you have cancer. You don't have much time. Did you understand what the doctor said yesterday?' But it was too late. The words just hung in the room like a piñata ready to explode all over him.

"My Dad stood still, back straight, shoulders squared. But, as he spoke, he dropped his chin and looked at the ground. I'd never, ever seen him do that before. At that moment, my father said, 'Yes, son, of course I do.' And with that, I could see his eyes well with tears. First time I'd ever seen my father cry.

"I walked over to him, and I put my hand on his back. Then I did something I didn't expect: I started to cry as well. Hard. And after about fifteen seconds, I couldn't catch my breath. You know that heaving kind of crying that kids do sometimes? That was me. I just kept crying. Doubled over, my back at my father's waist, I just lost it."

Donald sat back in his chair. "Right at that moment, I looked up at my father. And I saw this near terror in his face. His eyes were looking directly into mine, big as saucers, immobilized by what he saw in me, and probably stunned into stiffness over the drama of his life and my reaction to his pain. He literally could not move.

"But I could. I found some strength. Somewhere inside me, watching this man make an effort to comfort me after all these years of distance, I got up. I straightened my back and walked toward my Dad. Standing in between his arms, I put my arms around him." Donald stopped and began to cry. "I hugged my father.

"And then the most amazing thing happened. Right then, he hugged me back. For the first time in his life, my father hugged me.

"We stood there and cried together for about five minutes. When we let go of one another, we both put one arm around the others back. I looked at my Mom and she had her hands clasped together under her chin, tears streaming down her face."

Donald took a deep breath. "I learned something in that moment. I waited all my life for my father to hug me. And all I guess I needed to do was to hug him.

"Mind you, it took me a while. At some point in my life, I just took for granted that if he didn't offer any affection, I shouldn't either.

"I needed a moment, I guess, that I knew I wouldn't be rejected, that I wouldn't be told that my offer of affection would be wrong or inappropriate. And his cancer gave me that moment.

"Two weeks later, he died. And when he took his last breath, I had my arm around his shoulder, and he was holding my hand in his."

Donald started to cry again. "I got to hug my Dad. And he hugged me. Just doesn't get any better than that."

How it Works

In many situations, hugging has become somewhat rare. For a moment, in the seventies and early eighties, hugging was becoming more frequent and a little more common. Then it dropped off significantly. Today, we see people hug, but we have difficulty always knowing when to express ourselves by hugging someone.

In addition, the a form of hugging needs to be maintained. Actually, it is our preferred form of hugging. It is the chest-to-chest, both-arms-around-your-back hug. In short, the full frontal hug. This is, from our perspective, the heavyweight champion of hugs.

You can put one arm around the back of another person, and that's fine, and it qualifies as a hug. You tend to pat someone's back with one arm. You can do a "there, there" hug, also with one arm. And if that's all you can put together, that is far better than not hugging at all. The idea, however, is that you embrace the other person. A hug is being physically held. You are there to let that person know you love them, and hugging is the best way we know how to do that, in the most comprehensive and universal fashion possible.

Being hugged extends your vulnerability to the other person. The grasp you allow is an act of permission. It allows you to be connected with another, despite all your frailties and hurts, all your doubts and fears. Being hugged–for that moment–erases them all.

Hugging is affirming. It lets you know that, to that one person, in that one moment, you are loved and valued. It may be fleeting, it may even feel transitory. But that hug connects you to your core. Hugging is the physical reach into your heart. You open yourself when you allow yourself to be hugged. You give your full self to another when you reach to hug them.

Why this is Important

Research has found many benefits to hugging. Hugging produces oxytocin, a hormone released in our brain. Oxytocin, often referred to as the "Love Hormone," is linked to social bonding, creating a feeling of connectedness: "oxytocin floods our bodies with feelings of connection, trust, and contentment . . . Oxytocin is the secret to forming committed relationships, turning lust into long-lasting love. The oxytocin bond is the basis for lifelong relationships of all kinds that goes from parents love, partnership, and even two close friends."[104] This connectedness increases our feeling of security, and we feel less alone in the world. This alleviates the primal fears of loneliness and abandonment.

Leo Buscaglia, (who thought he should have been in the Guinness Book of World Records for the number of people he hugged in a lifetime, and made a point of hugging each person at every lecture who wanted a hug from him), said in his book Love, "We need others. We need others to love and we need to be loved by them. There is no doubt that without it, we too, like the infant left alone, would cease to grow, cease to develop, choose madness and even death." [105] Altogether, the positive feelings produced by hugging relieve stress and make people happier. Stress reduction lowers blood pressure and reduces the risk of heart disease, obesity, and diabetes, among other health benefits. Hugging is therefore fundamental to our lives. You should hug people as frequently as you possibly can.

---

[104] Kuchinskas, Susan. The Chemistry of Connection: How the Oxytocin Response Can Help You Find Trust, Intimacy, and Love. Oakland, CA: New Harbinger, 2009. Print. pg. vii

[105] Buscaglia, Leo. Love. New York: Fawcet Columbine, 1996. Print.

CHAPTER 5

REGENERATING YOUR HEART

To regenerate your heart is to take care of your physical self. Your biology, hormones, health, fitness, and mind are all synergistically connected; each part affects all other parts. We must create the optimal conditions to ensure a healthy physical self, using these keys:

Key One: Focus on your breathing

Key Two: Smile

Key Three: Laugh

Key Four: Exercise

Key Five: Know your Music

Key Six: Dance

Key Seven: The Red Nose

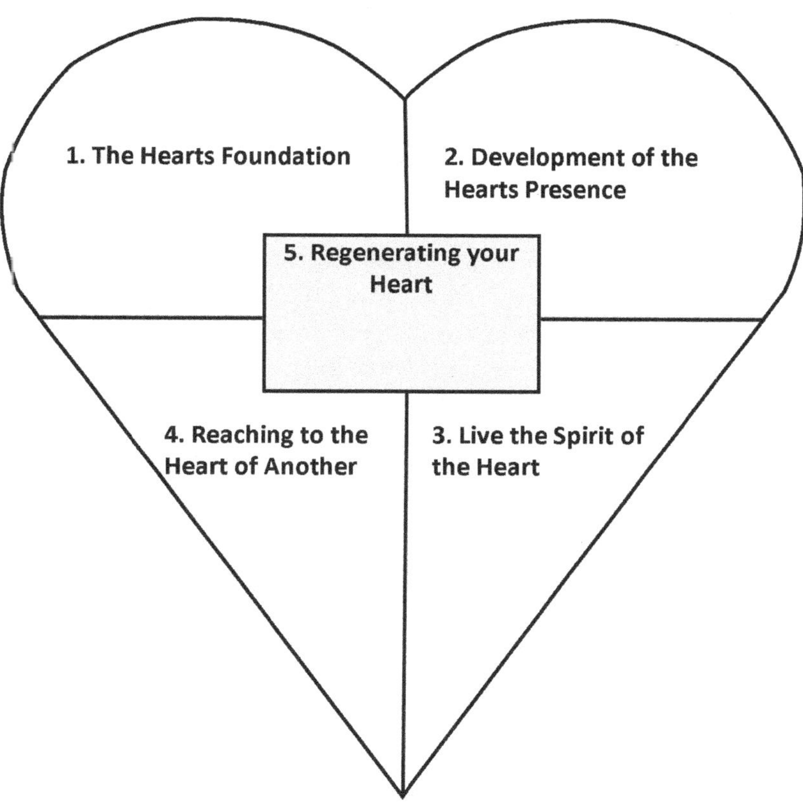
1. The Hearts Foundation
2. Development of the Hearts Presence
5. Regenerating your Heart
4. Reaching to the Heart of Another
3. Live the Spirit of the Heart

KEY 1

KEY ONE: FOCUS ON YOUR BREATHING

Focusing on your breathing is used in cultures around the world to re-center the mind in the midst of experiencing stress, confusion, and insanity. It is the singularly most effective way to put yourself back into focus, and is a single step to redirect your attention to the place of calm you familiarized yourself with earlier in the book.

You can focus on your breathing in any place, in any condition, or under any circumstances. You can literally do this anywhere, at any time of the day or night, as long as you're awake. Whether it is taking a deep breath, noticing how shallow or deeply your breathing flows, or just looking for the rhythm behind your breath, focusing on your breath builds your general ability to focus.

Sometimes it feels as if you're looking at the bottom of your nose. We have literally seen people look down and cross their eyes when they're trying to focus, and that works fine. Wherever you end up looking, give your attention to your breathing. The air is coming in, and held for a half second, and the air is going out.

Actually, that last sentence is what it sounds like inside your head when you focus on your breathing. At least, at first it does. You will tend to shorten that to "in . . . out" after a little bit, largely because the dialogue with yourself can become a little distracting. Sometimes a sound of any sort, often called a mantra, can accompany your breathing, but it doesn't matter. These are just different tools to allow you to lightly place your attention on your breathing.

You need to focus on your breathing any time you feel stressed or wish to be calmer. Focusing on your breathing is the universal technique to find your center and regain your emotional and spiritual balance.

A Story from the Heart

Reginald is a branch manager and loan officer in a local branch of a national bank.

We sat outside in his backyard, right next to his garden. It was raining, so we were camped underneath an overhang, watching the rain cover the plants and feeling the sharp wind sweep through the trees.

"Remember when you visited me at my office a few years ago? All that tension in the air, everybody-including myself-constantly on the phone, pressure to get the customers' loan documents put together, filed and approved? It's not like that anymore, not in the least. You wouldn't believe the place. After the hospital last year, everything changed."

A little more than a year ago, Reg started getting chest pains. "But not the kind that make you think you have a heart attack. These were across my ribs, as if someone was pushing me.

"I didn't think anything of it, at least not at first, but then one day I just couldn't breathe. Well, that's not exactly true. I think it was more along the lines of not being able to take a deep breath. But it was scary to me. I'd try to suck in as much air as I could, and it only went to a certain point.

"So I figured I'd take it easy, but at the same time try to increase my exercise. I took the dogs on longer walks. I got on the treadmill now and again. But no matter what I tried to do, my ability to breathe deeply didn't noticeably increase.

"Then, it was a Friday morning, right before work, and I became faint. I leaned on the car and slid to my knees. I called my wife, she called for an ambulance, and before I knew it, I was being wheeled into the emergency room of the hospital."

Reg stopped for a second, listened to the rain, and said, "As I was being rolled through those doors, I remember losing consciousness. The next thing I see is my wife and a doctor standing next to my bed. I'm in a hospital room and the weirdest sensation is coming through me. I'm breathing. But I have an oxygen cannula attached to my nose. I feel perfectly fine, I'm conscious, but I hear the doctor telling my wife that I may have to wear this tube on my face for the rest of my life.

"I sit up. Like I was being hurled from the bed, I sit up like a shot. I look over at the doctor, he looks at my wife, my wife then looks back at the doctor, and I say, 'Could somebody please look at me? There's this thing underneath my nose and I'd like to know what it's doing there?'

My wife said, 'Honey, the doctor said you may have had a heart attack, but the tests are inconclusive.' Then the doctor said, 'Reginald, what we do know is that your heart stopped for a few moments. We're going to run some more tests and see what happened and determine the next steps in treatment.'

"I fall back on the bed as fast as I sat up. I'm thinking, 'My heart did what again? Stopped? Are you serious?' And I've got this thing in my nose."

Reg smiled and said, "And now, here's the next thing that I thought of, and you're going to think I'm nuts, but I have to tell you. I'm thinking, 'Hey, I'm breathing. I'm feeling pretty good right now. Could somebody give me a mirror and see how I look in this thing because, hey, I'm a breathing stud right now and if I can get by without anybody noticing this thing on my face, I'm in good shape.' I completely forgot about my heart stopping. I just remember how much I loved feeling that I could breathe again!

"Now, I'm in the hospital for about three days, and the doctor comes back and said I had an irregularity in one of my heart valves. OK, great. All I know is for the last three days, I'm breathing great with my little cannula helper. So, they fixed the valve, chest pains were gone, and as I'm being discharged from the hospital, he takes me and my wife into his office and said, 'Reginald, you may have to wear this cannula for a while before we can make sure your heartbeat and your oxygen is regulated enough to resume daily activity. Please come back to me in two weeks and we'll see how you're doing.'

"Fine. Well," Reg paused, "not so fine, actually. Because the first day I stepped back into the bank, wearing my cannula and hauling a tank of oxygen behind me, the loan officers, the bank tellers and the bank president all looked at me like I had one foot in the grave. The bank President came over to me not an hour into my first day and said, 'Take a few weeks off and let us know when you're ready to come back to work.'

"I was livid. I felt pushed aside, discriminated against. But I loved my job and I loved the people. And I was determined to get back to work.

"So," he said, "I made myself breathe again.

"Every day, for about twenty minutes in the morning and twenty minutes at night, I concentrated on my breathing. I didn't know squat about meditation, I didn't even know that what meditation was! I just got quiet, shut off the phones and the TV, and concentrated on my breathing.

"My job was to get back to work. I had to get in touch with my most basic physical sensation, my breathing–the thing that really got my attention and put me into the hospital–if I was to get my life back again.

"Well, my friend," Reg said, as he turned to me, "I learned that what I was doing was, in fact, expanding my lungs and deepening my flow of oxygen. Little did I know that, at the same time, I was expanding and deepening my spirit.

"I got back to work in two weeks. In the process, I had begun to let go of external stimuli to make my happy. I lost five pounds because things like eating didn't have the same kind of attachment and meaning. I could regulate my feelings by just going back to my breathing. And every day, I come out here," as we waved his arm, showing me this beautiful, rain soaked yard, "to concentrate on my breathing and be at peace with myself and the world.

"And when I went back into work, everybody noticed the difference. They all asked how I did it. And, to make a long story short, the office is much less tense these days." Reg began to laugh and said, "Leading lunchtime breathing awareness exercises every day can even make my crazy work environment become a lot more peaceful."

How it Works

Think about the number of times in your life you've been asked to "take a deep breath." Then remember times in your life when you were relaxed, how regulated and deep your breathing became. Think, too, how you've recognized your breathing accelerate when under pressure. Noticing this take place is the first step to giving it your attention.

Then watch what happens.

When we begin to give our breathing attention, we can decide how we want it to change. For that moment, we feel a little more distant, more disconnected, from our stress. We have placed our concentration on our breathing and not on what we're thinking of or reacting to. We focus inwardly in an attempt to calm our feelings, instead of reacting to the outward stimulation.

Your breathing is the best place to focus because it is the fundamental beginning to any identifiable point of change in our behavior. In short, when we change our breathing, we calm down. We change our thoughts. We redirect our attention. And we begin an instantaneous change in our demeanor. We settle ourselves. We sit. We feel. And we breathe.

This process takes about five minutes. Even less. And the effects are startling.

And then things get really good.

See, when we continue to focus just on our breathing, then come back to our breathing whenever we get distracted, refocusing on the "breathing in . . . breathing out" rhythm of our breath, we begin to take the first steps toward meditation. Our body calms. Our intellectual and emotional focus returns to our breathing and it begins a deepening sense of relaxation and peacefulness. And all the benefits of health that meditation offers begin to take hold.

It only takes a few minutes to reset yourself from chaos to calm, no matter the situation. If you are standing in the midst of an emotional hurricane, you can detach and bring peace and focus back to yourself. Doing this daily, regardless of the stimuli you're facing, can begin to change the way you respond to stress in any situation. Merely concentrating on your breathing, noticing the changes in your body, and coming back to your breathing when distracted will change your life and your direction toward all things in your life.

And it begins with just a breath.

Why this is Important

The way you breathe affects your whole body. Your breath gives you life; it always has, and it will until you die. Your "breath is the bridge which connects life to consciousness, which unites your body to your thoughts. Whenever your mind becomes scattered, use your breath as the means to take hold of your mind again."[106] Although our breathing happens unconsciously, the way we breathe is an expression of our mood; "shallow and irregular breathing reinforces stress and can have negative physical consequences, whereas deep breathing induces relaxation and promotes circulation."[107] Your breath expresses your personal state. Shallow breathing holds in your tension. Deep breaths untie the knots of your contraction. Modifying the way we breathe can change our biology, which in turn affects our emotional state. Learning to take full breaths will increase our ability to relax. Breathe in deeply; feel yourself being alive, relax your muscles, and allow all aspects of your life to unfold in the present moment.

When your breath is shallow, you are rejecting or saying no to some aspect of your life. When you are "closed, feeling 'No' to some aspect of your experience, your world shrinks to the size of your refusal's clench. You become enclosed in the tightness of your 'No,' unaware of the openness beyond the drama of your contraction. Instead, you can fully feel your closure, breathe fully the texture of your pain, and open as whatever you are feeling, in any moment. Open and alive as love, you are free."[108] Focusing on your breath brings awareness to your inner state, and allows you to modify your feelings and be open to reality instead of closed-off, thinking about your deficiencies or negative things in your life.

---

[106] Nhất, Hạnh, Mobi Ho, and Dinh M. Vo. The Miracle of Mindfulness: An Introduction to the Practice of Meditation. Boston: Beacon Press, 1987. Print. pg 15

[107] Nhất, Hạnh, Mobi Ho, and Dinh M. Vo. The Miracle of Mindfulness: An Introduction to the Practice of Meditation. Boston: Beacon Press, 1987. Print. pg 15

[108] Deida, David. Blue Truth: A Spiritual Guide to Life & Death and Love & Sex. Boulder, CO: Sound True, 2005. Print. pg 17

KEY 2

KEY TWO: SMILE

This one is the game changer.

When you incorporate this into your life, every hour of every day improves. This sounds like a big promise but we assure you, smiling will absolutely change your life. Your emotional composition changes and improves permanently. You become a different, better, and happier person.

A smile shows the world your heart is engaged. It lets everybody know that you're physically affirming everything is all right. That life is good. That whatever comes up today, you will embrace with love.

A smile is the declaration. It is the statement to yourself and the world that everything is OK and it's going to be OK, too. It is the first step in making yourself available to speak from your heart. It gives another person the impression that you're safe, you're friendly, and you're kind. In short, it puts your heart on your face.

It is the beginning, the first overture of love and friendship, of every moment of your day, every day of your life.

It is an odd thing that we need to include this. You take for granted that a smile is just something you do, something that is just there. But think of it this way: A smile is your introduction to life. When you put a smile on your face, you are meeting the world with your best self.

A Story from the Heart

Jerry, a fifty one year old former short order cook and current chef at a four-star hotel, has one of the most beautiful smiles I've ever seen. I mean, when Jerry smiles, his face almost floats away from his head.

You could see that smile from a block away. His smile was actually the first thing I saw when I met him for breakfast at his hotel one Saturday morning. The sun had just come up and, although the street was still a little dark, Jerry's smile reflected the morning light.

When we sat down and I told Jerry what I'd wanted to write about, Jerry thanked me for choosing him for this essay, "But," he said, "It's been something I've done all my life. My mother used to insist that we smile, no matter what. It was what she did, and she did it all the time. She was just so happy. And it wasn't because her life was easy, not at all. She was a strong farm woman when she was young, and always worked some kind of manual labor job. But my Mom, she just kept at it. Big woman, about 240 pounds, but that smile just radiated. People would make fun of her when she smiled, but it didn't bother her. She just smiled anyway. It just made her feel good to smile. Always said that it reflected the 'sunshine in my soul.' Even when she died, she reached over to me and said, 'Come on now, Jerry, you give your Momma a smile,' and I did. It was the last thing she saw before she died.

"I was proud of that," Jerry said, and stayed quiet for a minute. I broke the silence, and asked a question about his mother. "You said that she smiled all the time but that people made fun of her when she smiled. Why was that?" "Oh, I forgot to tell you," Jerry said "my Mom didn't have any teeth."

I just sat there, not knowing what to say, so I said, "Oh, I'm sorry."

Then Jerry said, "You know, I'm glad you liked my smile. When I was a kid, and into my adulthood, I smiled and got made fun of just like my Mom.

"I didn't have any teeth, either. At least, not up until a few years ago."

Jerry said that he and his Mom had the same kind of gum disease. "It was a little rare, at least that's what I was told. We could've gotten dentures years ago but the money just wasn't there.

"Momma said, 'Jerry, that's OK. You don't smile with your mouth, anyway. You smile with your heart.'

"I always loved that–You smile with your heart. That always made me feel good. So I just kept on smiling, just like Momma. And, just like her, I took a lot of grief. The kids would call me names. The one that got me most was 'funny looking.' I never got that one. I mean, when you smile, it's a little like everything is funny, so that one never made a lot of sense." We both laughed over that one.

Then Jerry said, "You know what, though? Let me tell how I got these teeth."

Jerry said, "I was working as a cook at this wonderful little restaurant in the industrial section of town. Truckers, cops, hardworking, blue-collar guys used to come in there. Great people, too. I'd cook for them, talk to them through the years. They would become regulars in the place. And some of them became my friends.

"And when I say 'friends' I mean the kind of friend that never really meets outside of the restaurant. I know that because I put out feelers to see if any of those guys wanted to get together for a beer or coffee or something, but none of them did. They were busy, they had other plans. I always felt that they were avoiding me a little, but I just let it go. We had our friendship in the restaurant, and that was good enough. Still," Jerry said, "It would've been nice to go out with a friend now and again. See, Momma never got out much, outside of her job. She went to work, and she came home. We kids were her life. So, I didn't mind much. I didn't know any better, I guess.

"Anyway," Jerry said, "Not long after Momma died, one of the hostesses that poured the coffee and cleaned the tables in the restaurant was sick. I was back in the kitchen cooking, but it was a slow day. So, after I filled the orders, I went out front and helped clean the tables.

"At this one table sat a guy I'd never seen before. Nothing terribly distinct about him, just sat there drinking his coffee, barely made eye contact when he saw me. Well, I went over to see if he wanted any more coffee, smiling as always, and he looked up at me. He said that, yes, he'd like some coffee, but he kept looking at my mouth.

"Now, I was used to that," Jerry said, "it didn't bother me at all, but it was the way he looked. It was as if he just discovered something, something that he hadn't ever seen before. He then looked at my eyes, and I kept smiling, and now he smiled back at me. Mind you, he didn't say a word. Just looked at me, as if something came over him. You could tell his wheels were turning in his head, you really could. And, then he started to sip his coffee, and I went back to the kitchen.

"Well, a few minutes later, he got up to leave, and when he left he waved at me from the front door, smiled a big smile, got in his car and drove away. I cooked the next meal, put it out for the waitress, and went out to clean his table.

"And what I got there, he didn't leave a tip. Instead, he left his business card," he said, with that smile coming back to his face.

"On the front of the card, it said the man's name, and then D.D.S behind it. I didn't know what that meant, so I read the back. It said 'Jerry, call me to make an appointment. I will give you a smile. We'll work out the payments.'

"I had to ask a friend of mine what 'D.D.S.' meant. He said, "Jerry, that man is a dentist."

Jerry pointed to his teeth and said, "That's where I got these. Less than a year later, I got the job as Chef of this fancy restaurant. I know the teeth had everything to do with it.

"But," he said, "That's not the cool part," he said, "Let me introduce you to somebody." And, with that, Jerry waved to a young man in his late teens. "Jim, come on over here. There's somebody I want you to meet."

Jim came over and shook my hand. "This is my son, Jim." And while shaking my hand, Jim let loose a smile just like his dad.

"This job helped me pay for that smile. See, Jim had the same condition in his teeth that my Mom and I had in ours. So, once I had my teeth, I brought my son over to that Dentist.

"Oh, one last thing," Jerry said, "You know what the dentist said to my son once he got him in the chair? Hand to God, this is true. He said, Jim, you smile just like your dad. You two smile with your hearts.'

"It was as if my Momma was standing behind him, whispering in his ear."

How it Works

Most people run into three questions about smiling. When do I smile? Do I smile at everything I do? And, will people think I'm a simpleton for smiling all the time?

The short answer is a) Smile as often as you can, and be especially conscious if you're not smiling, b) Yes, smile at everything you do, and c) It doesn't matter if somebody thinks you're a whack job for smiling all the time.

Let's hit that last one first. Is there a better alternative to your expression? Do you think you'll actually live a happier life because your dour expression will make somebody else feel better? Yeah, we don't think so, either.

And as far as smiling all the time, we're advocating a grin or a pleasant expression. You should recognize yourself as smiling if you looked into the mirror, but not necessarily showing your teeth in an ear-to-ear explosion under your nose, twenty-four hours a day.

Your awareness of smiling could come from looking at somebody else whose expression is sad, angry or generally unpleasant. Observing that expression on someone else's face is a cue to check yourself and your own expression.

Watch for it. When you see how other folks walk through the day, holding that same flat expression, kick your smile into gear.

And watch for this, too. If they catch you smiling, see if they change their expression. See if they smile back. That connection alone makes smiling worthwhile.

Why this is Important

A smile is a powerful tool. As Zen teacher Thich Nhat Hanh says, "Sometimes your joy is the source of your smile, but sometimes your smile can be the source of your joy."[109]

A significant amount of research has proven that smiling effects your brain emotionally and physiologically. The physical act of smiling releases dopamine, endorphins and serotonin in your brain, just as we

[109] Thich Nhat Han

experience happiness with a surge of these chemicals.[110] This in turn reduces blood pressure, relaxes your body, lowers your heart rate, and increases your immune system.

A smile expresses happiness and joy to yourself and others. Studies show that smiling people are perceived as younger and more attractive. Smiles are contagious. Like jazz legend Louis Armstrong sang, "When you're smiling, the whole world smiles with you." This is due to "a previously unknown class of neurons — mirror neurons — [which] acts like a neural Wi-Fi system, monitoring everything the other person is saying and doing."[111] So when you see a person smile, mirror neurons in your brain create positive feelings in your mind. This makes you smile as well. We have all experienced this. As a practice, smiling makes you and everyone around you happier. Such a little act has far reaching positive effects. Manifest joy in the world.

---

110 R.D. (2000). Neural correlates of conscious emotional experience. In R.D. Lane & L. Nadel (Eds.), Cognitive neuroscience of emotion (pp. 345–370). New York: Oxford University Press.

111 Daniel Goleman Ph.D http://news.harvard.edu/gazette/story/2007/03/smile-and-the-world-smiles-with-you-but-why/

KEY 3

KEY THREE: LAUGH

The most direct path from your heart to another is through laughter.

Laughter affirms life. It lets our heart breathe and gives our spirit lift. Laughter gives life perspective.

When we're babies, we laugh as reflexively as breathing. Laughter is one of our most basic forms of expression at an unexpected surprise. As we get older, we widen our range on what makes us laugh, or what we see as funny. Our thoughts and experiences add to what makes us laugh, cultivating the garden of humor through everyday experiences.

Laughter lightens life. Herein lies its greatest value: When we laugh, we release tension. We relax. No matter our challenges, laughter eases the pain. In order to live a life that is centered in our heart, laughter must live in our eyes, in our smile, in our gait, in our posture, and in every movement of our being.

To laugh easily is to live happily.

There are times in this life when we need to be serious. But laughter reminds us that those times may be fewer than we think. Laughter lets us know that no matter how critical the circumstance may be, we can meet it with greater ease.

Laughter opens the door to joy. And joy gives us passage to love. Laughter is the effervescence of the heart.

A Story from the Heart

Saleem, or "Sal," is a nurse in a children's oncology ward in a hospital outside of my hometown, Chicago. He told me, "I have recently become a student of the techniques and humor of the great Wavy Gravy and Dr. Patch Adams. I try to apply this to my work with these kids." I met him in the cafeteria of his hospital, a large open area with leather chairs and couches throughout the floor. We sat on chairs near a window, and Sal brought over two vanilla milkshakes. "Yeah, I'm not a coffee guy. And this is what I bring to the kids upstairs. We drink coffee when we're adults. Kids, they never touch the stuff. So, if I want to connect with these boys and girls, I try to do what they do. Good for my spirit."

Sal is a clown. I mean, he's a nurse, but his passion is being a clown.

"I came to this somewhat by accident and, if I'm really honest about it, I pursued it with selfish motives. I had done some parties for kids when I was in college and my early twenties. And, in getting back into it, my intent was not to juggle tennis balls for twelve eight-year olds at birthday parties for some extra money. I started up being a clown again for one reason: to disconnect from my work at the hospital. I just needed a break. Four years in the children's oncology ward, and I was suffering from significant depression. I tried everything I could to get out of it–going to therapy, participating in grief groups, even getting on antidepressants–and nothing worked.

"So, I dusted off the old costume, got out my box of makeup and rented myself out as Tramp the Carnival Clown. Look it up. All I wanted to do was hear a little laughter once in a while, and I knew that these parties helped do that. The kids on the ward, well they didn't laugh much. They weren't there to 'party down,' you know what I mean? My job was, as I saw it, to speak in low tones, ask how they were doing, and try to ease their pain. I thought that mean keeping things slow, calm, and without any interruptive stimulation. I turned down the machines to a low hum so they wouldn't get disturbed by the beeps. That ward was kept like a church. It was what I really felt was best for the spirit of those kids, and what I thought would help them heal.

"And after you work three twelve-hour shifts, you need a little laughter. So that is what I did, I just created a little on my own.

"Well, during the fourth year, I ran across a book called Something Good for a Change by Wavy Gravy. And this, right here, was the turning point. I found this book in a bin where the volunteers kept their books for the patients in the hospital. Something drew me to it, I don't know what, but I was meant to read this book.

"In it, he talked about being a clown in the children's oncology ward in a hospital in Oakland. Turns out, he was the first and only person in the Bay area–or anywhere else, for that matter-that did this for these kids. He'd do all kinds of cool stuff–I mean, we're talking Wavy Gravy, here. Everything he does is cool, from teaching the kids songs to projecting movies on the back of the kids' heads. And they'd take turns being the movie screen! I mean, how cool is that?

"I know I sound like an absolute moron, but you'd think I would've gotten this a long time ago. I had an audience right underneath me, and a captive one at that! And, I figured, if I could make these kids laugh, I would be the best clown in the world and I'd put a little spark back into my life. I mean," Sal said, stirring his milkshake, "when I discovered this, I was still pretty selfish in my motives, so it took me a while to take the focus off my need for that spark.

"My first rule was the see to it that the kids didn't recognize me. I wanted them to see Nurse Sal as a different person from Tramp the Clown. So, I put on my clown makeup, red nose and added a wig, gloves, and big shoes. I changed my voice and went in to the ward during meal time. My first impression was sliding in on my stomach, making fart noises with animal balloons.

"They broke up laughing. Make a note on that one. If you need to make a kid laugh, farting noises are nearly a guarantee that they'll at least giggle. If you're a clown, and you've got an animal balloon, and you turn up its hind end while you're making farting noise, you'll have milk running out their noses.

"Then I started laughing with them. Man, to see all these kids just busting out, you just can't help but start laughing yourself. It was an amazing first day of this, let me tell you. And here's the thing: I would do this after my shifts. Those twelve hour, three day shifts? I got energized knowing that I'd have four straight days to make these kids laugh.

"And, you know," Sal said, "they all knew that the cancer was going to take their lives. But for those moments together, I got them to forget about it and just laugh. What better job is there than that? For the next five years, I was at the hospital nearly every day! I loved it.

"Something happened three weeks ago today that reminds me of why I do this. Amir, an eight year old, had liver cancer and was going to die. We knew it when he came in. He had maybe a month to go. And when these kids come in, being this close to death, I work extra hard being as entertaining as I can. I'd work with them for those three days shifts, but when it came to my Tramp the Carnival Clown days, I really turned it on for them.

"Amir was scheduled for surgery and it was nearing the end of the shift. My clown costume was in my locker at the hospital, so knowing that he was going in, I wanted to make him laugh one last time. He was getting pretty sick, and the surgery was a crap shoot. There was a better than average chance that he wouldn't survive the surgery, but it was a chance the doctors had to take to maybe work a miracle. I wasn't sure if I was going to see him again, so I asked his parents and they gave me the OK to see him in my costume before the operation.

"When I got to his bedside as they were wheeling him in, dressed head to toe as Tramp, I was making noises and the like, and Amir started to giggle. Then, just before he went in for surgery, I see him looking at my watch. Then he looked up at my eyes and said, 'Nurse Sal? Is that you?'

"I took off my wig, removed my red nose and said, 'Yes, Amir, it's me.' 'Oh, Nurse Sal,' Amir said, 'You're the best clown I've ever seen. Thank you so much for making me laugh.'

"And right at that moment, I did what any good clown would do: I made a fart noise.

"And it made Amir laugh, one last time."

<u>How it Works</u>

You can make yourself laugh, and mean it sincerely. There are even classes to teach you how to do such a thing. We can even laugh politely, or laugh to make another person feel like they are amusing or funny. It is well within our ability to do these things.

But laughing with sincerity means changing your attitude. It requires you to reframe a situation in a humorous light; to look at life as being slightly silly or little bit odd. This is one of the reasons that observational comedians, as they're called, have become so successful over the last 30 or 40 years. Anytime a comedian begins a sentence with the words, "Have you ever noticed," they are pointing out the peculiarities of life. And that's what makes us laugh.

This is, essentially, how laughter works. Our attitude toward life widens our observations. As this grows, we see things that are unusual, that are a little peculiar and, in fact, kind of funny. The horizon of life stretches, inviting and including all that is out of the ordinary, that which fits perfectly in the "theater of the absurd."

From this attitude, laughter is more familiar. It's easier to access. We look at life as having more fun, more color, more of the unexpected and unusual that sits outside of our "normal," day-to-day view. When we change our view of everyday life, we invite laughter at any given moment.

It is a little odd for us to describe the value of laughter. It should go without saying. But laughter is good for more than just your mood. Physiological and neurological data surfaces daily about its power to lower blood pressure and improve our awareness. Laughter is the best way to show you truly appreciate and value another person.

Why this is Important

Laughter brings joy to life. Laughter accentuates the best of times, and in the darkest of times, laughter can be the salvation. Viktor Frankl, referring to his lessons from the concentration camps, says "humor, more than anything else in the human make-up, can afford an aloofness and an ability to rise above any situation, even if only for a few seconds."[112] This ability to rise above a situation removes the person from suffering. During hard times, as Bob Newhart says, "laughter gives us distance. It allows us to step back from an event, deal with it and then move on."[113] This distance can, in the midst of suffering, release you from the prison of suffering.

A significant amount of medical, peer-reviewed research states the physical benefits of laughter, from reducing the risk of heart disease[114] to cancer treatment[115]. Research shows that the physical act of laughter has significant positive physiological effects such as the ability to "boost the immune system and circulatory system, enhance oxygen intake, stimulate the heart and lungs, relax muscles throughout the

[112] Frankl, Viktor E. Man's Search for Meaning. Boston: Beacon Press, 2006. Print.

[113] Newhart, Bob

[114] http://umm.edu/news-and-events/news-releases/2009/laughter-is-the-best-medicine-for-your-heart

[115] http://www.cancercenter.com/treatments/laughter-therapy/

body, trigger the release of endorphins (the body's natural painkillers), ease digestion/soothe stomach aches, relieve pain, balance blood pressure,[and] improve mental functions (i.e., alertness, memory, creativity)."[116]

You can allow laughter to enter into life more freely. Allow yourself the freedom to laugh and laugh often. "Why wait for reasons to laugh? Life as it is should be reason enough to laugh. It is so absurd, it is so ridiculous. It is so beautiful, so wonderful! It is all sorts of things together. It is a great cosmic joke."[117] To laugh more, you must look for the humor in the present moment. Laughter connects us to what is going on right here, right now in the present. In all situations, even the most mundane or serious, ask yourself, "What is or could be funny right now?"

Do not take life so seriously. Your perceptions, your opinions, feel so real right now, like they are you. But think about your thoughts and opinions from five years ago, ten years ago. How absurd! All life is change; we, along with the world, continue to change. Laugh along with the change.

Laughter's true wisdom bring more happiness, or at least relieves suffering. Nietzsche, often considered one of the darkest philosophers, says that true wisdom must bring laughter, "let that wisdom be false to us that brought no laughter with it!"[118]

---

[116] http://www.cancercenter.com/treatments/laughter-therapy/

[117] Osho, . Everyday Osho: 365 Daily Meditations for the Here and Now. Gloucester, Mass: Fair Winds, 2002. Print. pg 7

[118] Nietzsche, Friedrich W, and R J. Hollingdale. Thus Spoke Zarathustra: A Book for Everyone and No One. Harmondsworth, England: Penguin Books, 1969. Print. pg 23

KEY 4

KEY FOUR: EXERCISE

Exercise is just an absolutely awful way to begin your day.

It hurts. It is a pain in the ass. It takes willpower that most of us don't have in the morning. We are too preoccupied in the afternoon, and don't want in the evening. It's just a ton of time and trouble. We'd rather . . . well, do anything else. Wind our watch. Fold socks. Sit and look at the wall. On our list of priorities, on a scale of one to ten, exercise is about one-twelfth.

We figure that you can start your day with anything that isn't exercise, and it would be better than exercise. Moving around for the sake of keeping our body in shape seems like such a futile undertaking. We're going to age anyway. And we're just fine now, thanks. I'd like to sleep an extra ten minutes. That and a little coffee is about all the exercise I'll need.

But here's the deal: If you're going to live a life from the heart, and experience your life deeply and with fulfillment, you need to keep the vehicle that holds the heart in good working order. In short, if the body is healthy, the heart is healthy. If the body is in disrepair, we lose focus on our feelings. Our attention is on our pain, not on our fulfillment.

This is common sense, but we still meet it with resistance. We see this as gratuitous, at least, and completely unnecessary at most. We look at countless other people who do no more exercise than walking from their apartment to their bus stop and look just fine, thank you. Our grandparents didn't get up and do twenty pushups. And we all can name at least one person that has lived well into their eighties, sustaining themselves on not much more than gin, cigars, and profanity. They even occasionally stir their coffee with a stick of butter and still can recite Shakespeare while taking out the garbage.

We want to take for granted that we are going to age like them, especially that last guy. We want to be the person that just goes about their business, has a good time, and comes out the other end without a lot of pain, problems or concerns.

Yeah, well, we do, too. And exercise really improves those odds.

A Story from the Heart

Ann was a very successful personal trainer in a private health club, and she said she lived the saying by the late Jack Lalanne, "Exercise is everything."

So, at 42, when she was hit by a car, the paralysis in her legs kept her, as she put it, "limited in my lower limbs.

"I am a New Yorker. I used to dodge cars as sport. When you're raised in Manhattan, you don't cross the street, you navigate the traffic. So for this to happen, it's a hardship but it's almost a little more of an embarrassment." Laughing, she said, "I mean, seriously? I got hit by a car? I'm in the business of training people to make their bodies strong, agile, and flexible. And I get hit by a car! Doesn't that just piss you off?

"But," Ann said, scooting herself up in her wheelchair, "if I was to live by Jack's saying, I had to get back. I had to make it everything again . . .

". . . which seemed damned near impossible."

Ann wheeled around. "Let's look at all the ways you use your legs: walking, dancing, running, swimming, standing, squatting, kicking, and jumping. OK, now if we begin to associate all these activities with just the basic, daily movements that your legs support–and we're talking from helping you sit up in bed, to getting out of bed, to walking to the sink for water–we'd be here all day.

"Now, I lost my legs, my vehicle for exercise, my way to make exercise my everything. But," she said, tapping the wheels of her chair, "if everything was what I was after, then this new vehicle had to facilitate my exercise.

"And here was the first challenge: Throughout my career, I showed people what to do. I am an excellent teacher, but it was more than that. People knew that I lived what I taught. I 'walked the walk' in my profession.

"Now, that just went out the window. 'Walking the walk' became kind of pathetic."

Ann wheeled around and showed me the piece of paper she kept on her living room coffee table. "See this? I keep this here, at eye level, so I can see it every day. It's the definition of 'exercise.' Read what it says."

I took the piece of paper from her hands. "It means, 'Bring forth.' "

"I got that from a friend of mine," she said. "Then I looked up the root of the word 'exercise.' And two things popped out at me. First, it said, 'The act of bringing reality into action,' or in short, 'walking the walk.' Is that the coolest thing you've ever seen? Then," Ann said with gleeful excitement, "Check this out. When I was looking up the Latin root, I found this word."

Ann spun around in her wheelchair and, directly on the back, were the words Excelsior: Still Higher.

"It's the motto of the State of New York, my home state," she said. "It's my motto, too.

"The first day I rolled back into the gym, people looked at me with pity. And the first time I saw one of my clients look at me that way, I snapped back at them. 'Have you been training while I was gone? Do you not have the workout information I gave you? Get your butt back on that treadmill right now!' They knew I was back, and they knew I meant business.

"But I felt there were limitations. I taught a yoga class, and I stopped. I taught Qigong, and I did that in my chair, but it felt odd to me, so I stopped that, too.

"And then, let me tell you what happened. The first day into the gym, seeing a couple of clients, making sure they followed through my instructions, seemed weird. I wasn't participating. I was just yelling instructions. I felt hollow.

"As I got into my car, I saw the words on the back of my wheelchair as I was transferring it into the back seat: Excelsior: Still Higher." Ann shook her head. "I felt like such a jerk.

"The next day, I signed back up for my yoga class instruction and the Qigong. The guy that ran the gym didn't question me whatsoever. I did both of these classes from the chair. I would speak instructions, and show them what I could with my arms and my torso. Within weeks, they became the best attended class in the gym. Then I called the VA Hospital and asked if I could volunteer my services to the disabled veterans, to get them exercising in their chairs and giving them a new sense of their bodies, not only how they felt but what they could do with what they had. First class, twenty guys. Next class, thirty. And another class is scheduled to start in two weeks.

"I didn't know what to do with my arms, but I knew what to do with my mind. I was exercising through my knowledge, and I used my experience to communicate change."

Ann paused and said, "Then one day, a client I'd trained for years came over to me and said, 'Ann, I like you better now.' And, I immediately felt that he was patronizing me, trying to make me feel better or something. He must have seen my expression, and he said, 'What I mean is this: You care. You know what it's like to be me, I guess.'

"When I asked him what he meant by that, he said, 'Ann, sometimes I struggle to just get on a treadmill, lift a weight or, for that matter, show up to the appointment with you. But when I saw what you've gone through, how you came back and still showed up, still taught class, still gave instruction, I couldn't ever let you down. And then, when I saw you be more involved with me, asking me about my life and really showing interest in not just my goals in the gym, but my life in general, I thought that this is what I'd always wanted in a trainer. Somebody who really got me as a person. I guess what I mean is, you exercise your example in front of me, and in front of all the rest of us, too.'

"And then he said something that I'll always remember. 'Ann, don't take this wrong, but I think for the first time since I've been coming, I've seen you walk the walk.'

"So, yeah, I cried at that one," Ann said, "Exercise is everything. And I'm walking a better walk."

How it Works

Go to bed earlier. About a half hour. Get up earlier. About a half hour.

Use this extra time to exercise. Depending on your current level of fitness, it could be anything from a simple walk to training for a marathon, or even serious weight training.

For those beginning to exercise, start slowly. Set forth on a walk. That's how it begins. Start with twenty minutes a day. Yes, every day. A twenty minute walk–ten minutes out, ten minutes back.

It is a little better to exercise in the morning. Outside of the neurological benefits of the morning walk–particularly how it positively affects your mood–you get it out of the way. Most of us postpone exercise. We'll absolutely promise ourselves to exercise as soon as we get home in the evening, and then three days pass. Then we really commit to really, really do it this time and . . . you get the drift.

Walk in the morning. Ten minute out, ten minutes back. Getting by on as little as possible works for us. I heard a couple of people advocate doing this with a partner. We support that, although when you're partner's sick, busy, or oversleeps, it gives you an excuse to go back to bed. It's helpful to set an independent course on this whole exercise thing. The big habit is to change your sleep and to just get outside.

We have to. This isn't conjecture. The more we exercise, the better we feel, the better our bodies respond, and the faster we recover. When you exercise, all the rest of your concerns fade. When that happens, your heart has a little more room to move.

Move the body, and the heart will thrive. Your mood improves, and your ability and desire for compassion and love become second nature.

Get moving.

Why this is Important

Your time on earth is linked to your body. Your body can either be the source of vitality and energy or a limit to your personal freedom. It is up to you. Luckily, your body can be changed through the daily practice of a healthy diet and exercise routine. By keeping your body in good health, you tap into your physical source of vitality and energy.

Exercise, of course, improves your physical body by lowering body fat and increasing muscle, which increases overall health and energy. Scientists for decades have empirically proven that "training stimulates endorphins, neurotransmitters, and neurotropic growth factors your brain thrives on, making you feel good during and immediately following training. Scientists are now discovering long-term positive effects of regular strength training: it makes your neurons more robust while improving blood flow, oxygen and nutrients to your brain. Michael Craig Miller, M.D., editor-in-chief of the Harvard Mental Health Letter, summarizes what scientists have been uncovering for several decades, regular training 'improves your mood, decreases anxiety, improves sleep and resilience in the face of stress and raises self-esteem.' He adds that exercise itself makes for a 'pretty good antidepressant too, equal to drugs or psychotherapy in some studies.' "[119]

Not only can exercising make you feel physically and emotionally better, but research shows that a healthy diet and exercise can slow or even reverse the effects of aging.

[119] Phillips, Shawn, and Pete Williams. Strength for Life: The Fitness Plan for the Best of Your Life. New York: Ballantine Books, 2008. Print. pg 26

KEY 5

KEY FIVE: KNOW YOUR MUSIC

This list would not be complete without including listening to music as a basic step to access your heart.

Music helps us begin to define our identity. As a child, the music we hear from the radio, in church, and from our parents and siblings sets in motion our most basic recognition of what is available to our ears. From these references, even without us knowing about it, we start to hear things artistically. Our listening sharpens as we realize that certain types of songs stir our feelings of sentiment, loss, passion, and even anger. We literally feel the music pulse through our bodies. It is neurological excitement, firing all the electrical impulses throughout our being and engaging us in sweeps of emotion. We literally move our body and soul to Music. We can't help it. Music can move us into battle, make us march for a cause, rest our weary heart, and rock a child to sleep. Music generates the energy of life.

It is common that our musical references come from our youth, a time when we were most impressionable and felt things most deeply. As we grow, we become more selective about what we listen to, what resonates with who we are. Peer relationships affect our taste in music, as does popular culture. We can hear meaningful songs in our heads, especially ones we associate with more significant points in our lives. We can remember what songs were playing during the times of transition, loss, and events of change, as well as times of celebration. It is common for holidays and ceremonies to be deeply associated with music, and the meaning behind each note adds a texture and depth to the event.

And, with special brilliance, music is most often associated with love.

We remember the songs we heard when we found love, lost love, and searched for love. We heard the music that sent us soaring in joy and offered solace in heartbreak. Songs of love surround our senses and draw us back into our memory. We feel profound emotion when the right song brings us back to a time when we were young and happy, seeing love reflected back to us from another's eyes. Our hearts are drawn to the depth and magic that music stirs within us. We each have our own unique and beautiful soundtrack. Music, through the feelings it stirs and the emotions it brings forth, helps us define who we are and how we feel about ourselves.

<u>A Story from the Heart</u>

Anita was an orderly in a nursing home on the south side of Chicago.

"The orderlies are the ones that spend the most time with the clients," Anita said. "The nurses have to make their rounds, but the orderlies get them dressed, take them to the bathroom, get them in their wheelchairs or walkers, and prepare them for the day. They get their food to them, three times a day, and a snack in the evening.

"We're their friends. We become their family. And they become family to us, too."

Anita works the mornings. She has had the 6am to 3pm shift for years. I'm listening to her as she's getting patients ready for the morning routine. "I've seen so many people. And the conversations are always so bright. With most, even with those with some dementia, you just have to bring them back to a familiar point, and they follow your lead. You can talk about school, their career, or a family member, and a little light comes into their eyes. You see the ways that they remember. It's subtle, but their face tells you that their mind is where you've lead them, and you can always hear about that part of their life if you listen."

Anita folds the sheets on the end of a patient's bed. "It takes about a half hour, maybe forty five minutes, to get a patient ready for the day. And conversation just takes place. I'm a talker and I sing. I'll ask them things or, if they don't feel like talking, I'll hum a while or sing a little, and sometimes they come around. If I really want to hear about their day–and I'm a little pushy like that–then I rattle off questions about anything I can think of. I can bore them to tears with the best of them!" Anita let out a big belly laugh.

"And, sometimes, it's not a story or anything that brings them out. One guy surprised the heck out of me. Made me change the way I communicated with the patients."

Anita made a reference to a video I hadn't seen. "You remember that video about a guy named Henry, the nearly non communicative Alzheimer's patient who, when he heard a song, all of a sudden just came to life? Somebody played him a song he recognized, one that had meaning to him, and his face just about jumped off his head." Anita said, letting go another one of those laughs. "I mean, you could tell how it woke him up.

"Well, that happened to me." Anita kept making the beds and said, "One of the things this place does is, when they admit somebody as a resident, they get a history of just about everything. The social workers do an exhaustive search. What did they like to do? What do they read? What do they like to listen to? I mean," she said, tucking in a blanket, "it's a ton of information.

"I told you that, when somebody just doesn't feel like talking, I hum or sing a little under my breath. Well, every third day, we rotate our work in the facility. The A wing is where the dementia and Alzheimer's patients live. Some are slightly impaired, and some folks just live in their own little world.

"One morning I was assigned to one of my favorite patients. Amos had early onset dementia. Wasn't that old, maybe about 70, 71 at the time. Amos was one of those folks that just lived in his own world.

Always a smile, so pleasant, never complained. Just looked at me as if I was someone close to him. Such a loving expression on his face. He seemed like such a gentle man.

"But he didn't speak outside of 'hello' and 'thank you.' You could ask him how he was doing, and he'd just smile. Ask him if he'd like French fries or baked potato, and he'd do the same.

"I had a few extra minutes, and I looked through his portfolio. Turned out he grew up in Detroit, not far from Hitsville, USA. You know what that is?"

"That was the old Motown recording studio?"

"Correct," she said. "And that morning, I just felt like singing. Turned out, my husband and I had a huge fight and I was about this close to throwing him out in the street." Anita started wiping down the bathroom mirror. "We've been married thirty four years. This happens about two or three times a week," and Anita just howled with laughter.

"So this song was on my mind. Ever heard of 'Ain't Too Proud to Beg' by the Temptations?" I said I had.

"Well, check this out: When I went into Amos' room that day, I had that song on my mind. I was still mad at my husband, but he was apologizing before I went to work, so I was simmering down. And that song came to mind. So, with Amos, since he just kind of smiles a lot and doesn't really carry on a conversation, I started singing the first verse of that song: 'I know you want to leave me . . .'

"And," Anita said, her eyes getting a little bigger, "before I could get to the next verse, I hear this little voice from behind me sing, '. . . but I refuse to let you go.'

"Ha!" Anita let out a yelp and said, "It was Amos! I almost had a stroke right there! I've got my hand over my chest and I'm calling to my friend next door. I'm waving her in the room like I'm pulling a rope, and she stops at the door. I tell her to just stand there, be quiet and watch this. I sing, 'If I had to beg and plead for my sympathy . . .' and then I stop.

"And Amos sings, 'I don't mind, 'cause you mean that much to me.' And with tears coming down my eyes, I lean over and nearly touch Amos with my nose, and we both sing, 'Ain't too proud to beg, sweet darlin', please don't leave me, don't you go. Ain't too proud to plead, baby, baby, please don't leave me, don't you go.'

"I hugged that man so hard I thought I was going to kill him!" Anita said, laughing with tears in her eyes.

"But check this out: I had to know this man's music to reach him. The orderlies ended up doing this with all the patients, too. I mean, some of us were trying to sing Opera, Pat Boone, stuff we never in a million years would have sung. But it lit a light inside these folks. Not everybody, but enough so that we just kept doing it.

"Once we knew the music that touched their hearts, they came alive. The music that meant something to them when they were young means just as much today. It brought them back to another time. Now," Anita said, "the songs I sing to them mean something new to me. It reminds me of who they are, and makes me think of the life they lived. It brings me closer to them.

"I know the music that means something to me," Anita said, "and I love to share that with my friends and family. But finding the way to a person's heart is through their music. And, let me tell you, this place is full of song every single day. The music puts a smile on their faces and rekindles the meaning of life inside every one of them. And, I don't know if you notice, but I'm a pretty good singer, don't you think?" she said.

"You sing beautifully." I said.

"Yeah," she said, "I'm pretty sure Amos would agree."

How it Works

I refer to my friend, Hal Lingerman, in his book, The Healing Energies of Music for a succinct and balanced explanation:

"Music never stands still. Each note and phrase plays a part in building a continuously shifting array of shapes, colors, and consistencies which the total piece is vibrating into the atmosphere and the listener's consciousness." He goes on to say, "The more reverently and expectantly you can experience a piece of music, the more its mysterious beauty and hidden essences will open to you, revealing far greater depth and power."

Music stands alone in its ability to reach that deeply into our lives, literally changing our perspectives and experiences. When we associate a meeting, an event, a celebration, or a transition with music, we assign it a place in our lives. So when we hear that song, that associated event comes to us again. Our memories bring us to the place and time when that song was playing. It is the music that anchors our associative experience. It is within these experiences that the events give way to memories, and our memories come back to life. Music is as quick and direct a route to our emotional life as any other method we have.

Be mindful, therefore, of the power of music, in its strength and its gentleness. Pick music that stirs your essence towards goodness and peace, and those songs that put a smile on your face and movement in your shoes. Let your music be a record of all that is good in your life; moreover, may your music be a symbol of all the good that is within you.

Why this is Important

Although music is simply an organized collection of sounds, there is something magical about it. Nietzsche says, "Without music, life would be a mistake."[120] No matter which culture and which historical period, music has been a part of the human experience. In studies conducted by neuroscientists Dr. Robert J. Zatorre and Dr. Valorie N. Salimpoor, "when pleasurable music is heard, dopamine is released in the striatum — an ancient part of the brain found in other vertebrates as well — which is known to respond to naturally rewarding stimuli like food and sex and which is artificially targeted by drugs like cocaine and amphetamine."[121] This quote agrees with the statement made by Ludwig van Beethoven: "Music is the mediator between the spiritual and the sensual life."[122] Music is so essential to humanity that NASA scientists included a gold record entitled Music from Earth on Voyager 1, the interstellar space probe intended to introduce humanity to intelligent extraterrestrial life.

Beyond simple pleasure, music has a healing effect. As the physician Oliver Sacks says, "I regard music therapy as a tool of great power in many neurological disorders -- Parkinson's and Alzheimer's -- because of its unique capacity to organize or reorganize cerebral function when it has been damaged."[123] Music is therapeutic.

Jazz musician Charlie Parker says "music is your own experience, your thoughts, your wisdom."[124] There is truth in music. It can be a comfort when you are down, it can be motivational, it can create enthusiasm. A familiar song can transport a person to another place or time, to another emotional state. Allow music to open your heart.

---

[120] Nietzsche, Friedrich

[121] http://www.nytimes.com/2013/06/09/opinion/sunday/why-music-makes-our-brain-sing.html?_r=1&

[122] Beethoven, Ludwig van

[123] St, James J. When I Sit Down to Play: A Guide to Fulfilling Your Dream of Playing the Piano and Keyboard. New York, NY: Kensington Books, 2000. Print. pg 14

[124] Parker, Charlie

KEY 6

KEY SIX: DANCE

Dance is laughter for the body–a physical expression of happiness if there ever was one. Dancing takes the music in your heart and lets it travel all over your body. If any human action blares the exhilaration and excitement of life, it is dancing.

And in spite of its beauty and power, there's this one small thing about dancing: When we attempt to put one foot in front of another, with any consistent form or style, we're all bad at it. All of us. OK, maybe about five percent of us can dance with any predictable order. And if you can, you're probably female. Or you've had a ton of practice. The rest of us, not so much.

But that's OK. Dancing is a very individual, and very personal, sharing of your spiritual energy and internal happiness. So, the first thing we want to talk about is form. Most of us are bad at it, so don't worry about form when you dance. The only form worth having is the one that makes you feel best. One of my friends was dancing down the stairs and fell. Well, to the untrained eye, he fell. He said it was his "interpretive" dance of how he felt about his stairs.

The point is, if you call it dancing, it's dancing.

There is also no uniform or outfit that is more or less appropriate for this endeavor, but we feel that most of your dancing should be in your underwear or pajamas. There should be dancing when you get out of bed and into the bathroom. Make those your first dance steps. Then, take your next steps when you're flying around the kitchen, when you get out of your car, and when you come home from work. We would suggest that you dance on your way to work as well, although in consideration of your co-workers who may not have gotten on the dancing train, you may want to keep your steps a little less pronounced than, say, if you were dancing for the dog.

If you dance with your hands flailing, feet all over the place, and your butt out, wiggling to your neighbors through your window, you're dancing. If you dance with your arms straight to your side, head down, bobbing up and down on the balls of your feet, that's dancing, too. There is no form or fashion. As long as you're moving, and it's your moves, it's dancing.

A Story from the Heart

Randy is a dance instructor. Sixty two years old, he was born in the Dominican Republic and came to Illinois when he was a baby. He has the body of a thirty year old.

Recently, he noticed a change in the perception of dance, and he set out to do something about it.

"I've taught people how to do salsa, swing, tango, and hip hop," he said, sipping on iced tea in his studio above Michigan Avenue in downtown Chicago, "I've been a dance teacher since I was twenty years old."

Taking another sip of iced tea, Randy walked across the floor of his studio and sat down in his office. "When I first learned to dance, I was a little guy. Maybe four or five, I first remember dancing in the kitchen of my aunt's house, just down the street from where we lived. We had music on in that house all the time, and I remember seeing people moving. Didn't know what they were doing, but I thought I'd do it, too. They just seemed so happy.

"And at such a young age, I discovered that his is what dancing is all about. You hear the music, then feel it's spiritual, visceral effects, then you move.

"That was my first introduction to dance. And I've been doing it ever since.

"But, dance is so much more than that. To me, when people try to define dance, they first associate it with the body and then music, which is expected, but it's limiting. I mean, check this out: we use metaphors all the time about how the 'wind dances' or the 'light dances,' with no reference to 'body' or 'music,' only the implied wildness and lightness of its motion. You hear things like 'her fingers danced across the keyboard,' or 'the words danced across the page.' Dance, in this sense, means an effortlessness, with a certain arc of eloquence, but a happy, delightful air to it. This is dance. It's this arc, this air, you know?

"Now, remember, I'm a teacher. Which means I have students. And, I have these students at the end of their work day. Let me ask you something. How do you feel after a long day at work? If you said, 'I feel like dancing,' you'd be lying where you're sitting," Randy said, laughing.

"So, these people wanted to get in, know the steps, and get out so they could practice these steps on the dance floor Saturday night. OK, that's what they want, that's fine, but that's not dancing.

"Week after week of 'just show me the steps,' and I'd had it. I thought, 'I'm a dance teacher, and they are missing the energy and spirit that dance is all about.'

"So I tried something, and it's now a required course for every one of my students. They watch a group of experts in the field. Before they get any of these steps down, they are going to be shown the essence of dance.

"I had to enlist the help of some friends of mine, and right down the hall there's this class of, what I would call, experts in the field of dance. The expert class is right after theirs and, after their second class, they are going to stay a half hour later. When I put this idea into practice, I asked my experts and they said they would be thrilled to share their experience.

"Now, just before I started the next class, I said, 'tonight, before I begin the music, I am going to bring in the class of experts to show you exactly what I am looking for in a student. They will demonstrate with precision the spirit and joy within the context of each style of music. You will be asked to dance with them, in a group and with a partner, in order to demonstrate your ability to access your spirit.'

"Well," Randy said, rolling his eyes, "they had this expression of true disdain on their face. I stood there for a second, and I went down the hall, and I asked the experts to join me.

"And when the experts walked into the room, the faces of the students just lit up." Randy sipped his iced tea again and said, "See, the experts are five and six year old ballet students. They were told that they get to dance with the grownups if they're very good.

"I lined up the kids in a single file row. When I put on the CD, I said to the students, 'I want you to watch how the experts dance to the music, then I want you to copy each one of them exactly. I want you to copy their arm movements, their body motions, and particularly the expressions on their faces.'

"Well, as soon as the little ones heard the music, they just went at it. Just arms and feet and smiles all over the place. Then, so I could be heard over the music, I shouted, 'Now dance exactly like the experts!'

"All these adults started flailing away. Hands, arms, feet going in fifty different directions. And their expressions went from these awful, depressed faces to ones of delight. Smiles and laughter everywhere!

"I stopped the music and said, 'You see how this felt? You see how your self-consciousness, your need for precision, your expectations of your dancing just disappeared? This is how you dance. This is what dance is all about.'

"From that point on, they got it. They had more fun. They understood the lightness, the air, and the happiness I felt when I first listened to music at my aunt's house. They had a better time. They really enjoyed the class.

"And, I'll tell you this," Randy said, "in the end, they were really good dancers, in the best sense of the word."

How it Works

Dance requires a small change in your mindset. We don't dance if we're going to be observed, largely because we're so unaccustomed to doing it. That is entirely normal. We will always feel a little self-conscious doing something new in front of somebody else. Dancing doesn't have to be a public display.

However, if you can muster up the courage to dance in public, it is a freeing experience. Nobody is thinking of you or watching you; they are thinking of and watching themselves. They are as self-conscious as you are. Dancing outside of your comfort zone is giving your body permission to laugh with others doing the same thing, a little like a physical comedy club.

Dancing should be a daily event, something you do wherever and whenever you get the chance. In private is fine, but if you have a spouse, children, or especially pets, fire out a few moves for them when you enter a room.

Dance when you're happy. Dance when you're sad. Particularly then, because after a couple of minutes of dancing when you're sad, you'll be happy again. Dancing is a great antidepressant. It releases tension and expresses your feelings. It keeps the beat in your head and brings out the song in your heart.

Dancing helps you know who you really are again. You strip away so much pretense and ego. You allow yourself to be silly and courageous at the same time, expressing yourself with your whole body rather than words or deeds. Dancing literally brings a different dimension to letting yourself and the world know who you are.

Start Dancing. Begin Now.

And one, two, three, and one, two, three . . .

Why this is Important

For some, dancing is easy and fun, and for others, it is an anxiety-producing embarrassment. The beat is intuitive to some, yet elusive to others. Dancing can tap a person into the flow state; the dancer becomes one with the music and loses themselves in physical action, which reduces stress. Because dancing can be done as an individual, couple, or with a group, it can help strengthen relationships, or create new ones.

Here's stuff you already know, but it's worth repeating so you'll remember: Dancing as cardiovascular exercise has many physical benefits, helping the heart and overall fitness. Its physical activity burns calories, helping in weight loss. Dancing also helps a person stay flexible, and keeps their joints and muscles healthy. Dancing helps people learn to control their body, giving them better coordination, balance, and posture.

Dancing, because it uses the whole body, engages both hemispheres of the brain, increasing brain activity, and thereby increasing the complexity of neuronal synapses. Harvard Medical School psychiatrist Dr. Joseph Coyle says, "The cerebral cortex and hippocampus, which are critical to these activities, are remarkably plastic, and they rewire themselves based upon their use."[125] Dancing makes you smarter and helps your mind stay active.

[125] http://socialdance.stanford.edu/syllabi/smarter.htm

KEY 7

KEY SEVEN: THE RED NOSE

This works like a charm. It is as good as exercise and caffeine first thing in the morning.

Find yourself a red nose. They are usually made out of foam. The best places to get them are at toy stores, costume shops or, depending on the season, stores that are devoted to Halloween.

Put it on your face–where your nose is, duh–for a trial run. Now look into the mirror.

You're smiling. Admit it.

A red nose on the middle of your face makes us smile when we see ourselves in the mirror. We do the same thing when we see somebody else wearing a red nose, too: We break out in a smile.

A red nose is a universal symbol for humor. You can wear this in almost any part of the world and you will be recognized for your ability to have fun. You will be approached with the expectation of making somebody laugh. Since 1985, there has even been a Red Nose Day in Great Britain when people do "fun or funny things" to raise money for charity. Note that doing "fun or funny things" is associated with the red nose. Might want to make a mental note of that . . .

You wear one of these, you're expected to get a little silly. People are known to even make faces from time to time. You see one of these on someone else and, at the very least, you'll have a response. You see one of these in the middle of your face and you're going to have a bigger response, and we're betting the farm that the response is going to be positive.

This is foolproof. You see one on your face and you're going to smile.

And when you put this on first thing in the morning, you're guaranteed to begin your day happier than you were without it.

A Story from the Heart

I have been an advocate of wearing a red nose for most of my adult life. And when I met Mike, a friend, colleague, and another red nose advocate, for lunch, he relayed this story to me about his experience with the magic of the red nose.

"So I'm driving to work on a Saturday, and I'm listening to an interview with a guy named Moshe Cohen. He is a clown with the group Clowns Without Borders. He was talking about how he was entertaining children in a Nepalese refugee camp. He said that as he was driving around the town, he saw a group of children standing by the side of the road, motionless, watching his car go by. As the car slowed, he saw the children looking at him. He put on the red nose that he kept in his pocket for such occasions, and looked back at the children. With that, the children erupted, yelled 'Jōkara,' –which means 'Clown'–then leapt toward the car, laughing and chasing him.

"Over the years, I have always had a clown nose in my office. Usually I, like you, bring it out when a crying child needs comforting, or when the person sitting in front of me is suffering from terminal seriousness and needs to lighten their demeanor. And I use it in one particular situation more than any other: I put it on myself when I'm looking in the mirror, especially when I feel I need a lift, which is just about every other day.

"I'll give you an example of how profound the effect can be. I had a woman who was absolutely down. She didn't have a clinical depression; she had more of a chronic negative attitude. Yet, she ostensibly came to me to correct these feelings, to adjust that attitude, meanwhile fighting like all get out to hold on to these familiar negative feelings.

"So I gave her a challenge. I told her about my use of my red nose for both myself and my clients. I told her that, sometime in the next twenty-four hours, she had to wear a red nose, no matter where she was or what she was doing, for three hours straight. And, in order to give her some motivation, I told her that I would do the same. No matter what, no matter what I was doing, I would wear a red nose at the same time, for the same three hours, that she was wearing hers.

"She decided that she'd wear her nose from the hours of 6 to 9 pm that evening. She said that she was going to be at home and that she was going to watch TV and try not to look into any mirrors during that time. Fine. Three hours was all I asked, and she didn't seem to get the point of the exercise, but a deal is a deal.

"Well, at the same time she was going to wear the red nose, I was scheduled to attend a baseball game with a friend of mine.

"I explained to my friend, who thinks that I'm a little strange anyway, that I had to wear the nose to the ballgame and keep it on probably through the seventh inning. His only comment was, 'Good luck drinking a beer with that thing on your face.'

"The game started at 7 o'clock. I walked through the turnstile at 6:30, and the woman who took my ticket smiled at me. I got to the aisle, and the usher who escorted me to my seat smiled. I sat down, and the woman sitting next to me smiled.

"It could have been that they all thought I absolutely lost my mind. But the thing is, at that time it didn't matter. I was doing this to hold up an agreement, and I knew that this woman was in her living room watching TV with a red nose on her face.

"Now about that woman watching TV. What I didn't know what that she was watching baseball. The same game that I attended. The woman was watching my baseball game on TV.

"And something wonderful was about to happen.

"In the middle of the third inning, the cameraman turned his television camera toward me, and I saw the right light on the top of his lens get bright. And there I was on TV. Wearing my red nose. At the baseball game. In front of God and everybody. Including the woman at home wearing her red nose, in her home, watching the baseball game!

"She saw me. And the minute I saw that camera, I was thinking of her.

"Well, the next day, she called me. She said that when I was on TV the baseball announcer commented, 'Well, it looks like that guy is having a good time.' She said that when she heard that, she laughed so hard she almost wet her pants.

"She said she got up and immediately looked at herself in the mirror. When she saw her image, she laughed some more.

"She came back for one more session, mostly to tell me that she didn't need therapy anymore, that if she got a little too upset or serious or down, she would put on her red nose and look into the mirror. And she wouldn't feel so bad. Over the weeks, she'd call once in a while to check in. She says that, when she'd down, she wears that red nose and it brightens her spirits. The nose always brightens her spirits. And, she said, sometimes when she wears that nose, she can't help but think of me on TV at the ball game. She says that makes her laugh, too."

Mike went up to pay for the coffee and wanted to pay with a check. When the waitress asked for his ID, Mike did something I've seen him do often. He reached into his wallet, handed her his ID and with the other hand, put on his red nose.

But, on his ID, there's a little piece of foam covering his nose. On his driver's license, he has a piece of red foam glued over his nose.

The waitress looked down at the license, saw the red foam, and looked back up at Mike. When she saw that he now had a red nose on his face, she burst out laughing.

He looked over at me, smiled, and said, "Gets them every time."

How it Works

The red nose interrupts your conception of who you are. It changes your face so distinctly, but in such a colorful and cartoonish way, that you can't help but smile.

is the timing is critical, and if you want the biggest impact, it's imperative to put this on when you first start your day, before you put on your makeup or begin to shave.

But whenever you can manage it, put on your nose. And make sure you're looking directly at yourself in the mirror for ten seconds.

What you'll find is a lightening of your spirit, even a little. You can put on the nose with the thought of "OK, I'm going to do this, but I hate mornings, I haven't had coffee, and I really think this is stupid" and it doesn't matter.

When you put it on, and really look at your face, you're going to smile.

The red nose symbolizes lightness and ease. There is a gentleness and, probably most importantly, a disarming of your crabbiness when you see that nose on your face. Watch your expressions change when you have this red piece of foam highlighting your eyes and your mouth.

And we want to be clear on this: the red nose exercise is a private endeavor. This is something for your purposes only. The person that is to be entertained, that is to have spirits lifted, their eyes widened, and their face smiling broadly, is you. We are asking you to do this for your benefit first.

We ask this because the red nose is often associated with entertainment. And this exercise is not for show. Many of you would no more wear a Styrofoam nose than you would a pair of antlers to the grocery store. We are not asking, at first, you to share this with anyone.

We just know that this works. And there is no need for public displays of juggling, summersaults, or riding around in a little car.

Why this is Important

The whole point of wearing The Red Nose is to force you take yourself less seriously. That's it. Many cognitive behavioral therapy strategies accomplish the same result. But it can be as simple as putting a red nose on your face. This changes your perception and lightens your heart. Joseph Campbell says, "as you proceed through life, following your own path, birds will shit on you. Don't bother to brush it off. Getting a comedic view of your situation gives you spiritual distance. Having a sense of humor saves you."[126] So often we get caught up in our daily grind, our task list, our obligations, that we go from one thing to the next without taking a breather. Bad things inevitably happen; having a light heart decreases the mental resistance to unfavorable situations.

Putting on the nose may seem weird; it may seem corny. We ask you to think about it in the sense of a physical reminder to lighten up, to live from the heart. Stop for a second and find the spirit of life within the present moment. As Alan Watts says, "Man suffers only because he takes seriously what the gods made for fun."[127] Life is not meant to be taken so seriously.

Lighten up! Dr. Seuss says, "Nonsense wakes up the brain cells. And it helps develop a sense of humor, which is awfully

---

[126] Campbell, Joseph, and Diane K. Osbon. A Joseph Campbell Companion: Reflections on the Art of Living. New York, NY: HarperCollins, 1991. Print.

[127] Watts, Alan. Become What You Are. Boston: Shambhala, 2003. Print. pg 29

important in this day and age. Humor has a tremendous place in this sordid world. It's more than just a matter of laughing. If you can see things out of whack, then you can see how things can be in whack."[128] Put on a red nose; release your heart and your mind from the chains of stress.

[128] Nel, Philip. Dr. Seuss: American Icon. New York: Continuum, 2004. Print. pg 38

REFERENCES

Chapter 1
The Heart's Foundation

1. Trungpa, Chögyam, and Carolyn R. Gimian. Ocean of Dharma: The Everyday Wisdom of Chögyam Trungpa. Boston: Shambhala, 2008. Print. pg 151

2. Nisargadatta, Frydman, M., & Dikshit, S. S. (2012). I am that: Talks with Sri Nisargadatta Maharaj. Durham, N.C: Acorn Press.

3. Tolle, Eckhart. The Power of Now: A Guide to Spiritual Enlightenment. Novato, Calif: New World Library, 1999. Print. pg 90

4. Leonard, George. Mastery: The Keys to Success and Long-Term Fulfillment. New York: Plume, 1992. Print.

5. Tzu, Sun. Sun Tzu: The Art of War. S.l.: Pax Librorum Pub. H, 2009. Print.

6. Robbins, Tony. RPM

7. Osho, The Book of Understanding: Creating Your Own Path to Freedom. New York: Harmony Books, 2006. Print. pg 85

8. Robbins, Tony

9. Walsch, Neale D. Conversations with God: An Uncommon Dialogue. New York: G.P. Putnam's Sons, 1996. Print. pg 177

10. Holden, Robert. Happiness Now!: Timeless Wisdom for Feeling Good Fast. Carlsbad, Calif: Hay House, Inc, 2007. Print. pg 92

11. Buscaglia, Leo F. Love. Thorofare, N.J: Charles B. Slack, 1972. Print. pg 101

12. Branden, Nathaniel. The Six Pillars of Self-Esteem. New York, N.Y: Bantam, 1994. Print. pg 103

13. Branden, Nathaniel. The Six Pillars of Self-Esteem. New York, N.Y: Bantam, 1994. Print.

14. Emerson, Ralph W. Self-reliance. Seattle, WA: Domino Project/Amazon.com, 2011. Print.

15. Rand, Ayn. The Fountainhead. New York: Plume, 2005. Print. Chapter X

16. Merzel, Dennis G. Big Mind, Big Heart: Finding Your Way. Salt Lake City, Utah: Big Mind Pub, 2007. Print.

17. Einstein, Albert

18. De, Mello A, and J F. Stroud. Awareness. Collins Fount, 1990. Print. pg 74

19. Emerson, Ralph W, and Brooks Atkinson. The Essential Writings of Ralph Waldo Emerson. New York: Modern Library, 2000. Print.

20. Marcus, Aurelius, Charles R. Haines, and Aurelius Marcus. Marcus Aurelius. Cambridge, Mass: Harvard University Press, 2003. Print.

21. Deida, David. The Way of the Superior Man: A Spiritual Guide to Mastering the Challenges of Women, Work, and Sexual Desire. Boulder, CO: Sounds True, 2004. Print.

22. Bodhi, . The Noble Eightfold Path: Way to the End of Suffering. Chicago: Pariyatti Publishing, 2011. Internet resource. pg 80

23. Surya, Das. Buddha Is As Buddha Does: The Ten Original Practices for Enlightened Living. New York, NY: HarperSanFrancisco, 2007. Print. pg pg. 132-3

24. Csikszentmihalyi, Mihaly. Flow: The Psychology of Optimal Experience. New York: Harper & Row, 1990. Print.

25. http://www.psychologytoday.com/articles/200105/the-science-meditation

26. Brown, Daniel P. Pointing Out the Great Way: The Stages of Meditation in the Mahāmudrā Tradition. Boston: Wisdom Publications, 2006. Print.

Chapter 2
Development of the Heart's Presence

27. Dalai Lama and Howard C. Cutler. The Art of Happiness: A Handbook for Living. New York: Riverhead Books, 1998. Print. pg 13

28 De, Mello A. The Way to Love: Meditations for Life. New York: Image, 2012. Print. pg 4

29. Ben-Shahar, Tal. Happier: Learn the Secrets to Daily Joy and Lasting Fulfillment. New York: McGraw-Hill, 2007. Print. pg 7

30. Shimoff, Marci, and Carol Kline. Happy for No Reason: 7 Steps to Being Happy from the Inside Out. New York: Free Press, 2008. Print. pg. 89

31. Lyubomirsky, Sonja. The How of Happiness: A Scientific Approach to Getting the Life You Want. New York: Penguin Press, 2008. Print. pg 26

32. Lyubomirsky, Sonja. The How of Happiness: A Scientific Approach to Getting the Life You Want. New York: Penguin Press, 2008. Print. pg 110

33. Csikszentmihalyi, Mihaly. Flow: The Psychology of Optimal Experience. New York: Harper & Row, 1990. Print. pg 24

34. Seligman, Martin E. P. Learned Optimism: How to Change Your Mind and Your Life. New York: Vintage Books, 2006. Print. end of chapter 12

35. Covey, Stephen R. The 7 Habits of Highly Effective People: Powerful Lessons in Personal Change. , 2013. Print. Pg 70

36. Greene, Robert, and Joost Elffers. The 48 Laws of Power. New York: Viking, 1998. Print.

37. Greene, Robert, and Joost Elffers. The 48 Laws of Power. New York: Viking, 1998. Print.

38. Dalai Lama and Howard C. Cutler. The Art of Happiness: A Handbook for Living. New York: Riverhead Books, 1998. Print.pg 26

39. Dalai Lama and Howard C. Cutler. The Art of Happiness: A Handbook for Living. New York: Riverhead Books, 1998. Print.pg 26

40. Roosevelt, Franklin D.

41. Frankl, Viktor E. Man's Search for Meaning. Boston: Beacon Press, 2006. Print.

42. Frankl, Viktor E. Man's Search for Meaning. Boston: Beacon Press, 2006. Print.

43. Tolle, Eckhart. The Power of Now: A Guide to Spiritual Enlightenment. Novato, Calif: New World Library, 1999. Print. pg 220

44. Ralston, Aron. 127 Hours: Between a Rock and a Hard Place. New York, NY: Atria Paperback, 2010. Print. Pg 280

45. Millman, Dan, and Dan Millman. Body Mind Mastery: Creating Success in Sport and Life. Novato, Calif: New World Library, 1999. Print.

46 Dalai Lama

47. Lyubomirsky, Sonja. The How of Happiness: A Scientific Approach to Getting the Life You Want. New York: Penguin Press, 2008. Print.

48. Would You Be Happier If You Were Richer? A Focusing Illusion Daniel Kahneman, Alan B. Krueger, David Schkade, Norbert Schwarz, and Arthur A. Stone Science 30 June 2006: 312 (5782), 1908-1910. [DOI:10.1126/science.1129688]

49. Would You Be Happier If You Were Richer? A Focusing Illusion Daniel Kahneman, Alan B. Krueger, David Schkade, Norbert Schwarz, and Arthur A. Stone Science 30 June 2006: 312 (5782), 1908-1910. [DOI:10.1126/science.1129688]

50. Niv Bible. London: Hodder & Stoughton Ltd, 2007. Print. James 1:2-3

51. Dyer, Wayne W. Change Your Thoughts, Change Your Life: Living the Wisdom of the Tao. Carlsbad, Calif: Hay House, 2007. Print.

52. Merzel, Dennis G. Big Mind, Big Heart: Finding Your Way. Salt Lake City, Utah: Big Mind Pub, 2007. Print.

53. Socrates

54. Chödrön, Pema. The Places That Scare You: A Guide to Fearlessness in Difficult Times. Boston: Shambhala, 2001. Print.

55. Wilber, Ken. Grace and Grit: Spirituality and Healing in the Life and Death of Treya Killam Wilber. Boston: Shambhala, 1991. Print. Pg 159

56. Tolle, Eckhart. The Power of Now: A Guide to Spiritual Enlightenment. Novato, Calif: New World Library, 1999. Print.pg 37

57. Pattakos, Alex. Prisoners of Our Thoughts: Viktor Frankl's Principles for Discovering Meaning in Life at Work. San Francisco, Calif: Berrett-Koehler, 2010. Print. pg 4

58. Wilber, Ken. Grace and Grit: Spirituality and Healing in the Life and Death of Treya Killam Wilber. Boston: Shambhala, 1991. Print. Pg 159

59. Nhất, Hạnh. Teachings on Love. Berkeley, Calif: Parallax Press, 1997. Print. Pg 29

60. Aristotle

61. Mondo Zen Training Manual
http://www.mondozen.org/ literature 118189/Mondo Zen Training Manual for eReaders

62. Campbell, Joseph, and David Kudler. Pathways to Bliss: Mythology and Personal Transformation. Novato, Calif: New World Library, 2004. Print. xxx

63. Vogler, Christopher. The Writer's Journey: Mythic Structure for Writers. Studio City, CA: Michael Wiese Productions, 2007. Print.

64. Schwartz, David J. The Magic of Thinking Big. New York: Simon & Schuster, 1987. Print. pg 50

65. Robbins, Anthony. Awaken the Giant Within: How to Take Immediate Control of Your Mental, Emotional, Physical & Financial Destiny. New York, N.Y: Summit Books, 1991. Print. Pg 246-7

66. Robbins, Anthony. Awaken the Giant Within: How to Take Immediate Control of Your Mental, Emotional, Physical & Financial Destiny. New York, N.Y: Summit Books, 1991. Print. Pg 246-7

Chapter 3
Live the Spirit of the Heart

67. Laozi, , and Wing-tsit Chan. The Way of Lao Tzu (tao-Tê Ching). Indianapolis: Bobbs-Merrill, 1963. Print.

68. Butterworth, Eric. Spiritual Economics: The Principles and Process of True Prosperity. Unity Village, MO: Unity Books, 2001. Print.

69. Sharma, Robin S. The Monk Who Sold His Ferrari: A Fable About Fulfilling Your Dreams and Reaching Your Destiny. San Francisco: HarperSanFrancisco, 1998. Print. pg 169

70. Schwartz, David J. The Magic of Thinking Big. New York: Simon & Schuster, 1987. Print. pg 124

71. Maltz, Maxwell. Psycho-cybernetics. New York: Pocket Books, 1994. Print. pg 114

72. Lyubomirsky, Sonja. The How of Happiness: A Scientific Approach to Getting the Life You Want. New York: Penguin Press, 2008. Print. pg 206

73. Deida, David. The Way of the Superior Man: A Spiritual Guide to Mastering the Challenges of Women, Work, and Sexual Desire. Boulder, CO: Sounds True, 2004. Print. pg 37

74. Phillips, Shawn, and Pete Williams. Strength for Life: The Fitness Plan for the Best of Your Life. New York: Ballantine Books, 2008. Print. pg 6

75. Trungpa, Chögyam, and Carolyn R. Gimian. Shambhala: The Sacred Path of the Warrior. Boulder, Colo: Shambhala, 1984. Print. pg 51

76. Sharma, Robin S. The Monk Who Sold His Ferrari: A Fable About Fulfilling Your Dreams and Reaching Your Destiny. San Francisco: HarperSanFrancisco, 1998. Print.

77. Dalai Lama

78. Tolle, Eckhart. The Power of Now: A Guide to Spiritual Enlightenment. Novato, Calif: New World Library, 1999. Print. pg 40

79. Tolle, Eckhart. The Power of Now: A Guide to Spiritual Enlightenment. Novato, Calif: New World Library, 1999. Print. pg 40

80. http://www.oxforddictionaries.com/us/definition/american_english/practice

81. Leonard, George. Mastery: The Keys to Success and Long-Term Fulfillment. New York: Plume, 1992. Print. pg 74

82. Chödrön, Pema. The Places That Scare You: A Guide to Fearlessness in Difficult Times. Boston: Shambhala, 2001. Print. (2nd page of chapter 3)

83. Campbell, Joseph, and Diane K. Osbon. A Joseph Campbell Companion: Reflections on the Art of Living. New York, NY: HarperCollins, 1991. Print.

84. Coolidge, Calvin

85. Murray, W H. The Scottish Himalayan Expedition. London: Dent, 1951. Print.

86. Harris, Bill. Thresholds of the Mind: How Holosync Audio Technology Can Transform Your Life. Beaverton: Centerpointe Press, 2002. Print. pg 127

87. Ben-Shahar, Tal. The Pursuit of Perfect: How to Stop Chasing Perfection and Start Living a Richer, Happier Life. New York: McGraw-Hill, 2009. Print. pg 40

88. Rumi

89. Dewey, John. Democracy and Education: An Introduction to the Philosophy of Education. New York: The Free Press, 1966. Print. pg 360

90. Rogers, Carl R. On Becoming a Person: A Therapist's View of Psychotherapy. Boston: Houghton Mifflin Company, 1961. Print. pg 35

91. Millman, Dan, and Dan Millman. Body Mind Mastery: Creating Success in Sport and Life. Novato, Calif: New World Library, 1999. Print. 48

92. Goldman, Robert, and Stephen Papson. Nike Culture: The Sign of the Swoosh. London: Sage Publications, 2004. Print. pg 49

93. Vincent van Gogh

Chapter 4
Reaching to the Heart of Another

94. Aristotle

95. Maslow, Abraham H. A Theory of Human Motivation. , 2013. Print.

96. Gandhi, Mahatma

97. Dr. Seuss

98. Brady, Mark. The Wisdom of Listening. Boston: Wisdom Publications, 2003. Print. pg 25

99. Hamilton, Diane M. Everything Is Workable: A Zen Approach to Conflict Resolution. , 2013. Print. Pg 85

100. Einstein, Albert

101. Goleman, Daniel. Social Intelligence: The New Science of Human Relationships. New York: Bantam Books, 2006. Print. pg 54

102. Surya, Das. Natural Radiance: Awakening to Your Great Perfection. Boulder, CO: Sounds True, 2005. Print. pg 72

103. Karma-gliṅ-pa, , Sambhava Padma, and Robert A. F. Thurman. The Tibetan Book of the Dead, As Popularly Known in the West: Known in Tibet As the Great Book of Natural Liberation Through Understanding in the between. New York: Bantam Books, 1994. Print. pg 53

104. O'Brien, Conan

105. Covey, Stephen R. The 7 Habits of Highly Effective People: Powerful Lessons in Personal Change. , 2013. Print. pg 207

106. Kuchinskas, Susan. The Chemistry of Connection: How the Oxytocin Response Can Help You Find Trust, Intimacy, and Love. Oakland, CA: New Harbinger, 2009. Print. pg. vii

Chapter 5
Regenerating your Heart

107. Buscaglia, Leo. Love. New York: Fawcet Columbine, 1996. Print.

108. Nhất, Hạnh, Mobi Ho, and Dinh M. Vo. The Miracle of Mindfulness: An Introduction to the Practice of Meditation. Boston: Beacon Press, 1987. Print. pg 15

109. Nhất, Hạnh, Mobi Ho, and Dinh M. Vo. The Miracle of Mindfulness: An Introduction to the Practice of Meditation. Boston: Beacon Press, 1987. Print. pg 15

110. Deida, David. Blue Truth: A Spiritual Guide to Life & Death and Love & Sex. Boulder, CO: Sound True, 2005. Print. pg 17

111. Thich Nhat Han

112. R.D. (2000). Neural correlates of conscious emotional experience. In R.D. Lane & L. Nadel (Eds.), Cognitive neuroscience of emotion (pp. 345–370). New York: Oxford University Press.

113. Daniel Goleman Ph.D http://news.harvard.edu/gazette/story/2007/03/smile-and-the-world-smiles-with-you-but-why/

114. Frankl, Viktor E. Man's Search for Meaning. Boston: Beacon Press, 2006. Print.

115. Newhart, Bob

116. http://umm.edu/news-and-events/news-releases/2009/laughter-is-the-best-medicine-for-your-heart

117. http://www.cancercenter.com/treatments/laughter-therapy/

118. http://www.cancercenter.com/treatments/laughter-therapy/

119. Osho, . Everyday Osho: 365 Daily Meditations for the Here and Now. Gloucester, Mass: Fair Winds, 2002. Print. pg 7

120. Nietzsche, Friedrich W, and R J. Hollingdale. Thus Spoke Zarathustra: A Book for Everyone and No One. Harmondsworth, England: Penguin Books, 1969. Print. pg 23

121. Phillips, Shawn, and Pete Williams. Strength for Life: The Fitness Plan for the Best of Your Life. New York: Ballantine Books, 2008. Print. pg 26

122. Nietzsche, Friedrich

123. http://www.nytimes.com/2013/06/09/opinion/sunday/why-music-makes-our-brain-sing.html?_r=1&

124. Beethoven, Ludwig van

125. St, James J. When I Sit Down to Play: A Guide to Fulfilling Your Dream of Playing the Piano and Keyboard. New York, NY: Kensington Books, 2000. Print. pg 14

126. Parker, Charlie

127. http://socialdance.stanford.edu/syllabi/smarter.htm

128. Campbell, Joseph, and Diane K. Osbon. A Joseph Campbell Companion: Reflections on the Art of Living. New York, NY: HarperCollins, 1991. Print.

129. Watts, Alan. Become What You Are. Boston: Shambhala, 2003. Print. pg 29

130. Nel, Philip. Dr. Seuss: American Icon. New York: Continuum, 2004. Print. pg 38

ABOUT THE AUTHORS

Ed McShane, M.S.W., has over three decades of experience as a psychotherapist, coach, public speaker, and counselor.

Ed McShane uses Acceptance as his Foundation, Love as his Guide, and the Golden Rule for assisting and facilitating your Personal Growth.

From professional athletes, heads of corporations, physicians, attorneys, teenagers, students, ex-convicts, and the homeless, he has coached thousands of people to find a connection with their Heart and reclaim the meaning in their lives.

Grant Gavin, M.A.T., is a spiritual teacher, teacher, philosopher, and author. Through insights rooted in deep caring and depth of understanding of the nature of human reality, Grant has spent the majority of his life guiding students to personal transformation.

Grant Gavin has dedicated his life to pushing past perceived limitations. Grant is an avid adventurer, taking him to four continents; surfing, rock climbing, and mountaineering.

The core of his insight is that true happiness is found when guided by the wisdom of your heart, illuminated by Spirit.

10% OF BOOK PROFITS

YMCA HAITI LITERACY PROJECT

A Coach for your Heart will donate 10% of book profits to the YMCA of Haiti Literacy Project. There is a symmetry in writing a book and donating a portion of the profits from our book in support of literacy. Reading gives people access to a wealth of knowledge; through reading, individuals are able to understand the world more, learn new information, solve problems, and improve their overall wellbeing. Our goal for this book is to help people.

100% of the funds donated to the YMCA of Haiti Literacy Project go to the program. The primary objective of the Haiti Literacy Project is to jump start literacy skills for 1100 youth (early age/ not in school, after school, teens/young adults) and adults (particularly women and seniors) in three communities in Haiti in three years (2015- 2018 fiscal Year). The Haiti Literacy Project will be located at three YMCA Community Centers - Port au Prince, Laboule, and Croix des Bouquets in Haiti.

Specific Objectives

The primary objective of the Haiti Literacy Project is to jump start literacy skills for 1100 youth (early age/ not in school, after school, teens/young adults) and adults (particularly women and seniors) in three communities in Haiti in three years (2015- 2018 fiscal Year). The Haiti Literacy Project will be located at three YMCA Community Centers - Port au Prince, Laboule, and Croix des Bouquets in Haiti.

- With 9.7 million people, Haiti is the most populous full member-state of the Caribbean Community. It is the poorest country in the Americas as measured by the Human Development Index. There are 5 million children (18 years or less in age.) The Median age is 21 years. 4 million Haitians live in the diaspora.

- In January 2010, Haiti was struck by a 7.0 earthquake, leaving hundreds of thousands dead and hundreds of thousands more homeless.
- Nearly 80% of Haitians live in poverty and 54% in abject poverty. 75% of Haitians live on $2 or less per day.
- The average annual income is $653. Unemployment is 41%.
- Only 40% of Haitians have access to basic health care.
- Haiti's literacy rate is 53% and illiteracy is 47%.
- The educational system in Haiti is very weak, and ranks 177th of 186 countries for national spending on education. 90% of schools are nonpublic. Only 67% of children attend primary school, only 30% reach sixth grade and only 20% are in secondary schools.

The Haiti Literacy Project will offer literacy programs to 900 youth and adults plus 180 teen/young adults as volunteer tutors. These young adults will be trained as community leaders. In addition, 50-100 community volunteers, from partner organizations and other civic groups, will be recruited over three years at the Community Centers.

www.ingramcontent.com/pod-product-compliance
Lightning Source LLC
LaVergne TN
LVHW011342080426
835511LV00005B/107

* 9 7 8 0 6 9 2 5 2 8 3 2 7 *